Institutions, Partisanship and Credibility in Global Financial Markets

Increasingly integrated global financial markets have been shaken by a series of severe shocks in recent decades, from Mexico's Tequila Crisis to the upheavals in the Eurozone. These crises have demonstrated that signs of uncertain local economic and political conditions can result in market fluctuations, which in turn cause economic, social, and political instability. Such instability is particularly severe for developing countries that rely heavily on international financial markets for their financial needs. Building credibility in these markets is therefore important for national governments who wish to prevent market panic and capital flight and, ultimately, to achieve stable economic growth.

Earlier studies have argued that institutional arrangements that constrain governments and commit them to protecting private property rights and market-friendly policies can send a strong positive signal to the markets about a given country's sovereign credibility. This book argues, however, that the market perception of such credibility-building institutions is significantly contingent on which party governs the country. Formal institutions confer significant credibility-building effects on left-wing governments, whereas less or no significant effects are enjoyed by right-wing governments. And beyond that, any significant changes in a country's institutional landscape – such as a breakdown of democracy or joining an international organization that can influence domestic politics – have a particularly strong impact on the credibility of left-wing governments. This argument is supported by a quantitative analysis of sovereign credit ratings data collected from around 90 developing countries from 1980 to 2007, by case studies from South Asia, Eastern Europe, and Latin America, and by face-to-face interviews with 24 financial market experts based in Hong Kong, Seoul, and Paris.

Hye Jee Cho is Assistant Professor of Political Science at the Hong Kong University of Science and Technology, Hong Kong.

Routledge Research in Comparative Politics

For a full list of titles, please visit: www.routledge.com/Routledge-Research-in-Comparative-Politics/book-series/CP

64 **Citizenship and Democracy in an Era of Crisis**
Edited by Thomas Poguntke, Sigrid Roßteutscher, Rüdiger Schmitt-Beck and Sonja Zmerli

65 **Drivers of Integration and Regionalism in Europe and Asia**
Comparative perspectives
Edited by Louis Brennan and Philomena Murray

66 **Generations, Political Participation and Social Change in Western Europe**
Maria T. Grasso

67 **The Politics of Think Tanks in Europe**
Jesper Dahl Kelstrup

68 **The Statecraft of Consensus Democracies in a Turbulent World**
A Comparative Study of Austria, Belgium, Luxembourg, the Netherlands and Switzerland
José M. Magone

69 **Policy Change under New Democratic Capitalism**
Edited by Hideko Magara

70 **Rampage Shootings and Gun Control**
Politicization and policy change in Western Europe
Steffen Hurka

70 **Growth, Crisis, Democracy**
The political economy of social coalitions and policy regime change
Edited by Hideko Magara and Bruno Amable

71 **Think Tanks in the US and EU**
The role of policy institutes in Washington and Brussels
Christopher J. Rastrick

72 **Institutions, Partisanship and Credibility in Global Financial Markets**
Hye Jee Cho

73 **Health and Political Engagement**
Mikko Mattila, Lauri Rapeli, Hanna Wass and Peter Söderlund

Institutions, Partisanship and Credibility in Global Financial Markets

Hye Jee Cho

Routledge
Taylor & Francis Group
LONDON AND NEW YORK

First published 2018
by Routledge

2 Park Square, Milton Park, Abingdon, Oxfordshire OX14 4RN
52 Vanderbilt Avenue, New York, NY 10017

Routledge is an imprint of the Taylor & Francis Group, an informa business

First issued in paperback 2019

British Library Cataloguing-in-Publication Data
A catalogue record for this book is available from the British Library

Library of Congress Cataloging-in-Publication Data
A catalog record for this book has been requested

ISBN: 978-1-138-21485-9 (hbk)
ISBN: 978-0-367-27282-1 (pbk)

Typeset in Galliard
by Apex CoVantage, LLC

For my father, mother, sister, and Bosomi

Contents

Acknowledgements

This book would not have been possible without the support of people who have helped me at various stages of the project. I am grateful to Geoff Garrett and Ron Rogowski, who provided invaluable guidance on my research and training in international political economy at UCLA. Conversations with Geoff inspired me to study the subject and honed my thinking on the project. Ron gave me insightful critiques on my earlier drafts, allowing me to tap into his vast knowledge and experience in the field. Thanks to Geoff and Ron, I was able to pursue the project that I had in mind. I am no less thankful to Michael Ross for introducing me to various literatures that expanded my knowledge in political economy. Thanks as well to Ken Schultz for providing help that was crucial to the refinement of my econometric models and empirical analysis. From Dan Treisman, I learned that only hard work and dedication produce scholarship that meets rigorous professional standards, and I am grateful to him as well.

My sincere appreciation also goes to Jim Vreeland, who has been extremely generous with his advice and help with my research. His warm encouragement and thoughtful advice has helped me to address challenging issues I faced as an academic. My heartfelt gratitude goes to Ping-Sheng Koh as well for his invaluable support and thoughtful suggestions with various aspects of the project. I am also deeply indebted to J. Lawrence Broz for providing me with insightful comments that were critical in building and refining my argument and for his warm encouragement and advice.

My book has also benefited from valuable comments from folks at UCLA and the University of Rochester. I am grateful to Michael Chwe, Barbara Geddes, Jeffrey Lewis, Tom Schwartz, and Mike Thies at the Political Science Department of UCLA. I also thank Tom Dolan, Dan Epstein, Hein Goemans, Daniel Gillion, Mark Kayser, Martin Steinwand, and Randall Stone for their comments on the project during my post-doctoral fellowship at the Political Science Department of U of R.

I am also grateful to Ruben Atoian, Glen Biglaiser, Nancy Brune, Mark Copelovitch, Axel Dreher, Julia Gray, Alexandra Guisinger, Christopher Humphrey, Nathan Jensen, Dong-Hun Kim, Ed Malesky, Layna Mosley, Irfan Nooruddin, Chad Rector, and Stephanie Rickard for their helpful comments, encouragement, and making data available. Thanks as well to colleagues at the

Hong Kong University of Science and Technology (HKUST) for their support in the later stage of this project. I received particularly helpful comments from Yongshun Cai, Josh Derman, Wenkai He, Han Li, Kellee Tsai, and David Zweig. Earlier versions of the chapters have been presented at various conferences held by the American Political Science Association, International Studies Association, Midwest Political Science Association, Political Economy of International Organization, Western Political Science Association, Taiwan Insurance Guarantee Fund, and HKUST-Seoul National University, and talks at the University of Rochester, University of Vermont, HKUST, Korea University, and Ajou University in Korea, and I thank the participants for their comments. Simon Bates at Routledge has provided very thoughtful suggestions on my proposal, and I thank him for his feedback and patience. I would like to acknowledge the financial support by the UC Institute on Global Conflict and Cooperation, UCLA's Graduate Division, and HKUST.

Last but certainly not least, I am deeply indebted to my father, Kwang Won Cho, my mother, Kyung Sook Cho, and my sister, Hye Yeon Cho, for their unwavering support and belief in me. It is beyond my ability to fully describe the love and support they have given to me. This book could not have been completed without them.

An earlier version of Chapter 4 was published as: Cho, Hye Jee. 2009. "Democracy and Sovereign Credit Ratings: Do Democratic Institutions Boost Investor Confidence?" in *Korean Political Science Review* 43(5): 113–135.

Chapter 6 largely follows: Cho, Hye Jee. 2014. "Impact of IMF Programs on Perceived Creditworthiness of Emerging Market Countries: Is There a 'Nixon-Goes-to-China' Effect?" in *International Studies Quarterly* 58: 308–321.

1 Institutions, partisanship and market perceptions

What are the consequences for a country that loses the confidence of international credit markets? A series of severe shocks – from Mexico's Tequila Crisis to the recent Eurozone upheavals that have shaken markets around the world – have demonstrated that confidence lies at the very heart of international financial relations. Market confidence builds on policy credibility and predictability. Policy certainty is of critical importance in assuring investors. Increasingly, international investment has drastically diversified investors' country allocations so that local market fluctuations can now affect many countries at once, creating larger-scale market instability. Signs of economic or political uncertainty may result in massive asset sell-offs and financial market fluctuations, which in turn can cause economic, social, and political instability. The costs of market instability are particularly high for developing countries that rely heavily on international finance. Building credibility in international markets is thus an important task for national governments wishing to discourage capital flight and, ultimately, to achieve stable economic growth.

A key question for many cash-strapped developing countries is how to improve their creditworthiness in international financial markets. The extant literature has argued that political institutions that constrain governments, and thus work as a commitment mechanism, encourage investment. However, two important issues have been largely neglected in the literature. First, the markets' perception of the effectiveness of such institutions in fact depends crucially on the important domestic political environment – that is, which party governs the country. Furthermore, any significant changes in a country's institutional landscape – such as a breakdown of democracy or joining an international organization that influences domestic politics – are likely to have a significant impact on investor perceptions.

In this book, I address these important yet largely neglected questions by focusing on sovereign credibility – that is, a country's perceived ability and willingness to repay its sovereign debt. I argue that embracing institutional constraints has strong positive credibility-building effects for left-leaning governments while such effects are not likely to be significant for right-leaning governments.[1] Moreover, any significant changes in a country's institutional arrangements are likely to have greater impact on the credibility of left-wing governments.

This book specifically examines the "brand name" effect of government partisanship on market perceptions – that is, how a party's label affects markets' perception of the party when other important economic and political conditions are taken into consideration. The discussion will focus on *perception*, as investor confidence essentially builds on perceived risks and credibility. Perception is critical in international financial markets because it is an important determinant of market behavior and a major cause of contagion, whereby shocks propagate internationally, transcending their fundamental commonalities driven and exacerbated by investors' herding behavior (Obsfelt 1996; Pericoli and Sbracia 2003; Radelet and Sachs 1998).

Investors' perceptions of governments they regard as left-oriented are typically not favorable. Investors tend to associate them with higher inflation rates and larger public sectors, more expropriation risk, and less respect for debt obligations. They thus see such governments as less credible when it comes to prudent macroeconomic policies (Broz 2013; Broz and Weymouth 2013; Garrett 1998; Leblang 2002; Mosley 2003; Vaaler et al. 2005, 2006). This perception is largely due to the historical association between leftist governments and anti-market policies. Even today, the World Bank reports that the governments in the developing world that are classified as left-wing do indeed tend to expropriate private assets more often (MIGA 2013: 48). Extreme measures such as expropriation may have become less frequent over the years, but the policy risk that a government may suddenly change rules, regulations, and investment contracts still remains significant in many countries (Henisz and Zelner 2010; Sobel 2002).

The consequence of such negative market perceptions of left-wing governments is that even when political and economic conditions are controlled for, left-wing governments suffer stigma or a brand name effect whereby they receive a biased reaction in the markets, regardless of their stated intentions and actual policies. Although left-wing parties are not always market-averse or committed to expansionary policies, investors fear that they may behave opportunistically for political purposes.[2] As a result, investors are typically guarded and suspect left-wing parties of being less market-friendly than those farther to the right. It is indeed common to hear news reports that the election of a left-wing political leader has led to a drop in market indicators. Such concerns are particularly acute for investors in developing countries due to the greater policy uncertainty they face, the history of sovereign default and expropriations in such economies, and greater macroeconomic volatility overall (Bergoeing et al. 2004; Brooks and Mosley 2007; Broz 2013; Caballero and Krishnamurthy 2005; Gavin and Perotti 1997; Kaminsky et al. 2004; Lane 2003; Loayza et al. 2007; Mendoza 1991).

Holding such reservations about left-wing governments is rational for investors, who will tend to respond to information asymmetry and high information acquisition costs by using partisanship as an important shortcut for assessing the political environment (Broz and Weymouth 2013; Leblang 2002; Mosley 2003). Bankers and institutional investors may make more educated guesses about government policy than the general public, but it is still costly and time-consuming for them to unravel all of the aspects of the complex public policy issues facing the various governments in their portfolios (Brooks and Mosley 2007; Tomz 2007). Furthermore, investors are increasingly diversifying their portfolios to minimize risk, and have thus lost the incentive to gather costly information on individual countries (Calvo and Mendoza 2000: 102; Santiso 2003: 19). Political parties serve as labels that foreign investors use to anticipate the future course of government policy, and left-wing governments have to make extra efforts to establish their credibility in global markets.

In this context, the presence of domestic political and international institutions that constrain a country's political leadership from making arbitrary policy changes, and that make the future direction of policy more predictable, can send a strong positive signal to markets about the policy contents and future course of policy at the most fundamental level. I argue that such institutional constraints are likely to work as a *contingent signal*, so that they have a lesser effect on right-wing governments. Such governments are perceived as supportive of the business owners and capitalists who are their core supporters. They are perceived to oppose inflation and high taxes, and be more business- and market-friendly overall (Broz and Weymouth 2013; Hibbs 1977; MacRae 1977; Nordhaus 1975). They are not likely to be as threatening to investors as left-wing governments when other things are equal, as there is an expectation that property rights are more likely to be protected under right-wing governments than under left-wing governments (Broz and Weymouth 2013). Institutional constraints are therefore not as likely to be considered important with a right-wing government. Similarly, any significant changes in a country's institutional arrangements should have greater signaling effects on the credibility of left-wing governments than on their right-wing counterparts.

The argument that left-wing governments benefit more from constraining institutions is in accordance with the idea of "Nixon goes to China." This phrase, originally from the visit to China by a hardline anticommunist US President Nixon, has been used in the political science literature to describe a situation in which the policy proposals of a politician gain greater support when there is a greater perceived mismatch between the ideological position of the politician and the proposed policy (Cowen and Sutter 1998; Cukierman and Tommasi 1998). Because markets tend to perceive left-wing governments in the developing world to be more prone to expropriation, inflation, and populism[3] that often circumvents democratic rules, governments that are labeled as leftist can earn greater credibility by submitting themselves to institutional constraints designed to restrain unpredictable behaviors and protect private property rights.

The idea of Nixon-going-to-China in the political science literature has been confined to the domestic political settings rather than the international political economic context. The core of the idea, however, lies in perception, which is essential for understanding the behavior of international financial markets. The interactions between governments and investors are not much different in nature than those between governments and the general public, because investors also face significant information asymmetry and follow ideological clues in making decisions. Investors face significant difficulties in ascertaining governments' policy directions and preferences, particularly in developing countries (Mosley 2003; Santiso 2003; Tomz 2007). The domestic public may in fact have more local knowledge concerning their governments than foreign investors.

The international political economy literature, however, mainly focuses on the formal and informal institutions that structure collective choices, and surprisingly little attention has been paid to the question of how market perceptions of sovereign credibility are contingent on the dynamics between institutions, institutional change, and government partisanship, which is an important aspect of any domestic political environment.[4] This is probably inappropriate, as political parties are ubiquitous in real-world politics and have obvious influence over national and international policy choices. Moreover, previous studies that consider political parties in the literature focus on how institutions influence or shape their policies and behaviors to result in different economic outcomes.[5] These studies therefore neglect to address the dynamics of institutions and government partisanship in influencing market perception when other factors are taken into consideration.

Party labels serve as a powerful signal and information shortcut for the markets. Furthermore, investors tend to exhibit a negativity bias – that is, they tend to react more sharply to what they consider to be a negative event than to a positive one (Akhtar et al. 2011; Baumeister et al. 2001; Peeters and Czapinski 1990). The markets' perceptions of a political party, combined with such a bias, have a substantial and significant effect on market behavior, which has become an important consideration in current international market environment. Highly diversified and very complex financial markets discourage costly information gathering by investors and force them to rely considerably on risk perceptions based on information shortcuts and other investors' decisions (Bikhchandani and Sharma 2000; Gray 2013; Jegadeesh and Kim 2010). This reliance on perception has significant consequences, as it affects asset prices and may contribute to increased market volatility or even disruption.

The findings in this book suggest that credibility-enhancing institutions indeed send contingent signals to the markets so that they improve the sovereign credibility of left-leaning governments, whereas no such effects are found for right-leaning governments. Any negative development in institutional arrangements tends to have greater adverse effects on the credibility of left-wing governments than that of right-leaning governments. In the context that markets behave rationally to minimize costs given policy uncertainty, the brand name effects of a political party can be very influential. Brand name effects persist even when other important economic and political conditions are taken into consideration. The financial market experts interviewed for this study consistently noted that a political leader's party identity is very important for predicting the policy directions of a country and therefore developing investment strategies.

This book focuses primarily on formal institutions and their utility as an important signal in international financial markets. Recently, much attention has been paid to informal institutions such as norms, unwritten rules, and relational contracting practices as important influences on economic outcomes (Helmke and Levitsky 2004). It has been suggested that they shape political and economic outcomes by complementing or even substituting formal institutions (Helmke and Levitsky 2004). Some scholars even contend that so-called "best-practice" formal institutions, such as the court system and the rule of law that are designed to protect contractual and private property rights, incur high costs to build and maintain in developing countries (Dixit 2004; Rodrik 2008). Therefore, they argue, best-practice institutions can actually prevent developing countries from achieving reform and economic development, or at least require higher costs and efforts.

The findings in this book suggest, however, that formal institutions in fact play an important role by sending signals to the markets about sovereign credibility. Although informal institutions may complement or substitute for formal institutions, they cannot replace formal institutions as a fundamental solution (Helmke and Levitsky 2004: 731). More importantly, they cannot signal strongly and effectively because they are often not sufficiently visible to outsiders. The signaling effect of informal institutions has received little scholarly attention, probably because measuring their quality and international comparisons are difficult. Foreign investors cannot reliably assess the credibility of a government through its informal institutions. They may strengthen or complement formal institutions, but they cannot send a strong signal to the markets. It is also unclear how informal institutions affect sovereign credibility through their interactions with government partisanship. Brand name effects influence market behavior when future policy is unclear, and formal institutions ultimately work as a more effective commitment device to build credibility.

This book uses the idea of the Nixon hypothesis to explain the market behaviors. Previous findings on the relationship between institutions and financial markets are mixed, possibly because they do not consider that institutions' credibility-building effects are significantly contingent on the important domestic political condition of who governs.

Market perceptions of the left in developing countries: a lesson from Lula

Sovereign credibility reflects a country's perceived ability and willingness to repay its sovereign debt, and left-wing governments are often regarded as lacking in both areas. Of course, a party that is labeled left-wing will not necessarily always adhere to expansionary or market-averse policies. Furthermore, the left-wing emphasis on welfare measures, redistribution, and employment may help to address economic inequality and social problems caused by international market integration, which in turn may promote market stability. Regardless of what policies a left-wing party actually pursues, however, a leftist label tends to signal risk to investors, as they suspect that even if a left-wing political leader promises to implement business-friendly policies, he or she may later not hesitate to reverse direction in response to political needs. Leftist political parties therefore bear the burden of being perceived as a greater threat to investment than those further to the right.

Examples of such brand name effects are commonplace, but the case of the former Brazilian president Luiz Inácio Lula da Silva, or Lula, is particularly illuminating. As a founding member of the Workers Party of Brazil, he held and fought for strong left-wing beliefs, but once he became president, he adopted market-friendly policies. To many people, he is a stellar example of a successful left-wing politician who prudently managed the economy to win market confidence. Lula tried to reassure both foreign investors and local businesspeople that he was no radical and that he had in fact moved irrevocably to the center (*Institutional Investor*, December 2002). He focused on balancing budgets, giving the central bank independence, and promoting trade liberalization – tactics traditionally associated with more conservative, neoliberal politicians.

However, despite his proclamations and the largely market-friendly policy outcomes, there was constant suspicion of his true policy directions throughout his presidency. When Lula was first elected, analysts expected that the incoming administration would initially resist the temptation to boost government spending to stimulate growth, but that in the later years it would probably try to make good on some of the promises that had helped Lula to victory (*Institutional Investor*, December 2002). Then, with Brazil's economy lagging behind and growing only around 2 percent a year since Lula was elected, far below the expected growth rate of 6.5 percent for emerging markets, his administration eased spending controls as the new election approached (*Financial Times*, April 4, 2006). Lula pursued his expansionary policies thanks to high commodity prices and a buoyant international economic environment, but investors again suspected that he was likely to backtrack on the reforms he was pursuing and revert to a labor-friendly "populist" agenda to gain support (*Newsweek*, August 8, 2005).

Lula's landslide reelection reignited fears that he might attempt to pursue more populist and interventionist policies at the expense of fiscal austerity, as some powerful members of his Workers Party were urging him to increase government spending dramatically (*Globe and Mail*, October 31, 2006). For example, when the fiscally orthodox finance minister Antonio Palocci resigned amid a scandal, the Brazilian real fell 2 percent in a day and stocks on the Bovespa exchange fell almost 1 percent out of fear that expansionary policies might follow. The shock persisted for over a month as the total return of J.P. Morgan's Emerging Market Bond Index (EMBI) declined steadily for the following three months. Such a decline in response to political news is rare (*Associated Press*, March 28, 2006). The decline was a reaction to possible risks, as commentators doubted the true priorities of Lula's administration when the government granted a generous pay rise to public employees and increased the minimum wage by an amount significantly above the inflation rate (*Financial Times*, February 21, 2007). Analysts warned investors of a populist turn in Brazil, suggesting that Lula had in fact not betrayed the poor but rather the promise of growth (*Financial Times*, April 5, 2006). The market-friendly policies he pursued during his first term could not fully assure investors of his future policy directions.

Investors, of course, react sharply when left-wing leaders make policy promises that will undermine business interests, but they also keep a suspicious eye on left-wing governments for possible policy reversals, even when they appear to be on track with market-friendly policies. Lula's experience is a typical example of what left-wing governments face in international financial markets.[6] From an investor's perspective, assuming that leftist governments present a higher risk than right-wing governments is in fact a rational course of action. Information asymmetry and diversified portfolios leave investors ill-placed for gathering costly information on individual countries (Calvo and Mendoza 2000; Santiso 2003). Relying on information shortcuts is one effective response (Brooks and Mosley 2007; Gray 2013; Knight 1985), and a government's ideological orientation is one of the cues most frequently used by investors to overcome government policy uncertainty (Leblang 2002).

This type of information shortcut can be even more useful for those investing in developing countries. These countries pose a greater challenge for investors compared with advanced industrial democracies, as reliable information is much more difficult and costly to find. There is often a lack of good-quality data and little transparency in policymaking, making predictions about future policy difficult (Broz 2002; Sobel 2002; Vaaler et al. 2006). Furthermore, as the financial market experts that I interviewed noted, it is more difficult to predict the directions of policies in many developing countries because these countries lack experience in international financial interactions and tend to be deficient in the systems or institutional arrangements that provide a foundation for business activities. Those countries rely instead on their leaders for policy administration. The political leaders are more influential, as fast economic growth allows them greater power (Interviews 1, 3, 17, 20, 23, 24). In the context of such policy uncertainty, some leftist leaders propose moderate economic policies to ease investors' fears, but these proposals are generally ineffective in fully winning the confidence of the market.

Institutions as a *contingent* signal of policy predictability

When governments attempt to convince investors of their future policy directions, the domestic and international institutions that constrain governments to prevent arbitrary policy changes and commit them to private property rights and market-friendly policies may help to build credibility. What investors want to compensate for a lack of credibility is solid institutional structures that commit a government to its policy promises – a fundamental system or structure, such as the rule of law, that goes beyond individual political leaders so that policy is predictable regardless of who governs (Interviews 20, 24). Institutions constrain and shape political leaders' incentives and behavior (North 1990). Economic institutions enforcing property rights and functioning markets influence economic incentives in a society. The economic institutions are determined in turn by the society's political power dynamics, which are largely shaped by political institutions such as the form of government and the degree of constraints on political elites (Acemoglu et al. 2005). Governance structure and political institutions provide a predictable political foundation for markets, as institutions are expected to influence policymaking processes in such a way that some policy outcomes become more probable than others (Cukierman et al. 1992; Weingast 1995; Williamson 1994). Similarly, international institutions may shape economic institutions in a society through programs that force governments to adopt and commit to certain economic policies. As North and Weingast (1989) show, using the classic example of the effect of institutional changes on sovereign credibility in seventeenth-century England, domestic and international institutions that constrain arbitrary policy changes and enhance the predictability and stability of economic policy can improve the sovereign credibility of the countries that adopt them.

Economic policies are subject to time-inconsistency problems. Governments promise to protect private property rights, keep inflation and taxes low, and repay debt, but may renege on these promises later in the course. A firm institutional structure that commits a government to policy promises increases predictability, and therefore sovereign credibility, particularly for left-wing governments whose policies tend to lack market confidence.

As the counterintuitive conventional wisdom maintains, "only Nixon can go to China" – a left-wing government's submission to highly constraining institutions is likely to send a particularly strong positive signal to financial markets. The effects for right-leaning governments are likely to be much weaker, since their policy orientation tends to align better with business interests. This means that any changes that undermine the effectiveness of constraining institutions are also likely to have signaling effects on a government's credibility, and the effects are likely to be greater for left-wing governments.

This discussion will focus on the role of formal institutions in sending positive signals about the sovereign credibility of left-wing governments. More specifically, I argue that democratic institutions are superior to authoritarian governments in building credibility, and such credibility-building effects are greater for left-wing governments. Furthermore, improvements or deterioration in institutional quality may have greater signaling effects for left-wing governments. Compared with autocracies, various positive features of strong democracy make it easier to predict the course of future policies. In addition to the rule of law and respect for property rights, which are fundamental aspects for investors (Archer et al. 2007; Beaulieu et al. 2012; Biglaiser and Staats 2012; Jensen 2006; Schultz and Weingast 2003), democracies tend to more effectively control corruption through greater transparency in the policymaking process (Bardhan 1997; LaPalombara 1994; Lederman et al. 2005; Tanzi 1998). A system of checks and balances also appeals to investors, as it may prevent arbitrary policy changes (Jensen 2006; Kohlscheen 2004; North and Weingast 1989; Saiegh 2005). These features of democracy may be more effective in deterring populism, a significant concern for investors in economies run by left-wing governments. Moreover, a democracy may more effectively deal with a financial crisis if the transfer of power from a discredited political leader to a new successor occurs. Participatory politics allows for different concerns to be expressed and for economic problems to be solved through consensus-building (Rodrik 2008). All of this helps investors to better predict the directions and content of government policy (Interviews 11, 12, 14, 16, 23).

However, while a democratic system tends to reduce policy uncertainty, excessive political fragmentation can at times lead to policy gridlock in democracies (Haggard 2000; Haggard and Kaufman 1992; Keefer and Stasavage 2002). Excessive political constraints, often found in coalition governments, may negatively affect sovereign credibility if they are perceived as deterring efficient policymaking (Eichler and Hofmann 2013; Haggard and McCubbins 2001). Constraints may even promote corruption as different parties contend to win domestic political support. With a left-wing government, excessive constraints may be perceived as particularly risky, locking in leftist policies or blocking liberal market reforms if the chief executive is reform-oriented. Therefore, while foreign investors appreciate a certain level of institutional constraints against the executive rather than no political checks at all, too much political constraint can also undermine market confidence (MacIntyre 2001, 2003; Zheng 2011).

Constraining international institutions may also benefit left-wing governments. The International Monetary Fund (IMF) may be particularly helpful for left-wing governments because the IMF obliges its borrowers to follow policy prescriptions intended to stabilize their economies and to accept free-market policies (Vreeland 2003, 2007). The IMF's intrusive policy prescriptions and monitoring of implementation are designed to influence the economic policies and politics of borrowing countries. The IMF's enforcement of neoliberal market policies may result in its programs exerting a greater positive influence on investors' perceptions of left-wing signatories than on their right-wing counterparts, who are already more in line with the IMF's policy orientation.

I examine how these domestic and international institutional arrangements influence the relationship between government partisanship and sovereign credibility. Using quantitative and qualitative evidence, I demonstrate that although left-wing governments are perceived to be riskier than their right-wing counterparts, these institutional arrangements work as a contingent signal to improve their credibility. Such credibility-building effects are not pronounced for governments perceived as right-leaning.

Plan of the book and the findings

Chapter 2 is devoted to answering a few preliminary questions: Why is it important for countries to gain credibility in international financial markets? How do institutions and their changes influence credibility, and why do they work as a contingent signal? Why do formal institutions outperform informal institutions in building credibility? Investors face various types of risks, such as inflation, foreign exchange, and interest rate risks, among others, but political risks are always paramount where developing countries are concerned (MIGA 2013). While economic risks typically affect a government's *ability* to pay, political risk in sovereign debt markets is linked to a government's *willingness* to pay

(Tomz 2007: 16). Political considerations may lead governments to default, even when they have the ability to repay. A recent example is Ecuador's behavior under President Correa, where the left-wing executive decided to default on the country's sovereign debt, describing the debt holders as evil and claiming that the debts incurred by past governments were illegal. When a sovereign debtor does not repay, it is difficult for creditors to take coordinated action (Cole and Kehoe 1997; Tomz 2007). Private investors who have increased mobility can therefore simply withdraw their money if they are concerned about potential default (Broner et al. 2013; Santiso 2003).

In recent decades, the flow of private capital into developing countries has dramatically increased, with the rate of increase outpacing that of other types of investment (Arslanalp and Tsuda 2014). As the investor base becomes more international, governments must increasingly satisfy the high standards of foreign investors who are less likely to roll over and more likely to exit the market when policy uncertainty emerges (Broner et al. 2013; Cole and Kehoe 1997). Governments make various policy proposals to attract foreign investors, but they often find it difficult to convince markets of their sincerity.

Governments needing international credit therefore have a strong incentive to build a predictable and credible investment environment to earn investor confidence and develop market stability. In an emerging economy, important political and economic decisions are often at the discretion of a handful of political leaders. That increases policy uncertainty and political risk for foreign investors (Interviews 20, 24). Regardless of their actual policies, left-wing governments suffer from brand name effects, so that they are typically perceived to be less prudent economic managers and as more likely not to respect sovereign debt obligations. This makes formal institutions crucial for supporting their credibility in financial markets, because compared to informal institutions, they have greater visibility, stability, and comparability.

The subsequent chapters present empirical research designed to investigate the following questions: Do markets perceive left-wing governments to be riskier than others and accordingly give them lower credit ratings, even when important economic and political differences are taken into consideration? If so, then how do constraining institutions and their changes influence the relationships leftist governments have with their perceived sovereign credibility? The research involves quantitative data analyses that address potential endogeneity problems, face-to-face in-depth interviews with financial market experts, and country case studies. The research relies on sovereign credit ratings because they effectively reflect market perceptions and are crucial in international financial markets, providing the information on which investors base important investment decisions (Afonso et al. 2012). Ratings reduce investors' information costs and affect the behavior of the financial markets. They also exert significant influence by determining the terms of a borrowing country's access to the capital markets (Reinhart et al. 2003). Institutional Investor ratings are the main dependent variable and the ratings by Moody's, Standard and Poor's, and Fitch are used to check the robustness of the findings.[7] Institutional Investor is based on the evaluations of bankers and experts worldwide, and includes data on over 100 countries from the 1980s, providing a significantly wider coverage of countries and years than other major rating agencies. Moody's, Standard and Poor's, and Fitch generate ratings using their own analysts' assessments of the economic performance and political aspects of a country.

The data on government partisanship are obtained from the World Bank's Database of Political Institutions (DPI) (Beck et al. 2001), which classifies governments into left, center, and right, where applicable, based on the ideology of the chief executive. The classification relies primarily on the party name and description. This is an optimal variable for this research because it allows testing of the brand name effect on left-wing parties when other important politico-economic differences are controlled for. By indicating ideology but not policy, the variable picks up the effects of ideology on investor perceptions.[8] The database's coding decisions are carefully checked to ensure that they correspond with those of other sources.[9] This variable was chosen in light of a number of earlier studies using the chief executive's ideology to examine the relationship between government partisanship and investment (Archer et al. 2007; Brooks and Mosley 2007; Jensen 2006; Pinto and Pinto 2008; Vaaler et al. 2006), as decisions regarding sovereign debt repayment are largely executive decisions that need not be ratified by the legislature (Archer et al. 2007; Brooks and Mosley 2007; North and Weingast 1989; Vreeland 2006).

The quantitative findings are supplemented by country case studies from Latin America, South Asia, and Eastern Europe, and interviews with specialists in international investment and risk analysis. I conducted in-depth, face-to-face interviews with 24 financial market experts in asset and fund management and risk analysis. Each financial market expert was asked a structured set of questions during a 60- to 90-minute interview. The core questions focus on their perceptions and evaluations of how government partisanship and political and international institutions affect sovereign credibility. These experts are mostly at the executive level and are based in Hong Kong, Seoul, and Paris.[10]

Chapter 3 discusses the markets' perceptions of left-wing governments in developing countries. The extant literature on the partisan cycle model contends that left- and right-wing parties have distinct ideological goals and macroeconomic policy preferences. Left-wing governments tend to be more concerned about unemployment than about inflation, whereas right-wing governments have the opposite orientation (Alesina et al. 1997; Bagashka and Stone 2013; Blais et al. 1993; Brooks and Mosley 2007; Broz 2013; Castles 1989; Davis et al. 1966, 1974; Downs 1957; Hibbs 1977; Kramer 1971; Lange and Garrett 1985; MacRae 1977; Nordhaus 1975; Schmidt 1996; Tufte 1975, 1978). The converse view is that partisanship is not a useful proxy for government economic conditions, and with globalization, it is argued that leftist parties have given up their traditional policy preferences for more market- and business-friendly policies in an attempt to attract international capital in a competitive world market (Drezner 2001; Huber and Stephens 1998; Kurzer 1993; Mishra 1999; Moses 2000; Pierson 1995, 2001; Rodrik 1997; Ross 2000).

The debate on the policy differences between the left and the right continues, but market perceptions of left-wing governments seem to indicate that left-wing governments are seen as posing greater investment risks than right-wing governments, regardless of their actual policies. Such deep-seated negative market perceptions are particularly visible with respect to developing countries, associated perhaps with historical experience with previous left-wing governments who expropriated and nationalized international investment. Market indicators tend to fall significantly when a left-wing party comes to power, and the extent of the negative market response differs for developed and developing countries. Although the European debt crisis, and most recently the Greek debt problem, have alerted international investors to the risks associated with left-wing governments in more advanced economies, the market in general holds the belief that advanced democracies are more responsible in keeping their promises on policy and international investment.

The analysis of sovereign ratings in Chapter 3 shows that leftist governments are perceived to be riskier in developing countries, but not in advanced industrial democracies. They are seen as less creditworthy, even when other important economic and political conditions are taken into consideration. Furthermore, in a developing country, a left-wing government's extended tenure does not seem to reduce investors' generally negative perceptions. In face-to-face interviews, financial market experts agree that left-wing governments are generally perceived as riskier and admit that they do not fully trust any left-wing leader. Remaining in office for an extended period does not lessen the risk because a political leader can always change policies without warning, unless there are effective institutional arrangements to restrain such a leader (Interviews 3, 24).

Chapter 4 discusses the credibility-building effects of democratic institutions. Investor concerns about left-wing leaders are often strongly associated with fears of populism. Populism can arise from either the left or the right, but historically, leftist populism has been a greater threat to investors because it typically leads to radical measures to redistribute wealth and expand government control (Weyland 2013). Populism tends to flourish in weak democracies where populist strategies are less effectively checked and executive power can be extended by establishing direct links with the populace (Weyland 2013). The populist revival in Latin America in the twenty-first century, for example, is strongly connected to the political limitations and institutional weaknesses of the countries in the region (Roberts 2007).

Positive features of democracy, such as the rule of law, the protection of property rights, and checks against political leaders, of course appeal to investors (Archer et al. 2007; Balkan 1992; Beaulieu et al. 2012; Biglaiser and Staats 2012; Brewer and Rivoli 1990; Jensen et al. 2012; Saiegh 2005; Schultz and Weingast 2003; Sussman and Yafeh 2000; Stasavage 2003) and send positive signals about the sovereign credibility of a left-wing government. But does deterioration or strengthening of democracy affect the sovereign credibility? Deterioration may be a warning sign to investors about future policy directions and property rights protection. But the strengthening process can also involve instability or even chaos disruptive to the economy (Dahrendorf 1990; Haggard and Kaufman 1995; Przeworski et al. 2000). As both can affect sovereign credibility, I investigate how improvements and deteriorations in democracy affect sovereign credibility.

Financial market experts note that corruption is a major political risk, especially in emerging markets, and that it significantly increases policy uncertainty. Democracies are not wholly free of corruption, but they are at least more transparent in their policymaking compared to non-democracies, and their political leaders are accountable for their decisions, which reduces the probability of corruption (Bailey and Valenzuela 1997; Bardhan 1997; Laffont and Meleu 2001; LaPalombara 1994; Lederman et al. 2005; Linz 1990; Linz and Stepan 1996a, 1996b; Persson et al. 1997; Rose-Ackerman 1999; Tanzi 1998). Furthermore, attempts to achieve consensus through public deliberation help investors more accurately predict future policy directions (Elster 1998; Fung 2003).

Using statistical methods in Chapter 4 to address potential endogeneity problems, I find that democratic institutions are associated with better credit ratings for left-wing governments. I also test the effects of government transparency in policy-related information and find a significant and positive association between transparency and credit ratings for left-wing governments but not for their right-leaning counterparts. Analysis further shows that a democratic transition has a negative association with right-leaning governments' credit ratings, but not with leftist governments'. A deterioration in institutional quality significantly undermines the credibility of all governments. The negative impact does, however, seem to be greater for left-wing governments.

Venezuela and Peru illustrate the contrasting market responses to a deterioration in democracy under left-wing and right-wing populist governments. Both countries chose populist political leaders, but President Chávez of Venezuela represented strong left-wing populism whereas President Fujimori in Peru pursued market-friendly policies, often termed neopopulism. Both countries experienced a significant deterioration in democracy under those presidents. Chávez revised the constitution to extend his stay in power and circumvented the political institutions intended to check the president. Peru experienced a presidential coup, with the president closing the legislature and the courts. Despite this severe democratic deterioration, the market's punishment of Venezuela was harsher, as investors perceived the deterioration of democracy to be a greater threat under the Chávez administration than under the Fujimori government.

Checks imposed on political leaders sends a positive signal to investors about sovereign credibility. The nationalization of Yacimientos Petrolíferos Fiscales (YPF) in Argentina clearly shows that lack of political constraints undermines market confidence. The Argentine government's decision to nationalize the private oil company in 2012 shocked the markets not only due to the implied disdain for private investment, but also because Argentina had no effective checks on the left-wing government's actions undermining private property rights. However, while the markets favor a certain degree of political checks against the executive, excessive political constraints may also undermine market confidence, particularly when a left-wing government is in power. This is because markets may be concerned that left-wing policies they dislike may become irreversible, or that any market-friendly policy initiatives proposed by a reform-minded executive may get blocked by opposing actors.

Chapter 5 systemically examines how the level of political constraints affects investor confidence, and whether such signaling effects depend on government partisanship. I argue that political constraints on the executive that are either too rigid or too relaxed both undermine sovereign credibility of left-wing governments, whereas a moderate level of political constraints is more likely to send a positive signal to the markets. As seen from the findings in Chapter 4, although investors prefer to see a certain degree of institutional checks against a left-wing government rather than no constraints, flexibility in policymaking is also important for investors.

I conduct statistical analyses following on from these theoretical arguments and find that within the developing world there is a statistically significant, inverted U-shaped relationship between the degree of political constraints and a country's sovereign credit rating for leftist governments. More checks on a left-wing government tend to increase its credibility, but these effects become less pronounced when the checks become too rigid.[11] Additional tests show that such a trend is particularly true when a leftist executive pursues financial market liberalization. For right-wing governments, the results suggest that sovereign credibility is not significantly associated with the degree of political constraints. The financial market experts interviewed reveal that they perceive too much political constraint as undermining economic development. In particular, they report that policy gridlock in emerging market countries is more worrisome than in developed countries, because it often undermines liberal reform policies and thus increases policy uncertainty.

India is the country most frequently mentioned by the interviewees as having problems with excessive political constraints. Its coalition government is very tightly constrained, and the market's response to coalition politics in a left-wing government is more negative than in a non-left government. I examine two coalition governments in India: that of the United Front (UF) in 1996–98 and that of the National Democratic Alliance (NDA) in its early years in power (1999–2001). Both administrations had strongly reform-minded executives,[12] but each had to deal with vested interests and the internal conflicts created by coalition members who opposed economic reform. However, the coalition politics that caused greater concern among investors were those of the leftist UF government, rather than those of the center-right NDA government. Similar to the findings in the quantitative analysis, the case of India shows that the negative effects of extreme political constraints on credibility are particularly strong for left-wing governments.

Chapter 6 examines the effects of international institutions and government partisanship on sovereign credibility. Adopting an IMF program is likely to have an important influence on market perceptions, because IMF programs impose significant constraints on the borrowing government and shape policy outcomes.

I argue that adopting an IMF program benefits left-wing governments more than others. The IMF emerged at the end of the Second World War to maintain exchange rates and promote freer international trade. In the 1970s, when the old exchange regime collapsed, the IMF began to focus on balance of payments problems and became more involved in the developing world's domestic economic policies. In return for an IMF loan, a borrowing country must accept the IMF's conditions – a set of neoliberal policies that usually involve fiscal austerity, privatization, and trade liberalization (Vreeland 2003, 2007).

The IMF's enforcement powers enable it to reduce funding if countries sign an IMF agreement but later reverse their policy direction. Reneging countries also risk damaging their reputation in international markets (Stone 2002: 11). Thus, proponents of IMF conditionality believe that IMF programs act as a signaling device for investors, because the signing government signals its intention to implement the agreed economic reforms (Copelovitch 2010: 17; Marchesi and Thomas 1999). Such government pronouncements carry greater credibility, because investors expect that the IMF will effectively supervise the reforms.

While signing an agreement with the IMF can result in ideological costs for leftist governments, IMF intervention tends to be particularly effective for such governments in generating investor confidence. The IMF's conditions closely align with right-wing economic rhetoric – tight government budgets, limited social spending, privatization, and deregulation – so they are fundamentally incompatible with traditional leftist policy preferences. It is for exactly that reason that signing an IMF agreement can effectively boost investor confidence in a left-wing government. When a leftist leader agrees to accept IMF conditionality, investors are likely to take the signing as a decision of more serious consideration.

Using statistical analysis to address potential selection bias, I find that IMF programs have a positive influence on the credit ratings of leftist governments, whereas no such beneficial effects are found for their non-leftist counterparts. Hungary's experience in the early 1990s further confirms this. During its transition to a market economy, the Hungarian government borrowed money from the IMF, but the loan made to the center-right Hungarian Democratic Forum led to a downgrade in sovereign ratings, despite the loan having been intended to ease the transition. When the socialist government that followed signed an IMF agreement, however, the signing sent a positive signal to the markets about the country's sovereign credibility.

Contribution of the book

This book highlights political institutions as an important signal of sovereign credibility, the effectiveness of which depends crucially on government partisanship. Rival hypotheses in the study of sovereign credibility have largely focused on its economic determinants, contending that economic conditions and policy differences of borrowing governments – such as economic growth, inflation, fiscal balance, external debt balance, foreign reserves, trade balance, and investment levels – are important determinants of sovereign credibility.[13] However, the decision to default on sovereign debt involves a political decision rather than a decision based purely on economic grounds. Due to various political considerations, a debtor country often decides to default on sovereign debt, even though it has the ability to repay (Tomz 2007: 16; Reinhart and Rogoff 2009). International markets do not have effective enforcement mechanism to force a government to repay debt (Eaton et al. 1986), which makes it important to pay attention to political aspects, as willingness to pay is largely based on political and institutional factors.

The literature on the political determinants of sovereign credibility has thus focused on political institutions,[14] but earlier studies do not consider the effects of institutions conditional on domestic political conditions. My study shows that when important economic and political conditions are taken into consideration, political institutions play an important role in building credibility, and the effects are conditional on government partisanship. As explained by the idea of Nixon-Goes-to-China, left-wing governments benefit more from constraining institutions than right-wing governments do, due to the greater credibility problem they face to begin with.

One of the key aspects of the Nixon-Goes-to-China argument is that voters' *perceptions* matter. In a domestic political context, the Nixon framework focuses primarily on the signaling effect of policy proposals on credibility gains and on political support. The assumption is that the United States' policy to open up to China would have faced greater opposition had Hubert Humphrey, rather than the staunchly anticommunist Nixon, proposed it. More generally, political support for a policy proposal depends on both the policy and the policymaker who proposes it. The more atypical the policy proposal, the more credible the signal it sends to the public.

However, although frequently employed, the concept has rarely been tested rigorously, with only a few studies providing a theoretical explanation of the inherent paradox.[15] According to these studies, partisan politicians have better information about the state of the world and economic fundamentals than the general public, and thus are better able to judge the desirability of certain policies. The public, without knowing the exact preferences of politicians, must then infer whether a politician's proposed policy is in its interests. If, for example, a governing left-wing party proposes a strongly right-wing policy, then the public will think that it is doing so either because the government's private information suggests that such a policy is in the national interest, or because the policy is in accordance with the government's natural ideological tendency. Ultimately, the public will infer that the new policy must be a good policy for the objective welfare of the country, because a leftist government would not pursue extreme-right policies because of its ideological tendency. The credibility of such reforms increases when they are relatively extensive and rare (Cukierman and Tommasi 1998).

The Nixon framework is highly relevant to international financial markets because these markets are perhaps even more dependent on signals and perceptions than domestic politics. In analyzing the dynamics of institutional constraints and domestic political conditions, such as who governs, the Nixon idea suggests that the mismatch inherent in a left-wing government's pursuing prudent and market-friendly economic management makes a left-wing government's submission to institutional arrangements that promote such behavior all the more credible. This book is the first to apply this idea to the relationship between politicians and foreign investors in international financial relations. Moreover, no other study has tested the hypothesis using multiple methods of statistical data analysis, case studies, and interviews, as this book does.

The history of international financial markets is replete with stories of market panic and contagion leading to significant consequences nationally and globally, economically and politically, affecting tens of thousands of people's lives. This book examines the interplay between institutions and partisanship and its effects on market perceptions. Earlier work on institutions and partisanship has tended to focus on how institutions shape the behavior and subsequent policy outcomes of left- and right-wing governments, rather than on how institutions influence market perceptions of such governments differently, even when their actual policies may not be that different. Furthermore, earlier studies largely treat institutional settings as static, rather than taking into account the dynamic nature of institutional arrangements and how such dynamics affect market behavior. The discussion which follows demonstrates that investor perceptions are often formed by referring to partisan labels rather than to actual policies, and that institutional arrangements and their changes can serve as a powerful signaling mechanism for left-wing governments' sovereign credibility.

Some scholars have proposed that institutional constraints, such as the IMF and democratic institutions, may provide signals to markets, but they disagree about the effectiveness of signals. Results have actually been all over the map, with some scholars suggesting a positive signal, some a negative signal, and others finding no effect. My accounting for the differential effects of institutional signals across left and right governments is an original contribution, which solves the puzzling mixed bag of effects. Only left-wing governments can send a credible signal by accepting institutional constraints, because they have greater credibility problems regardless of their actual policies – what I refer to as a brand name effect. Earlier studies' neglect of the contingent nature of institutional signals has been unjustified, given that government partisanship is a fundamental aspect of domestic politics.

Conclusions: embracing constraints to build credibility

Financial globalization is not a new phenomenon, but today's market integration has reached unprecedented depth and breath. Developed countries have been actively participating in the financial globalization process, but developing countries are increasingly taking over. One of the fundamental economic problems that developing countries face is difficulty in mobilizing sufficient funds for investment. Further integration into global financial markets can thus provide developing countries with great benefits. Foreign capital can support domestic investment above the level that domestic savings would allow in recipient countries, aiding the development of the financial system. Financial globalization can, however, also bring market turbulence and contagion that accompany political and social consequences. Building market confidence and earning credibility are of great importance for governments seeking to attract foreign capital, because perceptions shape market behavior. With the rapid movement of international capital and the increased diversity of investor bases, perceived credibility plays a primary role in influencing investment flows.

Market participants need confidence in the direction of future policy before making investments, but it is often not easy for developing countries to provide policy certainty. Here, I show that the effects of the democratic system, a moderate level of political constraints, and IMF conditionality are contingent on the market perception of an important domestic political condition – the governing party – so that they allow left-wing governments to improve their policy credibility in the eyes of international investors.

The findings in this book suggest that the signals from so-called best-practice institutions about sovereign credibility are in fact crucial for maintaining market stability, which is important for economic growth. Informal institutions may reduce transaction costs, and such informal norms and practices may facilitate the workings of formal institutions. They cannot, however, send as strong a signal as formal institutions do, largely because they are less visible to outsiders. Furthermore, investor confidence is built on more fundamental and stable arrangements, rather than on those that are ad hoc or relational.

More importantly, this book contributes to the literature by analyzing the effects of political institutions and their changes on credibility that is contingent on government partisanship, an important political condition that shapes the financial market perception and behavior. The literature on the connection between financial markets and politics suggests that political factors in fact significantly explain emerging market crises (Bacmann and Bolliger 2001; Barber et al. 2001; Boni and Womack 2002; Drazen 1999; Martinez and Santiso 2003; Santiso 1999). However, there has been little effort to systematically analyze the dynamics between institutions, their changes, and government partisanship in influencing market perception.

The findings of this book also highlight the role of international institutions in international financial markets. Previous studies on the IMF have shown mixed findings on the catalytic effects of IMF programs. Some doubt that the IMF consistently helps countries in economic trouble. The discussion here shows that the IMF can help left-wing governments in economic crisis by reducing adverse market reactions, such as speculative attacks, and market disturbance caused by investor panic. By restoring market confidence, IMF programs can be a catalyst, enabling left-wing governments to improve their access to the financial markets. Left-wing governments may also be able to use the IMF programs to implement domestically unpopular economic reform.

Ironically, embracing institutional constraints may allow a leftist government greater policy autonomy in the long term without threatening the market. Traditionally left-wing governments emphasize employment, redistribution, and welfare policies for the less privileged. These qualities may be useful in addressing economic and social problems in many societies, but are often unwelcome by international investors. With the increasing criticism of the neoliberal economic order that has largely shaped the global economic system in recent decades, such leftist ideology may provide an alternative way to address economic and social problems ascribed to it. The findings presented in this book suggest that such ideological beliefs can in fact go hand in hand with stable market conditions, but only when a left-wing government has strong institutional foundations that constrain and commit its political leaders, enabling market participants to build confidence in them.

Notes

1 For the purpose of this argument, a left-wing party is defined as a party exhibiting labor-friendly and redistribution-oriented policies in its party identity as indicated by its name, description, and/or platforms. Although some studies argue that political parties in developing countries do not display the typical left-right distinctions shown in developed countries and that partisan cycle models are not applicable to developing countries, the parties still exhibit characteristics of more labor-friendly and more business-friendly policies. For example, scholars such as Broz and Weymouth (2013), Pinto (2013), and Vaaler et al. (2005, 2006) argue that a broader distinction of left-right is valid in developing countries around the world, and support their claim with empirical findings.

2 Work by Campello (2015), Drake (1991), Roberts (2014), and Stokes (2001) has addressed the question of when opportunistic behavior by left-wing governments in Latin America is likely, with diverse findings regarding the causes and directions of policy switches.

3 Populism has many definitions. Here I use the term to indicate a personalized political leadership that directly reaches the populace by circumventing representative institutions and pursues redistribution-oriented policies that are often manifested in private property expropriations and default on sovereign debt (Dornbusch and Edwards 1991; Roberts 2002; Eden et al. 2012).

4 Related work by Broz and Weymouth (2013) has shown that partisanship affects business owners' perceptions of property rights. Business owners view them as more secure under a right-wing government than under a left-wing government.

5 For example, Bodea and Higashijima (2015), Iversen (1999), Kaplan (2013), Pandya (2014), and Pinto (2013).

6 This was the case even though Lula was in fact a beneficiary of the favorable economic environment, as also noted by one investor that I interviewed (Interview 2).

7 Further tests used other measures of sovereign credibility, such as bond spread data from J.P. Morgan's Emerging Market Bond Index (EMBI) and credit default swap data, but the data coverage is too limited to yield meaningful comparisons of leftist with other governments.

8 Refer to Beck et al. (2001) for further details. This variable is recoded to classify centrist and rightist governments as non-leftist.

9 I referred to the data of Baker and Greene (2011) (which is based on Coppedge [1997], Wiesehomeier and Benoit [2009], and Pop-Eleches [2009]); Benoit and Laver (2006); Coppedge (1997); Stone (2002); and various other secondary sources, including encyclopedias and handbooks of political parties, academic journals, and monographs on different regions and countries. Further details on coding are provided in Chapter 3.

10 Further details about the interviews are provided in Appendix 1.

11 The quantitative findings in Chapter 5 suggest that the credibility declines beyond the degree of political constraints around the 75th percentile.

12 Nooruddin (2011) states that coalition governments better achieved economic reform and growth performance than the previous majority governments.

13 For example, Afonso et al. (2011), Cantor and Packer (1996), and Gelos et al. (2011).

14 For example, Archer et al. (2007), Jensen (2006), North and Weingast (1989), and Saiegh (2005).

15 Cukierman and Tommasi (1998) and Cowen and Sutter (1998) explain this paradox theoretically. Schultz (2003) and Bagashka and Stone (2013) incorporate the Nixon paradox into their explanations of peacemaking and exchange rate commitment, respectively.

2 Sovereign credibility in global financial markets

Perception is everything.

– A Senior Vice President of an investment bank on the importance of perceptions in financial markets

The fast and intense integration of the world economy has made building credibility more important than ever. Greater market integration allows borrowing countries to tap a larger pool of foreign capital and allows international investors to diversify their investments. The increasing scope of transactions, however, makes it difficult for investors to see the full picture regarding the condition of every country where they might invest because of the costs associated with gathering and processing information (Dornbusch et al. 2000: 183). Greater market integration makes the option of "exit" easier than ever for investors, so that when faced with uncertainty, they can simply decide to withdraw their investment and move elsewhere – which is often an easier choice for them than to raise their "voices" (Santiso 2003: 18), that is, express their dissatisfaction through various channels.

Investor confidence builds on perceived risks and credibility. As one financial market expert resolutely said, "perception is everything" in international financial markets. To improve perceptions of their credibility, governments in the developing world need to maintain macroeconomic stability, low inflation, and sustainable growth. More importantly, they need to convince investors that they offer a stable and safe market environment and investment profitability with manageable risks. Strong financial systems and regulations, credible contract enforcement and well-supervised financial institutions, a sound and stable environment for macroeconomic policy that minimizes any vulnerabilities in financial and monetary policy – these are the attributes of such environments (Summers 2000: 8).

At the base of such a credible and stable policy environment lie political institutions. Prior scholarship has discussed the role of political institutions in influencing financial markets. They shape the economic institutions that govern market activities and economic outcomes (Acemoglu et al. 2005). Financial markets thus respond to political institutions that constrain the executive, because such institutions help to keep their investments safe from political manipulation (Sobel 2002). Institutions that commit political leaders to honor agreements and adhere to the rule of law build market confidence (Sobel 2002: 41). Therefore, institutions that are conducive to market-friendly policies and protect private property may reduce political risk and policy uncertainty, ultimately increasing sovereign credibility.

Earlier published studies have, however, largely neglected two important aspects of the relationship between institutions and financial markets. The first is that the credibility-building effects of institutions depend on domestic political conditions. The signaling effects are not likely to be the same for all types of governments due to markets' overall different perceptions of governments of different types. The Nixon framework predicts that the effects of institutions should help left-wing governments in developing countries that have tended to lack market confidence. A party's label plays a signaling role in international markets so that when all things are assumed to be equal, left-leaning parties suffer greater credibility problems. Another important aspect that has received little scholarly attention is that any significant *changes* in the institutional landscape of a country may have a particularly strong impact on the credibility of left-leaning governments. Therefore, improvements or deteriorations in institutional quality, or joining an international organization that significantly influences government policies, are all likely to have strong signaling effects. That is because changes generate greater uncertainty about future policy directions when a left-leaning government is in power.

One way to measure the conditional effects of institutions on sovereign credibility is to analyze the institutional effects on sovereign credit ratings. Sovereign ratings are important for several reasons. They are provided by rating agencies and intend to reflect market sentiment towards different political and economic environments across countries. They also significantly influence financial market behavior because national governments are often the largest issuers in international financial markets, and also because government ratings affect the ratings assigned to other borrowers of the same nationality (Cantor and Packer 1996: 38). Sovereign ratings influence bond yields and stock market indicators, as well as foreign direct investment (FDI) (Albuquerque 2003; Kaminsky and Schmukler 2002).

Due to a greater integration and diversification of their investor bases, individual countries are exposed to greater external shocks and instability. In this chapter, I first address the characteristics of international financial markets that are prone to market fluctuations. I specifically discuss the brand name effect and the negativity bias (or negativity effect) – whereby investors tend to react more sharply to negative events than to positive ones – and their influence on market perceptions. I then discuss the role of domestic political and international institutions in influencing investors' perceptions in this context. The chapter ends with an explanation of the role of sovereign credit ratings as a means of estimating sovereign credibility.

Financial market integration and market volatility

Sovereign borrowing via government bonds has become an increasingly significant sector in global financial markets. Sovereign bonds are both an important source of finance for governments and a central part of large institutional investors' portfolios (Mosley 2003: 18). Sovereign bonds are the foundation of most fixed-income securities markets in both developed and developing worlds. They finance fiscal deficits, but trading them also promotes the development of securities markets and ultimately economic growth. They help to define a benchmark yield curve and to determine the overall credit spread (World Bank 2001). The yield curve for government securities is an important guide to the future movement of inflation and interest rates. It further determines the benchmark for the valuation of other fixed-income securities (World Bank 2001).

Private capital flow into bonds has dramatically increased in developing countries over the years. In the 1970s, when relatively few bonds were being issued, bank lending played a dominant role in the developing world. Today, the structure of bond markets in emerging market countries is similar to that in developed countries. Domestic and international bonds are issued by governments, corporations, and financial institutions. Most emerging market countries rely on government bonds. Net private capital flow to bonds in developing countries has steadily increased over the years, so that within just the ten-year period from 2001 to 2010, it rose from US$15.7 to 111.4 billion, almost a tenfold increase (World Bank 2012). Such a rate of increase in capital flow to bonds is remarkable compared to the increase in other types of investment such as FDI, which increased from US$158.9 to 506.1 billion over the same period (World Bank 2012). Bond trading has become a major component of international capital flows to developing countries. With the expansion of bond markets in developing countries, emerging market debt has become a separate category of investment.

With these changes, the collective action problem among investors has become more salient. In earlier times, sovereign debt was largely funded by a rather homogeneous group of lenders through bank loans and other syndicated loans so that the collective action problem was not a serious concern. Since the 1990s, however, there has been a change in the composition of international sovereign borrowing away from syndicated and bank loans toward tradable securities. The change has made coordination among creditors more difficult, because the number of creditors has increased and their interests have diversified (Krueger 2002).

Developing countries are finding international investors playing a larger role in their sovereign debt markets. Figure 2.1 shows that the shares of foreign investors in sovereign debt markets in emerging market countries have increased over the years. This trend is universal across all of the emerging markets that are developing their sovereign debt markets to attract foreign capital. Beyond that, the proportion of private investors among the foreign investors is increasing. In 2012, for example, about 80 percent of the total foreign holdings of emerging market debt were held by asset managers and other private investors (Arslanalp and Tsuda 2014: 19).

As foreign investors become more important, the possibility of abrupt capital outflow has become even more salient in the contemporary bond market. One of the major challenges posed by an increasing share of foreign investors in sovereign debt markets is that the borrowing countries become more sensitive

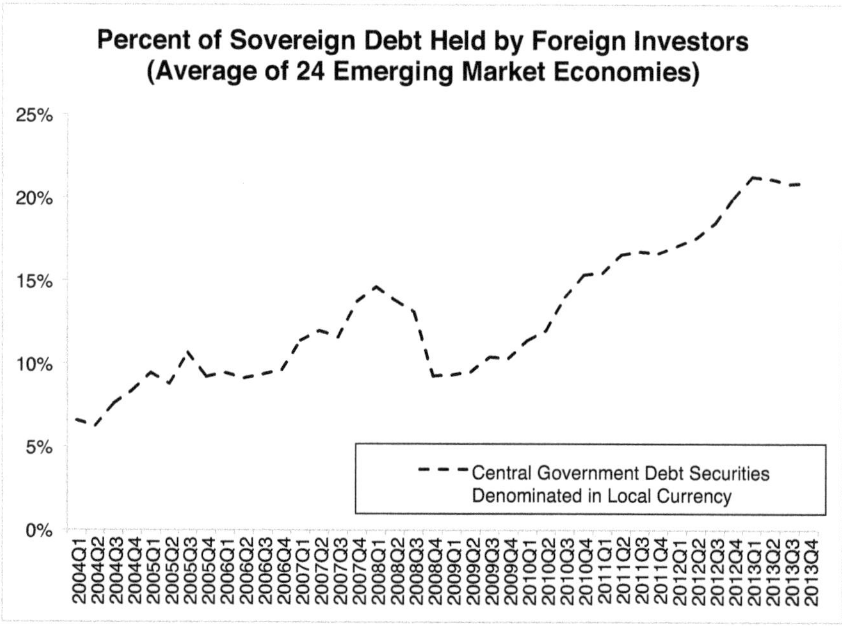

Figure 2.1 Proportion of sovereign debt held by foreign investors from 2004–2013
Source: Arslanalp and Tsuda (2014)

to external funding conditions (Calvo and Talvi 2005). As countries become more and more interconnected, market turbulence in one country almost instantly affects others. Foreign investors, especially foreign private investors, tend to be a significant source of market volatility, especially in times of economic difficulties, given the diversity of assets they invest in (Arslanalp and Tsuda 2014). They are typically less willing to roll over and more likely to sell and exit the market when a country is perceived to be in trouble and policy directions are hard to predict (Broner et al. 2013). Foreign investors tend to emphasize sound, safe, and robust market infrastructure and are sensitive to risks. Unlike domestic creditors, they have few resources to rely on if a government fails to honor its debt (Cole and Kehoe 1997: 21). As a result, with the increased mobility of capital, international investors may simply choose to withdraw their money if they become concerned about potential default.

In this regard, any political or policy uncertainty that can result in possible losses for investors can have a negative impact on a country's perceived creditworthiness. With the increasing internationalization of bond transactions, governments face greater challenges to satisfy the higher standards of foreign investors. In managing their portfolios, foreign investors can make national markets more vulnerable and volatile by abruptly withdrawing their investment (World Bank 2001: 21). As a consequence, reducing uncertainty and building sovereign credibility is an important task for borrowing countries. The fact that major emerging market countries have been seeing increasing shares of foreign investors in their debt markets proves that they have mostly managed to improve their credibility through sound and prudent management of their macroeconomic environment. Foreign investment has increased in tandem with improved credibility (Arslanalp and Tsuda 2014: 20). But most developing countries remain relatively risky, and one of the main risks is the political one.

Political risk in sovereign debt markets: perceived willingness to pay

Sovereign debt is generally considered to be the most secure type of debt because governments have the ability to take control of foreign currency reserves and print money. However, sovereign bonds are also subject to various types of risks. For example, investors in sovereign debt markets face interest rate and inflation risks. As investors often make a long-term commitment to a fixed nominal interest rate, they are subject to shorter-term changes in interest rates or inflation. Exchange rates can also pose risks for investors. In the case of foreign currency-denominated sovereign debt, a currency crisis can be a risk for investors, as a devaluation leads to heavy losses for local currency-denominated bonds.

Beyond all that, there is political risk. Political risk refers to the possibility that political decisions or events in a country will affect the business climate in such a way that investors will lose money or not make as much money as they expected when the investment is made (Kobrin 1982). Political risk constrains the property rights of foreign investors and can cause losses. Some examples are confiscation of property without adequate compensation, damage to property or action against personnel, government interference with the terms of privately negotiated contracts, breach of contract, adverse regulatory changes, changes in government that affect the legal system, and even civil unrest (Haendel 1979; MIGA 2013).

Political risk always ranks as one of the most important risks associated with foreign investment in developing countries. Surveys show that political risk is becoming more important each year in the assessment of investment risks (MIGA 2013). More specifically, uncertainty about the political leadership in national and international markets is pointed to as an important political risk that limits growth. Investors are most concerned about adverse changes in regulations, breach of contract, transfer and convertibility restrictions, and expropriation (MIGA 2013: 21).

Political risk in sovereign debt markets largely concerns the government's willingness to pay. Generally, national governments have an incentive to repay their debts on time to retain access to credit markets in the future, but domestic political considerations can sometimes tempt borrowing governments to think of abrogating their responsibility for repaying foreign debt. As the government may want to use scarce resources to obtain political support, domestic political conditions are important determinants of willingness to pay. It may decide to default on foreign debt at the expense of the economy's reputation, even when it has the ability to pay. The international markets have no effective enforcement mechanism which can force a government to repay debt. Sovereign bonds are backed by the "faith and credit" of the issuing government, not by physical or financial assets (World Bank 2001). This makes paying attention to politics an important precaution for investors in sovereign debt, because willingness to pay is often a function of political and institutional factors in a debtor country.

The concerns about willingness to pay apply to both developed and developing countries, especially since the recent European debt crisis has made investors jittery about political uncertainty in developed countries. Still, investors tend to be more optimistic about industrialized democracies, whereas they experience more problems with willingness to pay in developing countries. While examples abound of countries that have defaulted on their sovereign debts despite their ability to service them, Ecuador's decision to default in 2008 is a well-known example. Despite its ability to repay the debt, President Correa, a left-wing politician, decided to default on the country's sovereign debt. He said that the debt holders were "monsters" and declared the debt issued by previous governments illegal (*Reuters*, December 12, 2008). At that time, Ecuador's economy was doing well, with good economic growth rates driven by high commodity prices. The decision was predominantly political, based on the president's ideological and political position.

Overall, developing countries are considered as presenting greater default risk, which is still the major element that differentiates their government debt from that issued by developed countries. Politics is more important in developing countries because governments exert a greater influence over the economy than in developed countries (Interview 19). In particular, when the political power is highly centralized, it becomes difficult to predict outcomes, because even though the government may have a long-term plan, it can change the plan overnight without warning (Interviews 3, 14, 16, 23). Since political risk is one of the most difficult risks to predict (Association for Financial Professionals Risk Survey 2013), developing countries bear the burden of being considered risky for investors because the outcomes are often harder to predict in those countries.

The brand name effect, negativity bias, and institutions

Exacerbating such market suspicions is the fact that investors find it more difficult to get access to information in developing countries. International investors in particular face incomplete and asymmetric access to information, which is an inherent aspect of international relations. Every investor I have interviewed agrees that policy uncertainty is their biggest concern when investing in a developing country, because such countries usually lack transparency in their policymaking process and do not provide reliable economic data. Experienced institutional investors may be able to make educated guesses, but they still know much less about the political situation than local residents. These factors increase the international borrowing costs of developing countries. Faced with uncertainty, investor decisions are inevitably influenced by perceptions because of the diversification of investment allocation and information asymmetry.

A governing party's label is likely to be an important cue for investors in this context, who want to minimize information acquisition costs and use it as a shortcut in predicting policy directions. When it comes to sovereign default, left-wing governments, particularly in developing countries, are expected to default more often than other governments. This is because investors tend to associate them with a potential unwillingness to pay and reckless management of the economy. Left-wing governments, as a result, tend to suffer greater credibility problems.[1] The brand name effect suggests that a party's label influences international investors' perceptions regardless of what policies the party actually pursues.

For leftist governments, this brand name effect is reinforced by a negativity bias. The finance literature has discussed the psychology of market participants, and one influential argument is that markets tend to be more responsive to negative than to positive news. The psychology literature documents that bad news, bad emotions, and bad feedback have greater impact on individuals than good ones, and bad information is more thoroughly processed than good information (Baumeister et al. 2001). If, for example, good and bad events happened in the same intensity, bad ones prevail over good ones. That seems to be the innate predisposition of human beings (Baumeister et al. 2001). This idea of a "negativity bias" or "negativity effect" suggests that individuals regard the potential costs to be larger than potential gain when there is risk, and that negative information tends to have greater impact than positive information on overall evaluation (Peeters and Czapinski 1990; Akhtar et al. 2011). In other words, "bad is stronger than good" (Baumeister et al. 2001: 323).

The finance literature has discussed such negativity effects in market behavior. For example, Suleman (2012) examined the effects of political news on financial market indicators and showed that both good news and bad news influence market indicators, but bad news tends to have greater impact on volatility. Similarly, Beetsma et al. (2013) examined how news affected European sovereign bond markets during the crisis and found that markets respond only to bad news. Akhtar et al. (2011) showed that negative news about consumer sentiment has greater effects on stock returns.

Combined with the brand name effect, the negativity effect implies that investors are likely to act more sharply when a party with a leftist label comes to power than when a right-leaning party does. Still, the market response to a leftist leader in a developing country and in a developed country is different. Then what makes the difference in risk profiles between developed and developing economies? Investors point out that they have trust in developed economies because they are more deeply involved in the world economy, which compels them to act prudently. More importantly, at the fundamental level, such governments have institutional arrangements and systems which tend to ensure that regardless of who comes to power, the established consensus about how business should be carried out persists (Interviews 3, 14, 16, 23).

The economic policies of many developing countries tend to depend significantly on individual political leaders, because such countries often lack institutions which shield policymaking from arbitrary political manipulation. Such countries may perform well economically if they are lucky enough to have capable and dedicated leaders who successfully manage the economy. The trouble comes when a leader without the capacity to govern prudently comes to power and acts arbitrarily or seeks rent in the absence of institutional checks on the power. Financial market experts make the point that if a country has well-established political institutions that support market-friendly policies, it will tend to be able to maintain more stable economic growth regardless of who governs (Interviews 20, 24). This point has been recognized by scholars who study institutions in developing countries. Thus, for example, the governments in Africa have come to see that the economic growth of Asian countries was possible thanks to the rise of rule-based institutional arrangements (Diamond 2000). They understand that such arrangements reduce political risk by increasing transparency in policymaking.

Institutions as a contingent signal

Domestic political institutions and international institutions can serve as strong signals to international markets. Political institutions shape the incentives of political leaders and influence the distribution of political power, which in turn shapes economic institutions and the resource distribution (Acemoglu et al. 2005). Institutions make certain policy outcomes more probable and thus make policy directions more predictable (Cukierman et al. 1992; Weingast 1995; Williamson 1994). Political and international institutions that constrain the arbitrary actions of politicians signal to the market that investment will be less exposed to political manipulation. Market-friendly claims made by political leaders become more reliable when there are institutions that constrain them.

A financial market expert has opined that when making investment decisions about emerging market countries, ultimately the most important consideration is the political institutions. In an emerging market economy that needs to implement structural reforms, for example, one cannot decide how the reforms will unfold simply by looking at the economic aspects. The question is whether the country has economic institutions which can manage the reform, and the answer comes from looking at the political institutions (Interview 24).

Much has been published about the effects of institutions on investment decisions, but an important aspect that has largely been neglected is the question of how the effects of institutions may depend on domestic political conditions. Institutions that constrain political leaders and commit them to prudent management of the economy may be able to mitigate the brand name effect and the negativity effect for a leftist government. The greater the concentration of power, the greater the incentive for political leaders to renege on their policy promises. Strong institutions are one way to dilute that incentive. When investors are concerned that unconstrained leftist politicians may act opportunistically for political purposes, the outcome they fear is populist policies. Democratic political institutions are thought to promote policy credibility because there is normally greater transparency in policymaking and voters can hold political leaders to their policy promises (Haggard 2000; Przeworski and Stokes 1999; Schultz and Weingast 2003). Although some people argue that political business cycles increase policy uncertainty in democracies, the institutional checks and the rule of law play an important role in building credibility. In addition, democratic institutions are believed to give greater credibility in making agreements with other governments in the international arena, and such agreements also reassure international investors (Cowhey 1993; Fearon 1994; Gaubatz 1996; Leeds 1999). Democratic institutions have a natural affinity for economic freedom and secure property rights because the conditions needed for economic development are the conditions needed for democracy (Olson 1993). These characteristics of democracy are likely to be a more effective credibility-building mechanism for left-wing governments than for their non-leftist counterparts.

While it is generally agreed that such a "democratic advantage" exists, it is also widely known that too much political constraint on political leaders in democracies can actually lead to policy gridlock. Furthermore, although a system of checks and balances may provide policy stability by making policy changes more difficult (Tsebelis 2002), policy stability does not automatically correspond to more market-friendly policies for investors. Therefore, political constraints may be perceived as desirable as long as the policies they stabilize are favored by investors (Hallerberg and von Hagen 1999; Jensen 2006; Perotti and Kontopoulos 2002; Roubini and Sachs 1989a; Tsebelis 1995, 2002). Too much political constraint can be a particularly significant problem for left-wing governments, especially when they try to pursue market-oriented reform, because investors may worry that reform may get stuck because of policy gridlock.

Changes in institutional arrangements

Another point that has received little scholarly attention is how changes in a country's institutional arrangements affect market perceptions and how the effects depend on domestic political conditions. Earlier studies document the causes and consequences of institutional change, and the advance or retreat of democracy is one of the topics that has received extensive scholarly attention. Much research has been devoted to explaining the causes of such changes and how the changes affect economic outcomes, such as market liberalization and trade (Boix 2003; Giavazzi and Tabellini 2005; Milner and Mukherjee 2009; Papaioannou and Siourounis 2008; Persson 2005; Persson and Tabellini 2006; Rodrik and Wacziarg 2005; Stokes 2001; Weyland 2002). While the influential work by North and Weingast (1989) has documented how the rise of the system of checks and balances improved the sovereign credibility in England, surprisingly little attention has been paid to the consequences of institutional changes on investment decisions.[2]

Any changes that undermine the effectiveness of constraining institutions may have an impact on a government's credibility. Furthermore, negative institutional changes are likely to have a greater impact on credibility than positive changes. This is again due to the negativity bias. Thus, for example, a development strengthening democracy may influence credibility, but a breakdown of democracy is likely to have a far greater impact on sovereign credibility. Such effects are likely to be greater for leftist governments than for their right-leaning counterparts.

Joining an international organization can be an important signal for credibility, particularly when the international organization has great influence on domestic politics. A group of studies documented how international rules can affect a country's policies by influencing domestic political actors (Duffield 1992; McElroy 1992; Nadelmann 1990; Nye 1987). The General Agreement on Tariffs and Trade, for example, led to new rules developed in member countries (Cortell and Davis 1996). Government officials can even use international rules to their own advantage in domestic politics (McElroy 1992; Strange and Chang 1993). Strange and Chang (1993: 243) use the example of leftist governments in Spain and Greece who used International Labour Organization standards to back up their policies.

International institutions may also influence domestic politics by complementing domestic institutions. For example, investment treaties typically involve dispute settlement mechanisms that influence domestic politics. Investor claims often challenge executive decisions and thus work as an additional check on the executive and allow more information to be released about the executive's decisions. Such a constraint is important for countries that lack effective checks against the executive (Caddel and Jensen 2014). Such treaties address developing countries' lack of governance institutions and enforce the rule of law. An investment treaty then takes up the role of domestic institutions (Rosendorff and Shin 2015; Salacuse 2010). A country with credible domestic institutions and links with international institutions may look even more attractive as an investment destination (Ginsburg 2005; Tobin and Rose-Ackerman 2011).

In this regard, the IMF stands out as an institution that can work as an effective signal. The IMF binds political leaders because it has greater enforcement powers than other international institutions. IMF conditionality, a set of economic and financial policies prescribed by the IMF, has often been seen as a means of assuring lenders that a country in crisis will follow the Fund's economic policies (Edwards 2006; Stone 2002). IMF conditionality may act as a signaling device and reduce uncertainty about future policy and performance. The mismatch between left-wing ideology and the IMF's neoliberal policies sends a strong signal to the markets about the left-wing governments' will to implement reforms. By lending credibility, the IMF can help borrower governments gain investor confidence.

In summary, institutions can send strong signals to the international financial markets in support of a left-wing government. Politicians operate in an institutional context that constrains the range of feasible options available to them (Crisp and Escobar-Lemmon 2001). Submitting to constraining political institutions thus helps a left-wing government establish policy credibility and predictability, because such institutions shape policymaking process to yield more predictable policy outcomes favored by investors (Cukierman et al. 1992). Political institutions play a crucial role in building market confidence. As the effectiveness and coherence of economic policies depend on the effectiveness of the political institutions, institutional investors use the institutional arrangement as an important way to estimate sovereign default probability.

Formal versus informal institutions

This book focuses on formal institutions and their effects on sovereign credibility, conditional on government partisanship. The institutions discussed are formal in the sense that they impose written rules and operate enforcement mechanisms which formally commit a government to protect property rights and contracts. But it is useful to compare such formal institutions with informal institutions and to understand how they differ in their ability to build sovereign credibility.

Informal institutions have gained much attention in the past decade. This has been largely thanks to the experiences of transition economies and many developing countries which have gone through institutional changes. It spurred scholarly debate about the effects and limitations of institutional arrangements in achieving desired economic and political outcomes (Rodrik 2008). Informal institutions can broadly be defined as norms, embedded ideas, and unwritten rules specific to a social context and culture. They can play an important role in shaping political and economic outcomes. Informal institutions, and what others call the second-best institutions, may complement or accommodate formal institutions when the latter are effective, while they may substitute or compete with ineffective formal institutions (Helmke and Levitsky 2004). The Chinese *guanxi* (connections) is one example of an informal institution that often replaces ineffective formal institutions in Chinese business. Where formal legal institutions do not function effectively, informal personal relationships, or *guanxi*, help to solve disputes and promote coordination (Helmke and Levitsky 2004). Similarly, Rodrik (2008) discusses examples from many African countries where the courts are ineffective and corrupt to the point that they have ceased to function. Firms operating in such jurisdictions rely on relational contracting – that is, they build up long-term relationships with customers and suppliers based on trust.

Rodrik (2008) goes on to argue that although building what he terms first-best institutions (i.e. formal ones) is an appropriate and desirable goal for a developing country, an effective court system, the rule of law, and contract rights protection may be out of reach for a developing country in the medium term. Taking into account the complex problems such countries face, he argues that the best-practice institutions can actually prevent developing countries from achieving reform and economic development at otherwise lower costs and efforts. He also criticizes the approach of international institutions such as the World Bank and the IMF that promote these formal institutions.

The advocates of second-best institutions or informal institutions make valid arguments when they say that such institutions can play an important role in complementing and substituting for formal institutions, which are often inefficient in many developing countries. However, as some of them acknowledge, informal institutions are still second-best. They cannot replace formal institutions as a fundamental solution (Helmke and Levitsky 2004). They can be created because formal institutions are ineffective, but they are also created when political actors want to pursue goals that are not publicly or internationally acceptable (Helmke and Levitsky 2004). Politicians often create informal institutions because formal institutions are not to their benefit (Mershon 1994).

A major weakness of informal institutions is that governments cannot always rely on them as a credibility-building mechanism. There has been no significant study examining the signaling effectiveness of informal institutions, probably due to the difficulties in measuring their quality and their lack of international comparability. These characteristics also imply that foreign investors cannot rely on informal institutions when assessing the credibility of a government. They may help to strengthen the existing formal institutions or complement them, but they cannot send a strong signal to the markets. It is also unclear how informal institutions interact with government partisanships to affect sovereign credibility.

Assessing sovereign credibility: the role of credit ratings

One important indicator of market sentiment toward a country is its sovereign credit rating. Major rating agencies such as Institutional Investor, Moody's, Standard and Poor's, Fitch, and Euromoney provide investors with risk estimates. They differ somewhat in their methodologies, but most use a combination of qualitative and quantitative indicators to reflect various economic and political factors (Mosley 2003: 137).

There has been criticism that rating agencies make a large part of their revenue from governments that request ratings, and as a result that they provide a better rating to continue their business relationship with their government client (Beaulieu et al. 2012).[3] There have also been complaints that rating agencies failed to predict major financial crises, such as the Asian financial crisis and the US and European crises.[4] Rating agencies, however, have a reputational incentive to provide accurate information regarding which sovereigns are creditworthy (Mosley 2003: 138). If the agencies do not provide good-quality information, they will lose customers and eventually go out of business (Tomz 2007).[5]

Sovereign ratings play a crucial role in providing information on which investors base their investment decisions (Afonso et al. 2012). Sovereign credit ratings can reduce investors' information costs and also play a key role in the pricing of a sovereign debt (IMF 1998). Ratings are extremely important in setting bond prices and affecting financial market behavior. For example, bonds with lower ratings almost always have a higher risk premium than bonds with higher ratings (Cooley 2015: 4). If an agency lowers its ratings on a bond that has already been issued, the bond's price will fall.

Interviews with financial market experts further confirm the importance of credit ratings. All of the financial market experts I interviewed said that they refer to major credit rating agencies' ratings as a primary source and guideline when assessing country risk. Although those from relatively large financial institutions had their own research teams, they nonetheless referred to the credit agencies' ratings too. They further mentioned that other experts' perceptions of markets significantly influence their own perceptions, and such influence is even greater for mass markets. One of the experts added that most investors do not need to do their own analysis of individual countries when they choose investment destinations, because they rely on the ratings (Interview 17).

Perceptions of sovereign risk and ratings are crucial in determining developing countries' access to capital markets. Countries whose ratings fall below a critical threshold tend to lose access to private capital markets, whereas those with high ratings tend to have continuous access to capital (Reinhart et al. 2003). Earlier studies have shown that downgraded reviews and ratings lead to a significant drop in government bond yields and an increase in bond spreads. And such evidence is found for both developed and developing countries (Afonso et al. 2012; Kaminsky and Schmukler 2002; Reisen and von Maltzan 1999). Kraussel (2005) has shown that ratings by Moody's and Standard and Poor's affect the size of lending in emerging markets and that downgrades and negative outlooks have notably significant effects. Sovereign credit ratings affect not only investment decisions in the international bond and loan markets, but also the allocation of FDI, portfolio equity flow, and bank lending (Albuquerque 2003; Kim and Wu 2011). Furthermore, sovereign credit ratings also influence other markets, such as those for equities and for credit default swaps (Ismailescu and Kazemi 2010; Kaminsky and Schmukler 2002).

In this book, the Institutional Investor measure is used as the main variable of interest to analyze the effects of institutions on sovereign credibility. The findings are supplemented by reference to the ratings of Moody's, Standard and Poor's, and Fitch. Institutional Investor's measures are based on evaluations by bankers at 75 to 100 leading international financial institutions. They are senior economists and sovereign risk analysts at major international banks, money managers, and securities companies. The bankers are asked to grade each country on a scale of 0 to 100, with 100 representing those nations with the least chance of default. The bankers are not permitted to rate their home countries, and the individual responses are weighted, with more importance given to responses from banks with greater worldwide exposure and more sophisticated country-analysis systems (Mosley 2003). According to research by Butler and Fauver (2006: 55), who obtained more detailed information about Institutional Investor ratings, the market experts are asked to evaluate financial, economic, and political factors that have significant influence on the creditworthiness of a country. Financial and economic factors include balance of payments, current account balance, the stability of banking and financial systems, foreign reserves, debt-service ratio, absolute levels of debt, relationships with international institutions such as the World Bank or the IMF, export growth and diversity, gross domestic product (GDP) growth, and government fiscal policy. Political factors include the political system, regulatory regimes, the rule of law, corruption, government transparency, external security threats, internal strife, and terrorism.

In contrast to Institutional Investor, Moody's, Standard and Poor's, and Fitch rely on their own analysts' assessments for their country credit ratings. Moody's, for example, examines economic strength such as economic growth, institutional strength such as rule of law, policy credibility such as inflation rates, fiscal strength such as debt burden, political risk, and external vulnerability (Moody's 2012). Standard and Poor's similarly examines institutional and governance effectiveness, macroeconomic indicators, fiscal and monetary policies, and debt structure (Standard and Poor's 2013). Fitch considers debt burden and other external liabilities, the level of living standards, macroeconomic policies, and political risk (Fitch 2002).[6] Institutional Investor ratings have an advantage in that the dataset covers a much larger number of countries from 1980 than those from other agencies. Overall, the ratings are particularly useful for estimating investors' perceptions of uncertainty, because they rely on the perceptions of industry practitioners in corporate finance, institutional investing, commercial banking, and investment banking (Sobel 2002: 136).

Conclusions

Greater financial market integration has led to the growth of sovereign debt markets in developing countries. An increasing number of international investors, including a large proportion of private investors, now participate in developing countries' sovereign debt markets. Developing countries tend to pose greater political risks to investors, however, which significantly undermines their sovereign credibility. Investors can simply decide to withdraw their money from a country perceived to be troublesome if policy uncertainty persists. Therefore, borrowing countries have an incentive to improve their sovereign credibility to attract foreign capital and avoid financial market turbulence.

From an investor's perspective, investing in the government bonds of developing countries involves various types of risks. Among others, political factors play an increasingly significant role in determining the investment risks in emerging markets. The partisan label of governing party significantly affects investor perceptions about future policy directions, and leftist labels tend to undermine sovereign credibility. To assure investors that they can provide a safe and stable environment for investment, governments need to provide an institutional environment that provides credible policy predictability. Domestic political and international institutions that promote market-friendly policies and protect private property rights can help governments to send a positive signal to the markets about sovereign credibility. The effects of constraining institutions are likely to be greater for leftist governments. Furthermore, any changes in a country's institutional landscape, such as deterioration of institutions toward greater authoritarianism or joining IMF programs, are likely to have a greater impact on the sovereign credibility of leftist governments.

In Chapters 3 to 6, I examine how the left-right distinction affects investors' perceptions of sovereign credibility and present findings suggesting that the signaling effects of institutions are likely to be greater for left-wing governments. In Chapter 3, I elaborate on the relationship between governments and financial markets, focusing on the markets' perceptions of leftist governments. In Chapters 4 to 6, I test the effect of democratic institutions, the degree of political constraints, and IMF conditionality on sovereign credit ratings.

Notes

1 Chapter 3 provides empirical analyses of this point.
2 Resnick (2001) has investigated the effects of a democratic transition on FDI.
3 Institutional Investor ratings may suffer less from the selection problem in this regard, as governments do not request an Institutional Investor rating.
4 Refer to Abdelal and Blyth (2015) and Levich et al. (2002) for more discussion on the role of credit ratings.
5 Relatedly, Cantor and Packer (1997) studied US corporate debt ratings and found no evidence that firms seeking ratings from smaller rating agencies did so to achieve higher rating levels.
6 As noted earlier, I also tested other measures of sovereign credibility, including J.P. Morgan's EMBI bond spread data and credit default swap data. Because of their limited coverage of countries and years, they do not yield meaningful results on the institutional effects of a leftist government.

3 Leftist party government and perceived creditworthiness

Political events have a profound impact on the profitability of private investment. Not only do major disturbances such as civil wars, coups, protests, and riots significantly affect investor sentiment, but even such relatively minor disturbances as changes in cabinet members can have a considerable influence on investment decisions, causing market indicators to fluctuate. As investors need to assess policy directions amid a flood of political events and information, they tend to rely on information shortcuts to make investment decisions.

One important information shortcut that investors commonly rely on is the ideological orientation and professed beliefs of an economy's political leaders and government (Brooks and Mosley 2007; Gray 2013; Knight 1985). The general belief is that leftist governments tend to tolerate higher inflation and tax rates, have larger public sectors, and have a tendency to neglect debt obligations (Broz 2013; Broz and Weymouth 2013; Garrett 1998; Leblang 2002; Mosley 2003; Vaaler et al. 2005, 2006). Although some scholars contend that the typical left-right distinctions found in advanced democracies are not applicable to developing countries, other research has shown that a broader left-right distinction emphasizing more labor-friendly or more business-friendly policies is useful in developing country contexts (Broz and Weymouth 2013; Pinto 2013; Vaaler et al. 2005, 2006). In fact, market behavior shows that investors often predict the profitability of investments taking into account government partisanship, and that they tend to react sharply when a leftist party takes control of a country. It is not surprising to hear news reports saying that the election of a new left-wing political leader leads to a drop in market indicators.

A more careful observer of financial markets, however, would also notice that there are different degrees of market response to left-wing leaders from an advanced industrial democracy and one from a less developed country. The recent financial crisis in Europe has heightened the political risk of left-wing governments in developed countries, but in general, left-wing governments in advanced democracies tend to pose a relatively temporary and weaker threat to the market. Markets react more sharply to a similar change in a developing economy, and the disturbances tend to last longer.

Two cases illustrate the difference. President Barack Obama's reelection in November 2012 led to huge sell-offs in the markets and an increase in the risk premium. The yield on the ten-year Treasury bond fell the day after the election, and the Dow Jones index fell by 369 points, which was the biggest one-day fall in a year after the 389-point drop on Eurozone debt fears in November 2011. Moody's announced that a downgrade of its US credit rating was possible if the government did not address the country's deficit soon (*Dow Jones Newswires*, November 8, 2012). The market response was attributed to the defeat of the more business-friendly Mitt Romney and the continued gridlock in Congress that made it difficult to resolve fiscal debt problems (*USA Today*, November 7, 2012). The US economy was in fact in a difficult situation, as a "fiscal cliff" that would cause taxes to rise and decrease spending was coming and the fear of possible budget deficits had been looming. Concerns about new taxes and regulations were rising. The Dow Jones fell on seven out of ten days after President Obama's reelection, by a total of 457 points. However, the market jumped back within ten days, based on optimism regarding the budget problem's resolution.

In contrast, when Brazilian President Delma Rousseff was reelected in October 2014, the negative market reaction persisted longer. The market's hope that the more business-friendly Aécio Neves would defeat Rousseff had caused Brazilian assets to rally for weeks, but the reelection of Rousseff led to a fall in the market indicators. Brazil's currency, the real, suffered its worst sell-off in a decade, and shares in Brazilian companies, including some of the biggest in emerging markets, fell 5 to 10 percent, wiping $20 billion off the Bovespa index (*Reuters*, October 28, 2014). The market volatility continued into 2015. A J.P. Morgan Emerging Markets Investment Trust manager noted that even though President Rousseff appointed new ministers from the more market-friendly faction of her party, such as finance minister Joaquim Levy, a conservative banker, neither markets nor investors had confidence in President Rousseff (*Financial Times*, November 10, 2014). Rousseff announced that the administration would tighten Brazil's budget and increase investment and productivity in an effort to restart economic growth, but investors and analysts were skeptical that she could push through such economic reforms (*Wall Street Journal*, October 27, 2014).

It is not difficult to understand what causes such different market reactions. Simply put, developing countries present a wider range of risks to investors than developed economies (Mosley 2003). Earlier studies have shown that developing countries have greater overall macroeconomic volatility, such as in their economic growth, financial markets, and exchange rates (Bergoeing et al. 2004; Caballero and Krishnamurthy 2005; Gavin and Perotti 1997; Kaminsky et al. 2004; Lane 2003; Loayza et al. 2007; Mendoza 1991). Such volatility reflects deeper problems. For example, most developing countries have a shorter history of engaging in international financial markets and have less experience and weaker institutions managing their economies.

Politically, the risk of government predatory behavior is much greater and arises more frequently in developing countries, largely due to their governments' lack of institutional mechanisms to effectively check their political leaders. In many developing countries, individual political leaders exert disproportionate influence on policymaking by advanced economy standards. Developing countries typically lack effective institutional arrangements that constrain radical policies such as expropriation of private property, repudiation of contracts, and other kinds of property rights violations. Many developing countries have authoritarian governments, and such regimes have been linked to an increased risk of expropriation (MIGA 2012). The possibility of governments acting opportunistically by threatening foreign investors to win domestic political support is quite significant (Sobel 2002). The risk of what some scholars call "sovereign theft" becomes even greater when the country has economic problems. The risks of both sovereign default and expropriation are particularly significant during global economic slowdowns and periods of political instability (MIGA 2012).

A significant and lasting consequence of such market perceptions of left-wing governments in developing countries is that investments there are considered risky, regardless of the actual policy being pursued or promised. Being a leftist or socialist party carries a stigma such that even if the party actually implements market-friendly policies, constant doubt remains about the possibility of policy reversals. The findings in this chapter show that such brand name effects often lead to lower credit ratings than a non-leftist government would enjoy when other important determinants of credit ratings are held constant. This left–right distinction has less effect on the credit ratings of developed countries. These findings are further supported by interviews with financial market experts.

Earlier debates on government partisanship and policy differences

Many academic studies have examined the macroeconomic implications of partisan politics. They have explored the implications of partisan policymakers pursuing primarily ideological goals and have confirmed that different parties have different preferences about inflation, growth, and unemployment. Leftist parties tend to be relatively more concerned about unemployment than about inflation, while right-wing parties have the opposite concerns (Davis et al. 1966, 1974; Downs 1957; Hibbs 1977; Kramer 1971; MacRae 1977; Nordhaus 1975; Tufte 1975, 1978). Most studies in the literature have confirmed that left-leaning governments tend to tolerate higher levels of inflation, government spending, and deficits, and to be more willing to contemplate sovereign debt default. Right-wing governments are regarded as more committed to fiscal austerity and debt obligations (Alesina et al.1997; Bagashka and Stone 2013; Bearce 2003; Blais et al. 1993; Brooks and Mosley 2007; Broz 2013; Castles 1989; Lange and Garrett 1985; Schmidt 1996).

Other scholars have argued, however, that partisanship is not a useful proxy for a government's economic orientation. The so-called "third way" – the idea that social democracy can embrace neoliberalism – is cited as evidence. The assertion is that the changing international economic environment and deepening globalization have led leftist parties to give up their traditional policy positions in the face of mobile international capital (Huber and Stephens 1998;

Kurzer 1993; Mishra 1999; Moses 2000; Pierson 1995, 2001; Rodrik 1997; Ross 2000). Economic globalization manifested by increased international trade, foreign direct investment, and capital mobility has exposed national economies to significantly greater global competition, forcing national governments of any stripe to adjust their economic policies to attract international investment. Capital mobility allows such investment to quickly leave any country that does not provide a favorable market environment, so national governments must remain sensitive to the international market's evaluations and perceptions (Berger 2000; Cerny 1996; Mosley 2003).

For developing countries, for example, FDI is particularly important because it contributes to creating employment and often brings technology transfers. Although some developing countries, particularly those with a leftist government, once maintained hostile attitudes towards FDI and multinational firms, governments these days largely accept FDI as crucial for economic growth and thus are willing to adjust or change their economic policies to attract investment.[1] Some scholars discern a "race to the bottom" in wages and regulations as a result (Drezner 2001; Rodrik 1997). They emphasize how economic globalization tends to undermine welfare policies as governments try to provide investor-friendly environments by reducing funding for social services, lowering levels of taxation, and easing regulation. They provide evidence that the rise of neoliberalism since the end of the Cold War has contributed in emerging market countries to greater emphasis on minimizing government intervention in the economy and more investor-friendly and market-friendly policies.

The results of some academic studies support the argument that government partisanship is not an important determinant of policy differences between left and right. For example, Alesina et al. (1997) find no significant effect of government partisanship on budget deficits, and Franzese (2002) has presented similar evidence. Kontopoulos and Perotti (1999) find that the strongest effects of ideology on fiscal policy are in the areas of transfer spending and government wages, rather than the overall budget balance. They conclude that if market actors are unconcerned about microeconomic outcomes, they should be similarly unconcerned about ideology. Pinto (2013) further argues that leftist governments are actually more successful than right-wing governments in attracting certain types of FDI.

Government partisanship and market perceptions

When it comes to sovereign credibility, however, partisan effects on investor sentiment seem quite obvious.[2] The recent financial upheaval in Europe has demonstrated the impact of partisan politics on financial market sentiments, as in the case of the Syriza government in Greece. Scholars have investigated such a negative relationship between a leftist government and financial market reactions. Kurzur (1993), for example, has shown that leftist governments' expansionary policies lead financial markets to expect that future inflation rates will go above the rates of the country's main trading partners. As a result, expectations of expansionary policies lead to capital outflow. Similarly, Garrett (1998) found that countries with leftist governments and strong labor movements tend to pay higher interest rates than other countries. Such a relationship between government ideology and risk premium becomes stronger as a country's capital market becomes more open. Leblang and Bernhard (2000) contended that currency market participants rely on government partisanship and government formation to predict the probability of a speculative attack, and find that the probability increases when a left-wing party is likely to come to power.

Although the markets do display concern about left-wing governments in well-established democracies, the fact that they are advanced democracies gives investors greater confidence about government policy than a developing country could inspire (Mosley 2003). The markets have confidence that political leaders will not be able to resort to drastic measures, such as confiscating private property or instituting capital controls, because these countries are governed by institutions that provide the rule of law and investor rights protection. As a result, although investors are aware of policy variances across different governments in the developed world, their concern is relatively slight compared to the case of developing countries.

On the contrary, left-wing governments in developing countries tend to be perceived as posing greater risks to investors than their counterparts in developed countries. One of the financial market experts interviewed clearly made this point, noting that investors believe that the governments in so-called developed economies would not do something "stupid" to lose market confidence, because these governments are more deeply integrated into the world economy, and thus tend to be more responsible about the consequences of their policy choices (Interview 23). On the contrary, investors cannot be as confident about developing countries because these countries pose greater policy uncertainty. Similar points were made by other investors that more advanced and richer economies tend to act more prudently (Interviews 7, 21, 22). A study by Mosley (2003) supports this kind of market sentiment. She finds that the partisanship of leftist governments in developed countries does not affect their government bond interest rates, while leftist governments in developing countries must endure higher interest rates than rightist governments.

These points made by market experts and scholars seem to be supported by the very sharp market reactions to the prospect of a left-leaning government in developing countries. Plummeting value of financial instruments and asset sell-offs are often observed. For example, sovereign debt instruments fell significantly when Correa in Ecuador, Chávez in Venezuela, Lula da Silva in Brazil, and Zuma in South Africa won elections (*Tribune Business News*, April 10, 2001; *Financial Times*, November 19, 2006; November 28, 2006). Vaaler and his colleagues show that ratings agency assessments of sovereign risk are generally more favorable for right-wing governments (Vaaler et al. 2005, 2006), as their policies are more investor-friendly and decrease the likelihood of default. They also find that rating agencies downgrade a country when a left-leaning party is likely to replace a right-wing incumbent.

To invest for the medium to long term, investors need stability and rules that do not change. The greater political and policy uncertainties in developing countries affect investor confidence in those countries. Left-wing governments face greater suspicion because many investors equate leftism with populism. The political risks of expropriation and confiscation of property are often associated with left-wing populism in developing countries. Earlier research findings that expropriations are more frequent under left-wing than under right-wing governments (Eden et al. 2012; MIGA 2013) further confirm the market's negative perceptions of left-wing governments. Populism is a significant political risk, particularly in emerging market countries, because many developing countries lack strong institutional mechanisms that effectively check populist policies.

This negative perception is based on the history of many left-wing governments in developing countries that have frequently implemented macroeconomic programs with a populist flavor. While left-wing populist macroeconomic policies can be identified at various times in many countries, the best-known instances have been in Latin America. Populist leaders in Latin America have refused to repay debt, criticized the so-called Washington consensus and free trade, and supported nationalization. From as early as the 1930s, populist redistributive policies have been implemented in Latin America. Examples include Argentina under Peron between 1946 and 1949, Brazil under Vargas after 1945, Mexico under Cardenas between 1934 and 1940, and Peru under Velasco between 1968 and 1975. All were characterized by governments committed to having a strong role in setting prices, protecting workers and their wages, providing cheap food, state ownership of key industries, and state allocation of credit at low interest rates, which eventually led to extensive growth of the government sector, budget deficits, and pervasive corruption (Cardoso and Helwege 1991). Countries with a history of populist policies confront even more problems because, other things being equal, leftist governments and political systems with a history of populist attacks on business and property rights face greater difficulty establishing the credibility of their policy, regardless of their stated intentions (Haggard and Kaufman 1992). Investors suspect that leftist governments may behave opportunistically later in the course of their leadership.

In Venezuela, for example, Hugo Chávez said during his election campaigns that he welcomed foreign investment, would consider selling part of the state oil company's holdings abroad, and would not declare a debt moratorium unilaterally. Later, emboldened by his landslide reelection in December 2006, President Chávez brought major sectors of the economy under state control. He shocked the markets by declaring that the energy and telecommunications sectors were to be nationalized (*The Economist*, May 8, 2007). Soon after the announcement, the government acquired controlling shares in Venezuela's largest private telecommunications company and in a private electricity supplier. The government seized the majority equity share and operational control of four heavy-oil joint ventures in the Orinoco oil basin that had previously been controlled by six foreign companies (*The Economist*, May 8, 2007; *Business Week*, May 1, 2007). Chávez also extended state control over the banking and steel industries. The markets were unsettled by these radical nationalizations. President Chávez's threat to nationalize banks caused Venezuelan stocks to fall, and the government's decision to take over control of major oil projects hit the bond market (*Business Week*, May 4, 2007).

President Correa of Ecuador pledged to repay sovereign debt, but later changed his position and defaulted (*Financial Times*, November 19, 2006; January 3, 2007; December 5, 2006; *Business Week*, December 3, 2006). He tightened government control of the banking system and expanded the state's control of the production and commercialization of Ecuador's oil (*Business Week*, December 3, 2006). He also cut ties to international financial institutions, including the World Bank and the IMF. Furthermore, he threatened a moratorium on foreign debt repayment, requesting that foreign bond holders lower Ecuador's debt service burden by half (*Financial Times*, April 27, 2007). Investors' concerns about Correa's policies, including his threat to unilaterally limit payments on Ecuador's $16.8 billion foreign debt and use the money for social programs, hammered Ecuador's bonds (*Business Week*, December 3, 2006).

The problem with these governments is that they not only undermined their own sovereign credibility through policy inconsistency, but they also affected the markets' perceptions of other left-wing governments, which may in fact have been trying to pursue more market-friendly policies. In addition to the example of Lula da Silva discussed in Chapter 1, the markets were concerned that a policy reversal was a risk associated with socialist governments in countries like Poland and Hungary, where leftist governments had not previously been considered as serious a threat. Many post-communist European countries with a left-wing party in power implemented austerity policies because they wanted to dissociate themselves from the communist past (Tavits and Letki 2009). As they tried to pursue fiscal austerity while the general population expected the government to provide social assistance, they often faced difficulties. Privatization was one of the major reforms for those transition economies, and investors reacted sharply when these governments wanted to slow down privatization plans and reexamine the privatization deals (*Business Week*, December 15, 1997).

Investor concern about the risk of a policy reversal is particularly greater when the economy is in bad shape. A left-wing party's commitment to reform is tested when a country is in economic difficulties (Interview 24). And indeed, history teaches that any government faces greater risk of protests and even a coup when the economy is in recession (Acemoglu and Robinson 2001). The pressure for redistribution strengthens, which constitutes a threat for those with assets. A left-wing government is more likely to succumb to pressure in such situations, or at least investors assume that this will be the case. They form their expectations accordingly, and react sharply when they sense any sign of a policy shift likely to undermine their investments.

Anecdotes such as the above contribute to the amplification of brand name effects on left-wing governments in the developing world. Experienced investors confirm that any newly elected political leader definitely makes them uneasy due to greater policy uncertainty, but a leader with a less-than-market-friendly orientation surely makes them nervous. One investor said that a country "loses points" if a left-wing leader is likely to win an election (Interview 2). But they usually mention that while a political leader's ideological orientation matters, the country's political system is also important (Interviews 2, 12, 21). One investor noted that he would feel safer if the political system could bind the political leader so that the leader could not act arbitrarily. When asked whether a longer track record in office gives greater confidence in a left-wing leader, many interviewees disagreed. Experienced investors seem to emphasize that a person can always change, and whether he or she will do so depends on the political and economic environment (Interviews 3, 24). So risk boils down to the fundamentals. If a country has a well-established political system, it reduces investment risk because investors know that in the end, the institutions can deter arbitrary policy changes (Interview 20).

Therefore, left-wing governments seem to be at a disadvantage in attracting foreign capital, because there is no clear guarantee that these governments will not act opportunistically later. Investors are more cautious than ever these days. Even when a newly elected leader talks up his or her love of the free market, free trade, and growth, investors fear that the leader may fail to back up his or her proclamations (*Investor's Business Daily*, October 29, 2002). Such policy uncertainty and confusion leaves investors skeptical and can negatively influence investors' perceptions of those countries. These negative perceptions eventually lead to abrupt capital outflow, and economic as well as political instability.

Empirical findings

Thus far, I have discussed general market perceptions of left-wing governments by international markets using previous studies and various anecdotes. I test the effects of government partisanship on sovereign credit ratings empirically in my own research using the following hypotheses.

H3.1: In developed countries, government partisanship is less likely to have significant effects on sovereign credibility.

H3.2: In developing countries, leftist governments are perceived to be less creditworthy than governments which are not leftist.

H3.3: A country's credit rating is likely to fall when a leftist party replaces a right-leaning incumbent.

I test these ideas by creating regression models predicting Institutional Investor credit ratings over the period from 1980 to 2007. As has been explained in Chapter 2, the Institutional Investor data cover a much larger set of countries than ratings from other agencies. The ratings range from 0 to 100, with 100 indicating that a given country is least likely to default. I supplement the findings with additional analysis using Moody's, Fitch, and Standard & Poor's data. Following earlier research on sovereign ratings, I convert their letter ratings into numbers that range from 1 to 17, where 17 represents the countries with the least risk of default.

The main predictor tested is data on government orientation from the World Bank's Database of Political Institutions (DPI). It classifies governments as left, center, or right, where applicable, based on the chief executive's professed ideology. The classification relies primarily on the party name and description.[3] This variable is recoded to classify centrist and rightist governments as non-leftist. This is an optimal variable for this research because it allows testing of the brand name effects on left-wing parties when other important politico-economic differences are controlled for. By indicating ideology but not policy, the variable picks up the effects of ideology on investor perceptions.[4]

I include in the models control variables that are commonly regarded as important determinants of sovereign credit ratings. Those included are gross domestic product (GDP) growth, the government's budget balance, current account balance, foreign reserves, inflation, capital account openness, level of investment, and debt service.[5] A high rate of economic growth not only indicates that the economy is performing well, but also that the country is more likely to be able to service its existing debts, if any (Cantor and Packer 1996). The government's budget balance may also significantly affect government bond markets, because a large deficit undermines the government's ability to repay its debts. Accumulated deficits will tempt governments to use inflation to lighten their nominal liabilities (Turnovsky and Miller 1984). Similarly, a large current account deficit or a low level of foreign reserves reduces a government's ability to service its external debt. High inflation similarly reduces an asset's value, and it may imply structural problems in the government's finances. Many governments have relied on inflationary financing of a fiscal deficit when they are short of tax revenue or unable to cut government spending. That makes the rate of inflation a useful indicator of government discipline in some situations (Rowland 2004). Capital account liberalization also has a fundamental effect on improvements in macroeconomic and structural policies. And finally, a higher level of investment is likely to be negatively associated with government debt, while heavy debt service indicates that the country may have difficulty servicing its debt obligations, which leads to higher default risk.

In addition to these basic control variables, I also test for any influence of other variables which may be particularly relevant for the markets' perceptions of developing countries. One is the exchange rate regime. It has been shown to affect the level of inflation and fiscal discipline (Broz and Frieden 2001; Kastner and Rector 2003). A fixed exchange rate may impose fiscal discipline because expansionary fiscal policies will eventually exhaust reserves and put pressure on the rate. Abandoning a peg has a serious political cost for politicians, so fixed rates can discipline them. Others argue that fixed exchange rates actually make a country more vulnerable to speculative attacks and thus increase default risks (Sachs and Larrain 1999). Natural resource endowments are another element tested for their effect on market perceptions of developing countries, as investors may perceive natural resources to have a positive impact on a country's economic prospects. I also test the effects of regime types, as earlier studies find democracies to earn greater market confidence in financial markets. The effects of regime type depending on government partisanship will be further investigated in Chapter 4. And finally, I test for any effects of the tenure of the political leadership to explore whether a longer tenure in office helps to reduce perceptions of political risk, particularly with left-wing governments.[6]

I test the hypotheses using the feasible generalized least square (FGLS) model with Prais-Winsten transformation to address first-order correlation within each panel. I report panel-corrected standard errors to address panel heteroscedasticity (Beck and Katz 1996). I also include country and year fixed effects to capture cross-sectional variation and time trend. All control variables are lagged by one year to address any potential endogeneity problems. Lagging the dependent variable is also tested to addresses potential first-order serial correlations (Beck and Katz 2001, 2009).[7]

The basic model is specified as follows:

$$
\begin{aligned}
\ln \mathit{Credit\ Rating}_{it} &= \gamma_0 + \gamma_1 \mathit{Left\ Party}_{i,t-1} + \gamma_2 \mathit{Budget\ Balance}_{i,t-1} \\
&\quad + \gamma_3 \mathit{Capital\ Account\ Openness}_{i,t-1} + \gamma_4 \mathit{GDP\ Growth}_{i,t-1} \\
&\quad + \gamma_5 \mathit{Inflation}_{i,t-1} + \gamma_6 \mathit{Current\ Account\ Balance}_{i,t-1} \\
&\quad + \gamma_7 \mathit{Investment}_{i,t-1} + \gamma_8 \ln \mathit{Reserves}_{i,t-1} + \gamma_9 \mathit{Debt}_{i,t-1} + \epsilon_{it}
\end{aligned}
$$

Government partisanship and sovereign credibility

Table 3.1 presents the results of the relationship between government partisanship and sovereign credit ratings using Institutional Investor ratings.[8] The results of model 1 show that government partisanship is not significantly associated with country credit ratings in developed countries. Including other control variables, such as natural resources, fixed exchange rates, and years in office, also does not yield any significant association between government partisanship and credit ratings, thus the results are not reported here.

This finding is in line with some earlier studies contending that government partisanship is not an important determinant of economic outcomes and market perceptions when these governments, regardless of their ideological orientation, have already earned a certain degree of market confidence. What investors consider more important in those countries are other economic factors, such as economic growth, current account balance, and inflation. Thus, investors are mostly concerned about macroeconomic performance in these countries rather than the political ideologies of the government. The ratings in the previous year tend to have somewhat large coefficients. This is consistent with the literature noting that Institutional Investor ratings tend to be highly persistent over time.[9]

On the contrary, markets consider government partisanship an important determinant of sovereign credibility in developing countries, even when other important economic performances are taken into consideration. This suggests

Table 3.1 Government partisanship and credit ratings

	Developed Countries	*Developing Countries*				
	Model 1	*Model 2*	*Model 3*	*Model 4*	*Model 5*	*Model 6*
Left party	0.000	−0.020**	−0.019**	−0.021**	−0.020**	−0.007
	(0.002)	(0.009)	(0.009)	(0.009)	(0.009)	(0.011)
Natural resources			0.003***			
			(0.001)			
Fixed exchange rates				−0.006		
				(0.008)		
Regime type					0.001	
					(0.001)	
Years in office						0.001**
						(0.001)
Years in office * left party						−0.002*
						(0.001)
Budget balance	0.000	0.002**	0.001*	0.002**	0.002**	0.001*
	(0.000)	(0.001)	(0.001)	(0.001)	(0.001)	(0.001)
Economic growth	0.002***	0.005***	0.005***	0.005***	0.005***	0.005***
	(0.001)	(0.001)	(0.001)	(0.001)	(0.001)	(0.001)
Capital account openness	0.001	0.020***	0.021***	0.020***	0.020***	0.021***
	(0.002)	(0.003)	(0.003)	(0.004)	(0.003)	(0.004)
Investment	−0.000	0.001**	0.001*	0.002**	0.002**	0.001*
	(0.001)	(0.001)	(0.001)	(0.001)	(0.001)	(0.001)
Current account balance	0.002***	0.001	0.000	0.002***	0.001*	0.001
	(0.000)	(0.001)	(0.001)	(0.001)	(0.001)	(0.001)
Inflation	−0.001***	0.000	0.000	0.000	0.000	0.000
	(0.000)	(0.000)	(0.000)	(0.000)	(0.000)	(0.000)
Reserves (log)	0.000	0.042***	0.045***	0.040***	0.042***	0.044***
	(0.000)	(0.005)	(0.005)	(0.005)	(0.005)	(0.005)
Debt	−0.000	0.000	0.000	−0.000	0.000	0.000
	(0.000)	(0.000)	(0.000)	(0.000)	(0.000)	(0.000)
Previous year's rating	0.916***	0.796***	0.790***	0.798***	0.797***	0.791***
	(0.023)	(0.015)	(0.015)	(0.015)	(0.015)	(0.015)
Constant	0.366***	0.342***	0.326***	0.350***	0.333***	0.351***
	(0.094)	(0.072)	(0.073)	(0.074)	(0.072)	(0.073)
Observations	483	1,348	1,345	1,291	1,345	1,289
R-squared	0.98	0.97	0.97	0.97	0.97	0.97

Notes: ***$p < .01$; **$p < .05$; *$p < .10$ (two-tailed). The dependent variable is Institutional Investor and log-transformed.

that leftist governments in developing countries are likely to be associated with credit ratings lower than those of their non-leftist counterparts.

Models 2 to 6 in Table 3.1 report the regression results for developing countries. In models 2 to 5, leftist governments have credit ratings lower than non-leftist governments by approximately 2 points, and the coefficients are statistically significant.[10] Substantively, a change of 2 points looks rather small at first glance, but it is important to remember that what the model estimates is the effect of the partisan label or the brand name effect.[11] It is likely that leftist governments have greater effects that operate through economic outcomes.

Other determinants, such as the budget balance, economic growth, capital account openness, investment, and foreign reserves, have statistically significant associations with credit ratings in the expected directions in all models for developing countries. That is, countries with greater government revenues, faster economic growth, more open capital accounts, more investment, and larger foreign reserves are likely to have higher credit ratings. Model 3 includes natural resource endowments which correlate with better sovereign credibility, whereas fixed exchange rates in model 4 and regime type in model 5 are not significantly associated with sovereign credibility.

Model 6 in Table 3.1 tests whether a longer tenure in office predicts a better rating, perhaps by reducing policy uncertainty. The results show that longer time in office does have a positive relationship with the credibility of non-leftist governments. For leftist governments, the coefficient of the interaction between the leftist party and years in office shows a negative and statistically significant coefficient, suggesting that left-wing governments staying longer in power may actually have worse sovereign credibility. An additional year in office is associated with a 0.1-point decrease in credit ratings, and the coefficients are jointly significant at $p < .15$ (one-tailed).[12] The findings overall suggest that staying in office longer does not help a left-wing government build credibility. This seems to support the argument that regardless of a left-wing government's track record or past performance, investors tend to be wary of a possible policy reversal.

Governing party change and sovereign credibility

In Table 3.2, I further test the brand name effects by examining the effects of governing party change on the change of sovereign credibility. I use an ordinary least squares (OLS) model and adopt a first-difference specification of the basic regression model to examine how the change in government ideological orientation is associated with the change of Institutional Investor ratings. I create two variables to measure changes in government partisanship – the first one is coded 1 if a leftist political leader replaces a right-leaning incumbent; the other records the opposite cases. The dependent variable and control variables take the first-difference form.

The results once again show the negative association between leftist governments and sovereign credibility. The results of model 7 show that a leftist party's replacing a right-leaning incumbent is associated with a slower growth in credit

Table 3.2 Governing party change and credit ratings of developing countries

	Model 7	*Model 8*
	From non-left to left	*From left to non-left*
Governing party change	−0.039**	−0.010
	(0.019)	(0.019)
⊿Capital account openness	0.038***	0.038***
	(0.006)	(0.006)
⊿Investment	−0.000	−0.000
	(0.001)	(0.001)
⊿Budget balance	−0.001	−0.001
	(0.001)	(0.001)
Economic growth	0.008***	0.008***
	(0.001)	(0.001)
⊿Reserves (log)	0.065***	0.065***
	(0.008)	(0.008)
⊿Inflation	−0.000	−0.000
	(0.000)	(0.000)
⊿Current account balance	−0.001	−0.001
	(0.001)	(0.001)
⊿Debt	0.000	0.000
	(0.000)	(0.000)
Regime type	0.003***	0.003***
	(0.000)	(0.000)
Previous year's rating	−0.037***	−0.037***
	(0.006)	(0.006)
Constant	0.070***	0.070***
	(0.018)	(0.018)
Observations	1,289	1,289
R-squared	0.255	0.253

Notes: ***$p < .01$; **$p < .05$; *$p < .10$ (two-tailed). The dependent variable is Institutional Investor and log-transformed and first-differenced.

ratings (a 3.9-point difference in rating changes), and the association is statistically significant at $p < .05$ (two-tailed). When a right-leaning party replaces a left-wing incumbent, however, there is no statistically significant association between such a change of leadership and sovereign credit ratings. The sign of the coefficient for party change in model 8 is negative, although statistically insignificant. The negative sign might not be irrelevant to financial market experts' comments that a new political leader tends to generate concerns because there is no track record. The results in Table 3.2 thus suggest that market reactions are negative and sharper when a leftist political leader comes to power than when a right-wing leader replaces a leftist incumbent. These findings support the brand name effects and the negativity bias discussed in Chapter 2 – that is, markets are more responsive to what they consider to be bad events (i.e. a leftist party's coming to power) than to good events (i.e. a right-leaning government coming to power).

The empirical findings so far demonstrate that government partisanship plays a more important role in developing than in developed countries. The findings also suggest that leftist governments in developing countries are perceived as less creditworthy than non-leftist governments. But these findings represent only the tip of the iceberg. The following chapters will build on these results, testing the effects of political institutions that commit governments to market-friendly policies and policy stability. As we shall see, the effects of such institutions depend to some extent on the ideological orientation of the government.

Conclusions

The empirical findings demonstrate that government partisanship does not have a significant effect on the creditworthiness of developed countries. In developing countries, however, leftist governments tend to have lower credit ratings than non-leftist governments, even when other important economic and political factors are taken into consideration. A change in political leadership from a non-leftist to a leftist chief executive also has a negative association with sovereign credibility. These findings correspond with the observation that market actors perceive leftist governments to be riskier than other types of governments. Interviews with market experts also show that they tend to be more concerned when a left-wing leader comes to power. The results also suggest that a longer tenure in office does not increase the sovereign credibility of a left-wing government.

One of the market experts I interviewed proposed that even though left-wing governments may generate inflation and fiscal deficits, their focus on redistribution may be a good thing in certain situations (Interview 1). Earlier literature emphasizing the role of the welfare state is in line with such observation, as the argument goes that welfare policies can provide a safety net for people who suffer economically from globalization, so they may promote stable economic growth, which makes a country a more attractive investment destination (Garrett 1998). However, the findings presented in this chapter suggest that for left-wing governments to effectively convince investors about such advantages, they need to first assure investors about the safety of their investments from economic policies that may undermine their profitability or even sovereign theft.

Notes

1 Some countries have withdrawn from investment agreements out of discontent, but such withdrawal is exceptional and most countries remain within the system (Ryan 2009).

2 Studies on the history of the interaction between partisan politics and financial markets go back to the cases of England around the eighteenth century. In explaining how the British government earned its credibility in repaying debt, some scholars argue that the Whig party's control of parliament in the eighteenth century contributed to building credibility. The Whigs represented the so-called "moneyed interest" of merchants, businessmen, and financiers, whereas the Tories were mainly supported by the "landed interest" such as the Anglican clergy and the landed gentry (Carruthers 1996: 49). The differing positions of the Tories and the Whigs on issues such as debt and tax had an effect on financial markets. The Whig supremacy was associated with lower yields on government debt because the Whigs were deemed to be more reliable in dealing with the government's creditors (Stasavage 2003, 2007).

3 Refer to Beck et al. (2001) for further details.

4 As mentioned earlier, the coding decisions were checked to ensure that they correspond with those of other sources by referring to the data of Benoit and Laver (2006); Coppedge (1997); Baker and Greene (2011) (which is based on Coppedge [1997], Wiesehomeier and Benoit [2009], and Pop-Eleches [2009]); Stone (2002); and various other secondary sources. Some post-communist countries pose a challenge because they have so-called "dual executive" systems in which it is unclear who is in charge (Shugart 2005). For those countries, I followed Stone (2002)'s coding scheme and coded based on the most influential and relevant sources of executive power.

5 GDP growth is measured in annual percentage; government budget balance is government deficit or surplus as a percentage of GDP; current account balance is measured as a percentage of GDP; foreign reserves are measured as a percentage of total external debt (for developing countries) and total reserves (for developed countries); inflation data use GDP deflator in annual percentage; investment data are based on the investment share of GDP; and debt is measured by total debt service as a share of exports of goods, services, and income (for developing countries) and central government debt per GDP (for developed countries). The sources of these data are provided in Appendix 2.1.

6 The variable measuring exchange rate system is a binary one coding fixed exchange rate system as 1; natural resource endowments are measured by total natural resource rents as a percentage of GDP; the measure of regime type ranges from 0 (strongly autocratic) to 20 (strongly democratic); and tenure in office measures the number of years a party has been in office. The sources of these data are provided in Appendix 2.1.

7 Some contend that lagged dependent variables (LDVs) cause estimation problems, such as suppression of other independent variables' explanatory power (Achen 2000; Nickell1981). This is particularly a problem for datasets with a short time dimension (less than ten years), whereas such issues disappear when a time series is long enough to allow for stable results (Beck and Katz 2009). LDVs' suppression of explanatory power seems to be the case for the Moody's, Fitch, and Standard and Poor's ratings of developing countries, as those ratings cover seven to nine years on average. Including LDVs in their models suppresses the effects of some covariates, which makes it more appropriate to not include LDVs in analyses with those ratings, given the data structure.

8 The results using the credit ratings of other rating agencies are reported in Appendix 3.

9 See Cosset and Roy (1991), Haque et al. (1996), Altenkirch (2005), and Cruces (2006).

10 As the credit rating data are log-transformed, the coefficients are interpreted to fit the original rating scale of 0–100.

11 It is also important to note that the average yearly change in ratings in the sample is about 0.5 points.

12 The results using Moody's and Fitch ratings (reported in Appendix 3) further show that years in office do not have any significant effect on the negative relationship between leftist governments and their sovereign ratings. The results in Table A3.1 suggest that leftist governments' ratings are lower than their right-wing counterparts' by approximately 2–3 points in the original rating scale.

4 Democracy and sovereign creditworthiness

Do investors treat democracies as less risky than autocracies? How do markets react to institutional improvements toward greater democracy or deterioration toward greater authoritarianism? The notion that democratic political institutions help to foster investment, and thus economic growth, has gained much attention in recent years. Although some authoritarian governments have achieved very impressive economic growth within very short periods, many people have argued that democracies tend to have better performance in the long run. Theoretically, the relationship between democracy and investment seems to be intuitive. Investors make a long-term investment when they are confident that this investment will not be expropriated. Democracy embraces liberal principles, such as respect for private property rights, the rule of law, and checks on government, and better addresses corruption problems, all of which are believed to create a favorable environment for investment and a more stable foundation for long-term growth (Feng 2003; Huntington 1991; Olson 1993; Riker and Weimer 1993). Empirically, however, there is mixed evidence relating to whether or not democratic institutions promote investment. Whereas some researchers find that democracy improves access to capital (Beaulieu et al. 2012; Schultz and Weingast 1998), others show that democracy exhibits a negligible or even an adverse effect on investment, or at least that the so-called democratic advantage does not always apply in developing countries (Brewer and Rivoli 1990; Resnick 2001; Stasavage 2003; Sussman and Yafeh 2000).

More importantly, earlier studies have paid little attention to regime changes, such as a democratic improvement, or a recession. They have tended to treat institutions as static, examining how different levels of democracy affect policy outcomes and market reactions, rather than examining how changes in the quality of democracy may affect economic outcomes and market responses. Another important question that has been neglected is how any changes in the dynamics of institutions interact with other domestic political conditions to influence market perceptions. This neglect of the dynamics of democratic institutions is problematic, as countries experience institutional changes which shape market sentiment.

In this chapter, I systematically explore how the credibility-building effects of democratic political institutions may depend on the governing party's ideological orientation. I examine to what extent left-leaning democratic regimes are more effective than right-leaning ones in convincing investors in the bond markets. I further explore how institutional improvements toward greater democracy or deterioration toward greater authoritarianism affect sovereign credibility and whether such effects depend on government partisanship. Since investors tend to associate left-wing governments and political leaders with a greater risk of expropriation and property rights infringement, the characteristics of democratic institutions – represented by constraints on executive power, protection of property rights, and transparency in policymaking – may build investors' confidence more effectively with a left-wing government than with a right-leaning one. Furthermore, populism as manifested in left-wing politics has been shown to be detrimental to business interests, and well-established democratic institutions are likely to constrain populist leaders better than less democratic ones. Therefore, any improvement or deterioration in democracy may send a stronger signal about sovereign credibility under a left-wing government.

This chapter ultimately addresses the broader and overarching question of whether democracy helps to improve economic performance. Not only do scholars disagree on this major question, they disagree on an even more important one: do democratic institutions affect economic performance, regardless of any preconditions or political circumstances? Most studies which have examined the effects of democracy have declined to explore the possibility that the effects of democratic institutions may in fact be conditional on the political circumstances.

Methodologically, I address the potential endogeneity problem and selection bias in the relationship between democratic institutions and country credit ratings. The findings suggest that democracy is positively associated with country credit ratings and that democracy helps leftist governments to improve their creditworthiness. I further find that democratic transition is negatively associated with right-leaning governments, but no such negative relationship is found among left-wing governments. Deteriorating institutional quality has a negative relationship with the credit ratings of both left and non-left governments, but the negative effect seems to be stronger for a government regarded as left-wing. The experiences of Peru and Venezuela show that a deterioration in democracy under a left-wing government causes greater concern among investors than that under a right-wing government. Interviews with financial market experts confirm that they are mostly concerned about populism under a left-wing government and believe that democratic institutions may restrain populist leaders. Because democracy enhances the credibility of a left-wing government, any deterioration in democracy has a more pronounced impact on investment when the government is on the left of the political spectrum.

"Democratic advantage" and sovereign credibility

The question of whether a democratic regime provides a better investment environment and promotes economic growth is an important one to ask. Some scholars argue that democracy requires immediate consumption for public spending and redistribution, thus reducing the resources available for investment. The poor – who comprise the majority of the population in most developing countries – could favor a candidate who promises to reduce the economic, political, and social privileges enjoyed by the middle class (Huntington and Dominguez 1975). Redistributing wealth to benefit the poor undermines wealthier people's incentive to save and invest (Alesina and Rodrik 1994; Dornbusch and Edwards 1991; Persson and Tabellini 1994). Voters may also prefer that a government not repay its sovereign debt, hoping for higher government spending financed by foreign borrowing (Drazen 1997; Saiegh 2005). They may see loan default as promoting both the national interest and their personal welfare (Tomz 2002: 2). When combined with populism, a democracy may expropriate capital when the poor have extensive political power (Alesina and Rodrik 1994; Dornbusch and Edwards 1991; Persson and Tabellini 1994).

However, an authoritarian regime "may have the appearance of government stability but generally lacks the fundamental social basis for regime stability" (Feng 2003: 159). Authoritarian governments are usually one-party dictatorships existing for decades with irregular government changes accompanied by fundamental alterations in the constitution and the rules of the political game (Feng 2003). The irregular changes often involve a coup d'état, and a successful coup significantly increases the possibility of other future coups (Londregan and Poole 1990). Such unpredictable government changes greatly increase the policy uncertainty of an authoritarian regime (Feng 2003).

When it comes to sovereign credibility, democracies are usually considered more likely than autocracies to honor international agreements. For example, Schultz and Weingast (2003) argue that democracies are predicted to be more creditworthy because the domestic audience costs are higher for elected officials than for authoritarian leaders so that voters will punish elected officials that do not honor debt obligations. Representative institutions enhance a country's borrowing power because they constrain a democratic government to honor its debts. Such democratic advantage is expressed through the rule of law and the protection of property rights (Biglaiser and Staats 2012; Jensen et al. 2012), which help democratic countries to maintain better access to credit than their undemocratic counterparts (Schultz and Weingast 2003).

Scholars have discussed how conditions favoring economic freedom go along with liberalization of the political order (Olson 1993; Riker and Weimer 1993). Olson (1993: 572) points out that,

> The conditions that are needed for maximum economic development are exactly the same conditions that are needed to have a lasting democracy . . . the same court system, independent judiciary, and respect for law and individual rights that are needed for a lasting democracy are also required for security of property and contract rights.

Denzau and North (1994) have shown that political freedom and the protection of property rights are both correlated with shared values and a common culture, and are therefore naturally compatible. Accordingly, they argue, economic performance is a consequence of the institutional framework of the polity and the economy.

On the link between democratic institutions and sovereign creditworthiness, the financial market experts that I have interviewed all agreed that the characteristics of democracies, such as the rule of law, greater transparency in policymaking, and protection of private property rights, are very important in reducing policy uncertainty and political risk. An interviewee who had recently retired from the industry but nonetheless requested strict confidentiality of his identity said that in many developing countries where there are no democratic rules, "the government acts like the Mafia" in that political leaders use their power and influence to confiscate private property at will. Other interviewees made a similar observation, saying that some authoritarian emerging-market countries, such as China, have a great potential for economic profit, but their success despite a lack of democracy has largely been due to their rapid economic growth rates, which has been high enough to compensate for the political risk such countries pose. They predicted that when the economies of such countries stop showing stellar economic growth, they will face severe problems because investors will find that the returns on their investments no longer compensate for the political risk posed by those governments and will stop investing in those countries (Interviews 7, 10).

Corruption, transparency, and democracy

Democratic governments are believed to control corruption better than authoritarian ones, which too appeals to many investors. Corruption, defined as the abuse of political authority or public power for private benefit, is regarded as a major hindrance to investment and economic growth in many developing countries. Corruption undermines investment and growth because a corrupt political and economic system does not allow market participants equal and open access to the market. Such access itself becomes important, and those wanting access need to bribe government officials (Habib and Zurawicki 2002: 293).

Despite some observations that corruption may promote economic growth in certain contexts (Acemoglu and Verdier 2000; Huntington 1968; Leff 1964), corruption is generally believed to undermine economic development by increasing the cost of business and investment, reducing the productivity of public expenditure, and distorting the allocation of resources (Brunetti 1997; Brunetti and Weder 1998; Kaufmann et al. 1999; Mauro 1996; Mo 2001; Poirson 1998). Thus, acknowledging the importance of reducing corruption and increasing transparency for stable economic development, numerous initiatives, most notably those of the IMF and the World Bank, have been introduced since the 1990s to combat corruption in developing countries. But corruption tends to feed on economic under-development and is often deeply embedded in a society, making it difficult for many developing countries to fight corruption.

Financial market experts I have interviewed all agree that corruption is indeed one of the most severe problems faced by developing countries and is an important cause of policy uncertainty, which increases the investment risks associated with those countries. Corruption raises the premium on retaining power because the best way to personal wealth in a corrupt political system is to control political decisions and allocations (Diamond 2000). This, in turn, significantly increases policy uncertainty. Indeed, corruption can be viewed as a tax that is destructive by nature, because investors need to make payments to government officials and yet cannot be sure that they will get the outcome they have paid for (Mauro 1996).

Democracies are not free from corruption, but corruption tends to be more prevalent in countries in which laws and processes are less transparent and the administrative apparatus has excessive power (LaPalombara 1994; Tanzi 1998). Transparent political processes and institutional structures that oversee and make political leaders accountable for their decisions are likely to reduce the probability of corruption (Bardhan 1997). Lederman et al. (2005) argue that political institutions that increase accountability tend to reduce corruption. The accountability of a political system is, in turn, determined by its degree of competitiveness, its checks and balances, and its degree of transparency (Lederman et al. 2005). In a system with a high degree of political competition, checks and balances, and transparency, politicians are punished when they seek payments or enact policies that are not approved by the general public. Democratic systems are therefore likely to be less corrupt than autocracies. Bhattacharyya and Hodler (2010) have shown that an abundance of natural resources tends to increase corruption in a country, but a better quality of democratic institutions tends to reduce it. Other scholars find that characteristics of democracy, such as greater government accountability, competitive elections, and checks and balances, reduce the incidence of corruption (Bailey and Valenzuela 1997; Laffont and Meleu 2001; Lederman et al. 2005; Linz 1990; Linz and Stepan 1996a, 1996b; Persson et al. 1997; Rose-Ackerman 1999).

Illiberal democracy, deliberative democracy, and sovereign credibility

The fundamental element of a representative democracy is the election of its political leaders. Of course, many undemocratic countries hold elections, but such elections are tightly controlled and have a different function than the competitive elections characterizing democracies. The investors I have interviewed were clearly aware that some countries have a political system which superficially resembles that of a democracy but in reality does not function democratically. Some scholars refer to these as competitive authoritarianism (Levitsky and Way 2002) or electoral authoritarianism (Diamond 2002; Schedler 2002). These types of government are neither fully democratic nor fully autocratic. Elections are held regularly, but the dominant party or dominant political leader always wins, typically by oppressing and coercing the opposition. The elections are not completely fraudulent; the opposition does have a chance to win, but that chance is typically very slim (Howard and Roessler 2006). Russia is an example frequently mentioned by financial market experts I have interviewed. Its institutions, such as electoral rules, resemble those of a democratic system, but they do not function democratically (Interviews 3, 16, 21, 22, 23). The financial market experts recognize that true democracy involves more than institutional structures; the institutions must actually operate in a democratic way.

Another important aspect of democracy that is not widely discussed in the political economy literature but was mentioned by several interviewees is that deliberation and consensus in a society, operating through democratic procedures, are important signals for investment decisions. Decision-making through discussion between free and equal citizens – deliberative democracy – may help a government build legitimacy and improve its efficiency while at the same time educating the general public about important issues (Elster 1998; Fung 2003). Discussion of deliberative democracy has flourished for some years, but studies of its effects on investment and economic growth have been few.

The investors I have interviewed note that the process of deliberation enhances policy predictability because public debate allows investors to get a sense of the significance of the issues and the direction of policymaking (Interviews 11, 12, 14, 16, 23). Other interviewees have also noted that a democratic political mechanism that allows discussion among the citizens and government is important for reducing policy uncertainty (Interviews 1, 2). This influences sovereign credibility, because deliberative democracy is an indicator of transparency in policymaking, and to some extent of social harmony and stability.[1] In many authoritarian governments, a main cause of policy uncertainty is the lack of public debate on important policy issues. Policy decisions are announced without consultation, thus rendering the direction of government policy much more difficult to predict (Interview 23).

The process of deliberation is also important because it provides an opportunity for different actors to better understand their own interests and work to find a solution that may reduce conflict. In this respect, democratic systems have characteristics that better promote social dialogue and conflict resolution in a peaceful way than do autocracies. Rodrik (2007), for example, argues that because participation and the rule of law in democracies provides better ways to regulate and manage social conflict, democracies are also better at managing external shocks to the economy. That is because when a society experiences economic difficulties, it needs an institutional mechanism that will lead to an outcome that will benefit the society's different interests, and democratic systems tend to provide institutions that encourage participation, negotiation, and compromise (Rodrik 2007).

One finance expert has commented that, of the Asian countries affected by the Asian financial crisis, Indonesia experienced the most difficulties because of its political system (Interview 24). Indonesia did not have a political system that mediated economic problems through political discussion. In such circumstances, economic complaints become political complaints, which can be expressed as violent protests against the government. Thus, the market expert continued, the country had a greater risk of political disorder when the economy was not performing well.

Left-wing governments, populism, and democracy

One of the major reasons why left-wing governments in developing countries are perceived as risky is that investors tend to associate left-wing governments with populism. Populism has many definitions. Some define it as a personalized style of political leadership in which the leader appeals to various social groups with a distinct economic development strategy (Roberts 2002). Others define it in a narrower economic sense, stating that populist programs frequently overlap with those of socialism, and that redistributive goals are central to populist beliefs (Dornbusch and Edwards 1991). Populism in that sense emphasizes income redistribution while neglecting the problems of inflation, deficits, external constraints, and investors' response to less market-friendly policies (Sachs 1989; Dornbusch and Edwards 1991). Populism may be based on either leftist or rightist ideology, but this narrower definition has been particularly relevant to left-wing populism as left-wing governments tend to expropriate more readily than others (Eden et al. 2012).

Populism arising from left-wing leaders has been more of a threat to democracy and investment in recent decades (Weyland 2013; Aytac and Onis 2014).[2] Left-wing populism is more disconcerting for investors because it often takes the form of property expropriation and default on sovereign debt. Its best-known instances have arisen in Latin America and appealed to the poor through demagogic advocacy of redistribution and expansionary policies (Castaneda 2006). Such left-wing populist demagogues have expressed radical opposition to Western-sponsored neoliberalism. Because some of their policy positions have inherent affinities with left-wing policies, some authors even argue that socialism is intrinsically populist (March 2007: 65).

Populism tends to gain greater strength when a democracy is less consolidated or is weaker (Mudde and Kaltwasser 2012). This is because weak democratic institutions do not effectively prevent populist strategies from exerting executive power through establishing direct links with the populace, which stands in tension with democracy (Weyland 2013). The revival of populism in Latin America, for example, in the twenty-first century is also closely related to the political limitations and institutional frailties of the region (Roberts 2007). Lack of trust in democratic institutions, such as the party system, legislature, and the judiciary, has also engendered populism in recent years (Doyle 2011). Strong democratic institutions are more effective in keeping political leaders in check and thus are more likely to reduce the likelihood of populist leaders emerging.[3] When a solid democratic institutional context is present, popular chief executives are less likely to fall victim to populist temptations (Navia and Walker 2009).

Populism tends to gain even greater strength when an economy is in difficulty. One financial market expert I have interviewed noted that investors may tolerate a left-wing government in good times, but when the economy goes bad or certain political events occur, it becomes unclear what the government will do (Interview 24). In that situation, the existence of effective institutional mechanisms that constrain left-wing leaders may reassure investors about future policies.

The accountability mechanism of democratic regimes limits the abuse of executive power, and its institutional constraints are important in discouraging populism. The checks and balances in the power distribution and the democratic process that requires transparency and auditing ("institutionalized suspicion") keeps abuse and waste under control (Bardhan 1999: 102). Such systems of checks and balances may thus offer better protection of property rights (Olson 1993; North and Weingast 1989; Bates 2001).

Institutional changes and perceived creditworthiness

An important aspect of the discussion on democracy that has received little attention is how institutional improvements toward greater democracy or deterioration toward greater authoritarianism may influence sovereign credibility, and how such changes interact with other domestic political conditions. If investors respond to regime types, they are likely to react to changes in regime as well. The signaling effects of such changes may in fact be stronger than those of more stable institutions, such as a stable democracy or autocracy.

There is empirical evidence suggesting that democratic transitions lead to economic growth (Giavazzi and Tabellini 2005; Persson 2005; Rodrik and Wacziarg 2005; Persson and Tabellini 2009; Papaioannou and Siourounis 2008), and that they correlate with greater trade openness and market liberalization (Milner and Mukherjee 2009; Boix 2003; Weyland 2002; Stokes 2001). If democratic transitions indicate greater market liberalization, less corruption, and better protection of property rights from populist leaders, it is easy to see how they might promote sovereign credibility.

While improving democracy may be a good sign that a country is reaching toward greater respect for the rule of law, investors' rights, transparency, and other desirable aspects of democracy, the transition process itself can be destabilizing, at least for the short term. That would normally undermine market confidence.[4] Transitions may retard economic growth, which would undermine sovereign credibility. For example, Przeworski et al. (2000) have shown that regime transitions divert resources and energy away from production and thus affect the growth of an economy. Dahrendorf (1990) has presented evidence confirming that political transitions usually result in instability and unrest. Resnick (2001) has demonstrated that democratic transitions undermine FDI inflow into developing countries. A transition to democracy may occur during an economic crisis or after an authoritarian government has made economic adjustments. In the former case, economic policy demands from different groups may impede reform; in the latter, reform may be associated with the interests of the previous authoritarian government, which may lead to limited political freedom (Haggard and Kaufman 1995). In all cases, from an investor's perspective such transitions involve uncertainty and instability.

Any deterioration of democracy as manifested by undermining existing institutional arrangements and the democratic culture may be perceived as a threat by investors and thus also affect sovereign credibility. Populist leaders are more likely to rise to power in weak democracies (Navia and Walker 2009), so deteriorating democracy may thus be perceived as increasing political risk. Indeed, a deterioration in democracy may have a greater effect on sovereign credibility than improvements in democracy. Furthermore, the negative effects of any deterioration in democracy may be felt more strongly under a left-wing government because of the initial credibility problems of such governments.

Earlier findings on democracy, investment, and sovereign credibility

Scholars have reached contradictory conclusions about the relationship between democracy, investment, and sovereign credibility. Helliwell (1994)'s empirical work indicates that democracy tends to promote investment, which has a positive effect on growth. Using data on developing countries in Latin America and elsewhere, Pastor and Hilt (1993) and Pastor and Sung (1995) found that democracy has a positive relationship with private investment. Feng (2003) found that greater civil liberty strongly predicts a larger share of investment in GDP. Li (2009) confirmed that democracies tend to expropriate less than autocracies. Acemoglu et al. (2014) argued that democracy leads to economic growth by increasing investment, providing better education and other public goods, inducing economic reform, and reducing social unrest. On the other hand, a cross-sectional regression analysis published by Levine and Renelt (1992) showed that democracy is not a robust predictor of growth. Barro (1996) found evidence of a nonlinear relationship between democracy and growth, such that greater democracy enhances growth at low levels of political freedom but undermines growth once a moderate level of political freedom is attained. Buthe and Milner (2008) showed that democracy has no effect on FDI inflows when some forms of trade policy, World Trade Organization (WTO) membership, or a preferential trade agreement are controlled for.

Regarding sovereign credibility, Jensen (2006) has shown that democracy correlates with better credit ratings when the economy's level of development, current account balance, debt, and GDP growth are controlled for. Other scholars too have confirmed that democratic countries tend to have better access to capital (Schultz and Weingast 1998; Beaulieu et al. 2012), though there are some who have concluded otherwise (Brewer and Rivoli 1990; Sussman and Yafeh 2000; Stasavage 2003). Democracies can be shown to have defaulted either less often or more often than authoritarian states, depending on the samples and statistical techniques used (Balkan 1992; Saiegh 2005). Controlling for selection effects, Saiegh (2005) found that democracies are more likely to reschedule their debts, and that there is no significant difference between the interest rates they pay and those paid by non-democracies. Archer et al. (2007), however, could find no association between democracy and creditworthiness. Taken all together, these observations suggest some further speculations.

In this chapter, I capture both objective and subjective aspects of democracy by using alternate measures of democracy. I specifically test the following hypotheses:

H4.1: Democratic institutions are likely to correlate with better sovereign credibility, and the correlation is likely to be stronger for left-wing governments than for other types of governments.
H4.2: Government transparency is likely to be positively related with sovereign credibility, and the correlation is likely to be stronger for left-wing governments.
H4.3: Institutional changes, particularly deterioration toward greater authoritarianism, may undermine a country's sovereign credibility and the effects are likely to be greater for left-wing governments.

Quantitative and qualitative evidence

Addressing the relationship between democracy and economic outcomes requires careful examination of the causal directions, as it is the subject of considerable controversy. Some commentators contend that democratic institutions emerge as a result of economic and political development (Lipset 1959; Boix and Stokes 2003), whereas others argue that democracy does not induce development and neither does development induce democracy. Democracy does tend to survive better in wealthier countries (Przeworski et al. 2000), but some argue that democratization in Africa and Eastern Europe has largely been due to the external international environment, such as the Western world's foreign policy agenda and aid (Krueger 1999; Saiegh 2005). To correct for potential endogeneity and selection effects in the relationship between democracy and sovereign credit ratings, I first use a treatment effects model.[5] The results show no endogenous relationship between democracy and creditworthiness.[6]

Therefore, I use the basic model shown in Chapter 3 and incorporate a difference-in-differences design by interacting democracy and leftist party government to examine whether the effects of democracy on sovereign creditworthiness are more positive for leftist than non-leftist governments.[7]

I use two different measures of democracy and generate several different estimates from these. Because one of the goals of this chapter is to contrast the effects of democracy with those of non-democracy, I first use a dichotomous measure by coding democracy as 1 and non-democracy as 0. This dichotomous measure of democracy is from Cheibub et al. (2010), which classifies a regime as a democracy if it meets all of the following requirements: (1) the chief executive is popularly elected or selected by a popularly elected body; (2) the legislature is popularly elected; (3) more than one party competes in the elections; and (4) a new regime can come to power under the same rules used to choose the incumbent. This defines democracy empirically, based on observable facts.[8] It also nicely reflects switches between democracy and autocracy, whereas continuous measures better reflect incremental changes in democracy.

While a dichotomous measure for democracy is most suitable for the present purpose, I also test using a continuous measure of the Polity scores from the Polity IV (Marshall et al. 2009). The original scores range from –10 (strongly autocratic) to +10 (strongly democratic). They are based on six aspects of a country's political institutions, with a focus on executive powers, executive selection, and the freedom of elections. They estimate the existence of institutionalized constraints on the exercise of power by the executive and also measure the citizens' civil liberties in their daily lives and in their political participation. Other aspects of pluralist democracy, such as the rule of law, systems of checks and balances, freedom of the press, and so on can be regarded as means to or specific manifestations of these general principles. I modify the original scale to the scale of 0 (strongly autocratic) to 20 (strongly democratic).

As in the previous chapter, the major dependent variable is the credit ratings from Institutional Investor. I also include economic growth, government budget balance, current account balance, inflation, capital account openness, foreign reserves, investment, and debt service. Country and year fixed effects are also included. The FGLS model with Prais-Winsten transformation and panel-corrected standard errors is described as follows:

$$
\begin{aligned}
&\ln Credit\ Rating_{it} \\
&\quad = \gamma_0 + \gamma_1 Democracy_{i,t-1} + \gamma_2 Left\ Party_{i,t-1} \\
&\qquad + \gamma_3 Democracy_{i,t-1} * Left\ Party_{i,t-1} + \gamma_4 Budget\ Balance_{i,t-1} \\
&\qquad + \gamma_5 Capital\ \ Account\ Openness_{i,t-1} + \gamma_6 GDP\ Growth_{i,t-1} \\
&\qquad + \gamma_7 Inflation_{i,t-1} + \gamma_8 Current\ Account\ Balance_{i,t-1} \\
&\qquad + \gamma_9 Investment_{i,t-1} + \gamma_{10} \ln Reserves + \gamma_{11} Debt_{\ i,t-1} \\
&\qquad + \gamma_{12} \ln Credit\ Rating_{i,t-1} + \epsilon_{it}
\end{aligned}
$$

Effects of democracy on sovereign credibility

Table 4.1 reports the effects of democracy on credit ratings. Model 1 uses the dichotomous measure by Cheibub et al. (2010), while model 2 uses the continuous measure by Polity IV.[9] The results for model 1 confirm that left-wing governments do tend to be perceived as riskier than others, but being a democracy benefits their credibility. Democratic left-wing governments have significantly higher credit ratings than left-wing governments which are undemocratic (by 5.4 points[10]). The joint significance of the interaction term and democracy is significant at the 5 percent level (two-tailed). For non-leftist governments, however, being a democracy does not have a significant relationship with credibility.

Model 2 also suggests that left-wing governments tend to have better credibility when they are more democratic – a 1-point increase in the Polity IV score is associated with a 0.4-point increase in sovereign credibility. The joint significance of the interaction term and democracy is significant at the 1 percent level (two-tailed).[11] For non-leftist governments, the findings once again show that there is

Table 4.1 Democracy, government partisanship, and credit ratings of developing countries

	Model 1 *Democracy Indicator by Cheibub et al. (2010)*	*Model 2* *Democracy Indicator by Polity IV (Marshall et al. 2009)*
Left party	−0.064***	−0.083***
	(0.021)	(0.028)
Democracy	−0.002	0.000
	(0.011)	(0.001)
Left party* Democracy	0.056**	0.004**
	(0.023)	(0.002)
Budget balance	0.002**	0.002**
	(0.001)	(0.001)
GDP growth	0.005***	0.005***
	(0.001)	(0.001)
Capital account openness	0.021***	0.020***
	(0.003)	(0.003)
Investment	0.002**	0.002**
	(0.001)	(0.001)
Current account	0.001**	0.001**
	(0.001)	(0.001)
Inflation	0.000	0.000
	(0.000)	(0.000)
Reserves (log)	0.041***	0.042***
	(0.005)	(0.005)
Debt	−0.000	−0.000
	(0.000)	(0.000)
Rating in the previous year	0.795***	0.796***
	(0.014)	(0.015)
Constant	0.347***	0.347***
	(0.072)	(0.072)
Observations	1,348	1,345
R-Squared	0.97	0.97

Notes: $^{***}p < .01$; $^{**}p < .05$; $^{*}p < .10$ (two-tailed). The dependent variable is Institutional Investor and is log-transformed. Model 2 reports results using the FGLS model. Two-stage model results are presented in Table A4.2 in Appendix 4.

no significant association between the level of democracy and sovereign credibility. Other control variables, such as budget balance, economic growth, capital account openness, investment, current account balance, and foreign reserves, are also important determinants of sovereign ratings in both models.

Table 4.2 Democracy, government partisanship, and credit ratings of developing countries (summary)

	Government Partisanship		*Difference*
	Leftist	*Non-leftist*	*(Leftist) – (Non-leftist)*
Democracy			
No	43.66	50.06	**-6.4**
Yes	49.06	49.86	-0.8
Difference			
(Democracy) – (Non-democracy)	**5.4**	-0.2	**5.6** (Difference-in-Differences)

Notes: The effects are presented as the number of points on Institutional Investor's 100-point rating scale, with other covariates at their mean values. Statistically significant figures are in bold.

Table 4.2 summarizes the results of model 1 in Table 4.1 as a simple table. The numbers are calculated from the coefficients in the model under the assumption that the other control variables have their mean values. Because the credit rating data are log-transformed, the numbers have been converted to fit the original rating scale of 0–100. Left-wing governments that are democracies tend to have ratings higher by about 5.4 points than those which are not democratic, but for governments which are not leftist, the credit ratings do not differ significantly between democracies and non-democracies. Looking just at undemocratic governments, left-wing governments are again perceived to be much less creditworthy than their non-leftist counterparts (with credit ratings on average 6.4 points lower). Among democratic governments, however, the sovereign ratings of left-wing governments almost catch up with those of non-leftist governments. Most importantly, the difference-in-differences value shows that the credit rating difference between left-wing democracies and autocracies is 5.6 points larger than that between right-leaning democracies and autocracies, a statistically significant difference. Figure 4.1 illustrates the effects reported in Table 4.2, with the difference in the slopes for the leftist and non-leftist governments representing the differing effects of democracy on the ratings of leftist and non-leftist governments (difference-in-differences). Being a democracy gives a credibility boost for left-wing governments, but not for others.

One of the financial market experts I have interviewed noted that the reason democratic rules may provide greater assurance to investors regarding left-wing governments is that when circumstances are unfavorable, any government tends to resort to measures that support its core constituency. For a leftist government, such measures are typically less market-friendly (Interview 24). That is, such measures aimed at gaining popularity are often populist policies that significantly undermine private investment, and the leaders are tempted to circumvent

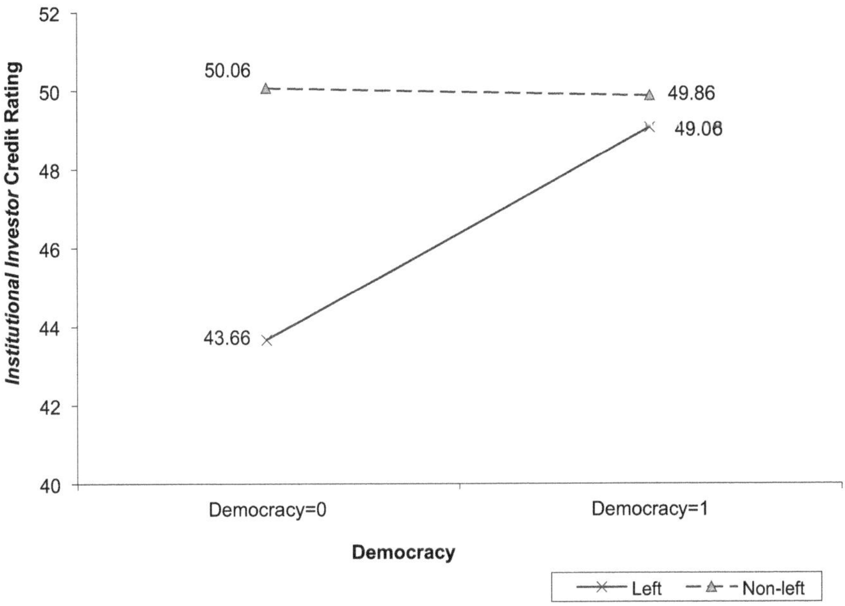

Figure 4.1 Effects of democracy on perceived creditworthiness

institutional constraints to gain political support. Therefore, having more democratic institutions enables investors to have greater confidence, because strong democratic institutions should be better able to deter populist leaders.

Government transparency and sovereign credibility

Given the earlier discussion linking democratic governments to less corruption and greater transparency, I take an additional step to test the effects of government transparency on Institutional Investor ratings. One question regarding the study of corruption and transparency is whether they are something that can be measured and, if so, how they can be measured (Rohwer 2009). It is difficult to measure them directly, and existing measures tend to be based on perception surveys and rankings based on evaluations. Because my models examine the determinants of market perceptions of sovereign credibility, it is more appropriate to use an objective measure of corruption and transparency than using other available measures that rely on perceptions.

I use the measure of government transparency by Hollyer, Rosendorff, and Vreeland (Hollyer et al. 2014). They estimated governments' willingness to disseminate policy-relevant data. Their index (hereafter the HRV index) is based on World Bank data provided by national governments to international organizations such as the IMF and International Labour Organization. I use this measure because it estimates a narrow and precise concept of transparency – a government's disclosure of policy-related information – and thus provides an objective measure of transparency. Some of the HRV data are missing because national governments failed to provide them or they were deemed unreliable and deleted (Hollyer et al. 2014). The HRV index ranges from –11 to 10, with a higher value indicating greater transparency.

Table 4.3 reports the results.[12] Government transparency is positively associated with sovereign credibility of leftist governments, as the coefficients for transparency are jointly significant at the 5 percent level (two-tailed). A one-point increase in the HRV index is associated with a 1.3-point increase in sovereign credit ratings. However, no such association exists for right-leaning governments. The interaction term is also statistically significant, suggesting that the effects of transparency on the credibility of leftist and non-leftist governments are significantly different. Transparency is considered to be an important element of democracy and has conditional signaling effects on sovereign credibility, which once again supports the Nixon-going-to-China framework.

Institutional changes and creditworthiness

If investors respond to regime types, they are also likely to react to regime changes. The signaling effects of such changes may be greater than those from stability, regardless of the level of democracy. Therefore, another way to understand how investors value democracy is to look at how they react when a country's democracy improves or deteriorates.

While improvements toward greater democracy may be a good sign for a country in the sense that it is reaching toward greater respect for the rule of law, investor rights, transparency, and other desirable aspects of democracy, the transition process can nevertheless be destabilizing for society, at least in the short term. One might nonetheless expect investor reactions to be sharper when a democracy deteriorates than when it improves. This is again due to the negativity bias, according to which negative events typically tend to generate sharper market reactions. Furthermore, such reactions may be stronger when the government concerned is left-wing.

To estimate the institutional improvements and deterioration, I use the Polity scores from the Polity IV (Marshall et al. 2009) to create two different sets of variables representing institutional changes. I create two *Institutional deterioration* variables based on score changes in the past five and ten years. First, I code 1 if there was a negative change in the Polity score in a given country-year, and 0 if there was a positive change or no change. I then count the number of deteriorations in the past five years and ten years. *Institutional improvement* is measured similarly. These variables include all improvement and deterioration episodes, and a country experiencing changes may remain an autocratic or a democratic regime during the whole sample period. Institutional changes may be driven by economic shocks which also affect credit ratings, so I create variables measuring the number of economic crises in the past five and ten years.

Table 4.3 Government transparency, partisanship, and credit ratings of Developing countries

	Model 3
Left party	–0.032**
	(0.013)
Transparency	0.005
	(0.004)
Left party* Transparency	0.008*
	(0.005)
Budget balance	0.001*
	(0.001)
GDP growth	0.005***
	(0.001)
Capital account openness	0.019***
	(0.003)
Investment	0.001**
	(0.001)
Current account	0.001*
	(0.001)
Inflation	0.000
	(0.000)
Reserves (log)	0.043***
	(0.005)
Debt	–0.000
	(0.000)
Rating in the previous year	0.799***
	(0.015)
Constant	0.340***
	(0.074)
Observations	1,283
R-squared	0.97

Notes: ***$p < .01$; **$p < .05$; *$p < .10$ (two-tailed). The dependent variable is Institutional Investor and is log-transformed. The results are based on the FGLS model. The results using a two-stage model are presented in Table A4.3 in Appendix 4.

It is based on the data published by Laeven and Valencia (2008), which record banking, currency, and debt crises.

Table 4.4 reports the coefficients of models representing the effects of institutional deterioration on investor perceptions using Institutional Investor ratings.[13] Models 4 and 5 report the results of institutional deterioration in the past five years, with model 5 including a crisis in the past five years. Similarly,

Table 4.4 Institutional deterioration, government partisanship, and credit ratings of developing countries

	Deterioration in past 5 years		*Deterioration in past 10 years*	
	Model 4	*Model 5*	*Model 6*	*Model 7*
Left party	−0.019**	−0.017*	−0.016*	−0.014
	(0.009)	(0.010)	(0.010)	(0.010)
Deterioration	−0.024***	−0.024***	−0.010**	−0.010**
	(0.008)	(0.008)	(0.004)	(0.004)
Left party* deterioration	−0.005*****	−0.001****	−0.003****	−0.001†
	(0.015)	(0.016)	(0.008)	(0.008)
Budget balance	0.001*	0.001	0.001*	0.001*
	(0.001)	(0.001)	(0.001)	(0.001)
GDP growth	0.005***	0.005***	0.005***	0.005***
	(0.001)	(0.001)	(0.001)	(0.001)
Capital account openness	0.019***	0.020***	0.021***	0.020***
	(0.003)	(0.003)	(0.004)	(0.004)
Investment	0.002**	0.002**	0.001**	0.001**
	(0.001)	(0.001)	(0.001)	(0.001)
Current account	0.001**	0.001*	0.001*	0.001*
	(0.001)	(0.001)	(0.001)	(0.001)
Inflation	0.000	0.000	0.000	0.000
	(0.000)	(0.000)	(0.000)	(0.000)
Reserves (log)	0.040***	0.045***	0.041***	0.046***
	(0.005)	(0.005)	(0.005)	(0.005)
Debt	0.000	0.000	0.000	0.000
	(0.000)	(0.000)	(0.000)	(0.000)
Crisis in past 5 years		0.001		
		(0.004)		
Crisis in past 10 years				0.001
				(0.003)
Previous year's rating	0.788***	0.782***	0.784***	0.776***
	(0.015)	(0.015)	(0.016)	(0.016)
Constant	0.377***	0.374***	0.397***	0.392***
	(0.071)	(0.071)	(0.074)	(0.074)
Observations	1,325	1,299	1,278	1,257
R-squared	0.97	0.97	0.97	0.97

Notes: ***$p < .01$; **$p < .05$; *$p < .10$; **** jointly significant at $p < .10$; ***** jointly significant at $p < .05$ (two-tailed); † jointly significant at $p < .10$ (one-tailed). The dependent variable is Institutional Investor and is log-transformed.

models 6 and 7 report the results of institutional improvement in the past ten years, with model 7 including a crisis in the past ten years. The results suggest that both leftist and non-leftist governments tend to be associated with lower credit ratings when they experience a deterioration in institutional quality in the past five and ten years. The negative effects of deterioration are likely to be greater for leftist governments, as their ratings tend to be lower by 0.1 to 0.5 points.[14] The results further suggest that for both left and non-left governments, the negative effects of institutional deterioration are likely to be greater when such negative changes happened relatively recently. This seems to make sense, as more frequent institutional deterioration in the relatively recent past are likely to have greater impact on market perceptions.

Table 4.5 reports the effects of institutional improvement on credit ratings.[15] Improvement is associated with lower ratings for right-leaning governments in models 8, 9, and 10, but there is no statistically significant association of the two for left-wing governments in any of the models. The findings may suggest that investors regard institutional changes – even though they are toward greater democracy – worrisome, because such changes often involve instability in a society. For left-wing governments, however, improvements toward greater democracy may be seen as a relatively good sign, which may dilute the negative perceptions associated with transition.

As expected, the results overall show that investors react more sharply to institutional deterioration than to improvement. Negative responses to institutional deterioration are evident for both leftist and non-leftist governments, and the negative effects of institutional deterioration are likely to be greater for left-wing governments than for others. Market disturbance caused by institutional improvement is likely to affect right-leaning governments only.

Cases: Venezuela under Chávez and Peru under Fujimori

The cases of Venezuela and Peru nicely illustrate how deterioration in democracy under a left-wing government and a right-wing government send different signals to investors. The two cases clearly show that investors react more sharply when a deterioration in democracy occurs in a left-wing government than in a right-wing counterpart.

President Chávez of Venezuela and President Fujimori of Peru were both populist leaders, and both significantly undermined democracy in their country. However, they differed in the nature of their populist policies. The populist qualities of "Chavismo" in Venezuela under Chávez was characterized by very strong leftist rhetoric, anti-globalization, and a distaste for market-oriented reforms (Hawkins 2003). Hugo Chávez was one of the strongest left-wing populist leaders in Latin America. In common with other well-known leftist populists in Latin America, such as Evo Morales in Bolivia, Rafael Correa in Ecuador, Daniel Ortega in Nicaragua, and Nestor Kirchner and Cristina Fernández de Kirchner in Argentina, he attacked the shortcomings of capitalism and democracy, and framed politics as a struggle between the "people" and the

Table 4.5 Institutional improvement, government partisanship, and credit ratings of developing countries

	Improvement in past 5 years		*Improvement in past 10 years*	
	Model 8	*Model 9*	*Model 10*	*Model 11*
Left party	-0.020**	-0.017*	-0.016	-0.015
	(0.010)	(0.010)	(0.012)	(0.012)
Improvement	-0.012**	-0.012**	-0.006*	-0.006
	(0.005)	(0.005)	(0.004)	(0.004)
Left party* Improvement	-0.002	-0.002	-0.002	0.000
	(0.010)	(0.010)	(0.008)	(0.008)
Budget balance	0.001*	0.001	0.002**	0.001*
	(0.001)	(0.001)	(0.001)	(0.001)
GDP growth	0.005***	0.005***	0.005***	0.005***
	(0.001)	(0.001)	(0.001)	(0.001)
Capital account openness	0.020***	0.021***	0.021***	0.021***
	(0.004)	(0.004)	(0.004)	(0.004)
Investment	0.002**	0.001*	0.001*	0.001*
	(0.001)	(0.001)	(0.001)	(0.001)
Current account	0.001*	0.001	0.001	0.001
	(0.001)	(0.001)	(0.001)	(0.001)
Inflation	0.000	0.000	0.000	0.000
	(0.000)	(0.000)	(0.000)	(0.000)
Reserves (log)	0.043***	0.047***	0.042***	0.047***
	(0.005)	(0.005)	(0.005)	(0.005)
Debt	0.000	0.000	0.000	0.000
	(0.000)	(0.000)	(0.000)	(0.000)
Crisis in past 5 years		0.001		
		(0.004)		
Crisis in past 10 years				-0.001
				(0.003)
Previous year's rating	0.784***	0.778***	0.787***	0.780***
	(0.015)	(0.015)	(0.016)	(0.016)
Constant	0.390***	0.385***	0.391***	0.382***
	(0.075)	(0.075)	(0.077)	(0.076)
Observations	1,330	1,300	1,278	1,257
R-squared	0.97	0.97	0.97	0.97

Notes: ***$p < .01$; **$p < .05$; *$p < .10$; **** jointly significant at $p < .10$ (two-tailed). The dependent variable is Institutional Investor and is log-transformed.

"oligarchy." Such leaders tend to nationalize industries and use social spending to reward their supporters and create clientelist relations with the poor. They centralize power in the presidency by arguing that representative democracy must yield to a more personalistic system. They denigrate the United States and globalization, which tends to make their rhetoric and policies quite nationalistic (Brands 2009). In contrast, the presidency of Fujimori involved what some scholars call "neopopulism," in which free-market policies are supported (Weyland 2006; Roberts 1995).

Latin America as a region experienced severe economic problems in the 1980s and 1990s. Most countries in the region were heavily indebted and were dealing with the aftermath of currency and debt crises. Venezuela was no exception. The country had been one of the wealthier countries in the region until the early 1980s, with a relatively stable democracy. However, it was not able to fully recover from its debt and currency crises in the 1980s and 1990s, and its economic situation even worsened in the 1990s. Venezuela suffered high inflation, unstable economic growth, and increasing unemployment. Low oil prices strained the economy, and the government could not reduce its deficits.

These economic problems, together with corruption scandals involving mainstream Venezuelan politicians in the 1990s, undermined public support for the government. Widespread discontent with the government's austerity measures and the officials involved in corruption resulted in anti-government protests and the defeat of the government's party in regional elections. Venezuela had previously maintained a relatively stable democracy with a two-party system. The two major parties, Accion Democratica and Comité de Organización Política Electoral Independiente (COPEI), shared largely similar macroeconomic policies, so changes in government from one party to the other did not result in big policy changes (Kaufman and Stalling 1991). The continuing economic problems and increasing rate of poverty among Venezuela's citizens led to their disenchantment with the established politics.

In that context, President Chávez's criticism of the two-party system and political corruption won popular support. Chávez became president at a time when economic hardship in Venezuela was being borne disproportionately by the lower and middle classes. His leftist rhetoric took advantage of the situation to mobilize underprivileged people by promising redistribution (Roberts 2012). During his electoral campaign, Chávez attacked the notion of representative democracy by associating it with the interests of the wealthy. His radical trajectory throughout his presidency has led many observers of Venezuelan politics to question the democratic nature of his regime.

Despite Chávez's electoral victory, opposition parties remained significant in the congress and the judiciary. To limit the power of the opposition parties and increase his own power in the congress and the judiciary, Chávez held a series of referendums to gain popular support for his goals. For example, he created a new National Constituent Assembly (ANC) dominated by members of his own party to draft a new constitution and replaced the congress. The opposition challenged these moves as a form of dictatorship, but Chávez defended them, saying they were needed to combat corruption and implement reform. The congress and the ANC signed an agreement on political coexistence, but Chávez empowered the ANC by asking it to approve his budget proposal while ignoring the congress' opposition to it.

The ANC also endorsed the new constitution, which was then approved through a referendum. The new constitution significantly strengthened executive power through several measures. It extended the presidential term from five to six years, removed the senate, and increased the government's control of the economy, including giving the government a monopoly in oil. The opposition criticized this centralization of power, but Chávez had strong public support. In 2000, new presidential, legislative, and other regional elections were held under the new constitution, and Chávez won the presidency with especially strong support from the poor. The newly elected national assembly further strengthened presidential power by allowing presidential decrees without legislative checks.

Judicial independence was also undermined, with a Judicial Emergency Commission being set up to investigate the judiciary. The government's control over the judiciary increased as it appointed judges to suit its own political interests, and judges were not guaranteed job security. Although Chávez promised to implement social reform by attacking corruption and making government policymaking more transparent, the measures he actually took made the government less transparent and less accountable.

Chávez reversed the trend toward privatization observed under the previous Caldera administration. He suspended privatization of the health system and nationalized important industries. Especially after winning another presidential election in 2006 with more than 60 percent of the vote, Chávez further radicalized his policies. For example, he altered the new constitution to allow perpetual reelection of the president. This was accompanied by anti-party discourse attacking Venezuela's then-existing institutions. He expanded the role of the state in the country's key economic sectors still further and gave the executive branch power over institutions. He further discouraged private investment in all sectors, depressing productivity, especially in the oil sector, and employment. Lack of fiscal discipline led to inflation problems, and the ensuing price controls led to scarcities of goods.

Venezuela's Institutional Investor ratings fell significantly for the first five years after Chávez took office. The downgrades were based on a combination of slow economic growth and political concerns about his administration (*Institutional Investor*, September 2002, September 2003). Specifically, after Chávez's reelection in 2000, the rating fell by 4.6 points the following year, despite most macroeconomic indicators being similar to the previous year's. Institutional Investor (September 2001) clearly stated that the reasons were political. In the following few years, higher oil prices were able to "offset unease" about President Chávez's reckless behavior, but Venezuela again experienced a large fall in its 2009 ratings due to "populist policies" (*Institutional Investor*, September 2009). Fitch commented on Chávez's plan to accelerate social spending only in states which had elected pro-Chávez governors by stating that such policies undermined democracy and the business environment. Fitch assigned Venezuela the lowest business environment ratings in the region, based on the decreasing foreign investment and increasing long-term political risk (*Business Monitor International*, October 14, 2008).

Contrast Venezuela's experience with that of Peru under Alberto Fujimori in the 1990s. When Fujimori was running for the presidency, he had to create his own party because he was an outsider to Peruvian politics and was not able to secure nomination from an existing party. Being an outsider to the established political system worked in Fujimori's favor, because at the time, people's distrust of the political system and parties was extremely high. It was Peru's problems at the time which enabled Fujimori to become president. Specifically, Peru had experienced an economic crisis in the late 1980s that led to a deep recession. This in turn led to a political crisis, as the political parties were accused of managing the country poorly. This was an ideal context for an outsider (Roberts 1995).

Some scholars argue that political leaders such as Fujimori, Menem, and Collor belong to a neopopulist group that pursues neoliberal reforms and are thus distinct from the classical forms of populist leaders like Perón, Cárdenas, Vargas, and Haya de la Torre (Weyland 1996). Fujimori pursued neoliberal economic policies using populist political strategies. Populism had traditionally had a greater affinity with left-wing ideology, but the neopopulism practiced in countries such as Peru reveals that populism and neoliberalism can operate together during times of economic crisis. People accepted harsh austerity measures imposed by the government because they preferred austerity to total economic collapse (Weyland 1999b). Like other neopopulist leaders such as Collor and Menem, Fujimori dissociated the societal interests that had close ties with public agencies. He established a central control of government apparatus to implement neoliberal policies and of private sectors which did not cooperate with him (Weyland 1999b). The Ministry of Finance pursued fiscal discipline and market reforms, which seemed to lead to a deep recession, lower wages, unemployment, and cuts in public spending, hurting most people in the country. Poverty increased, while at the same time, some business people made considerable profits through buying state enterprises. Thus, income inequality in Peruvian society increased (Weyland 1999b).

Politically, Fujimori's measures significantly undermined Peru's democracy. He attacked the political elite and establishment institutions they controlled (Levitsky and Loxton 2013). The legislature and the judiciary were both dominated by the existing major parties, so Fujimori challenged them through excessive decrees to circumvent the legislature and carried out a presidential coup (*autogolpe*) in April 1992. He dissolved the constitution, closed the congress, purged the judiciary and other state institutions, and ruled with quasi-dictatorial powers. He announced that the immediate suspension of the constitution and the congress was required to combat corruption and increase efficiency. He established an Emergency and National Reconstruction Government to implement free-market economic policies. After closing down the legislature, he exercised legislative power with the consent of the Council of Ministers. Major media outlets were occupied by the military.

The deterioration of democracy in Peru was so significant that Peru's Polity score fell significantly from 8 in 1991 to –3 in 1992. However, Fujimori claimed that he had installed true democracy, terming the earlier system a "partyarchy." He believed that to solve Peru's severe economic problems, he had to pursue efficiency at the expense of liberal democratic procedures and consensus (Levitsky and Loxton 2013, quoting Conaghan 2005). Even though Fujimori's political actions dismantled democracy in Peru, his initiatives remained well supported by the populace because he had risen to power through populist tactics.

Despite all, the breakdown of democracy in Peru did not cause a sharp reaction from investors. After Fujimori took power in 1990, Peru's sovereign credit ratings steadily increased every year during his presidency. Peru received IMF-supported programs from 1993, which became a turning point allowing the country to produce an impressive economic performance. However, during the early period of his presidency, before the advent of the IMF programs, Fujimori had already instituted drastic economic reforms to tackle economic problems (Pop-Eleches 2009). For example, in 1990 he announced the removal of consumer subsidies, which led to significant price increases. Furthermore, Fujimori used his emergency legislative powers to announce economic decrees that eliminated the state control of telecommunications, railroads, and postal services, allowed privatization of the health care system, and reformed the social security services, among others. Although those moves met popular resistance, they were able to address investors' concerns about political instability and poor economic growth, which fell by 3 percent compared with the previous year. Peru's Institutional Investor rating was higher than that for the previous year by 1.1 points.

The market's reaction to Peru at that time contrasts with its treatment of Venezuela, where the Institutional Investor rating fell by nearly 5 points in 2001 following the reelection of Chávez in 2000, despite Venezuela's macroeconomic performance remaining similar to that of the previous year. The political risk perceived as surrounding the Chavez government and fear of his predatory economic policies that threatened private investment clearly ruined the market's appreciation for Venezuela. Investors feared that Venezuela's declining democracy would go hand in hand with greater threats for private and international investors. Conversely, although the democratic breakdown in Peru disturbed political stability, investors were less concerned about their investments being at risk of sovereign theft, reassured by Fujimori's market-friendly policies. These two cases show how populism and democratic breakdown can lead to quite different outcomes for a government's sovereign credibility, and that the effects largely hinge on the leader's ideological orientation.

Conclusions

This chapter has examined the relationship between democratic institutions and sovereign credit ratings. There is no consensus about the effects of democracy on economic performance, as theories and empirical findings point in different directions. In relation to sovereign credibility, the democratic advantage argument states that democracies build sovereign credibility among investors because the accountability mechanism induces democratic governments to be more responsible in dealing with their debt obligations.

Democracies have positive qualities that appeal significantly to investors. A democratic system has greater accountability and representativeness that increase policy predictability. Democracies better address corruption because they are more transparent than autocracies in their policymaking. Corruption tends to be more prevalent in less transparent situations and where the administrative apparatus has excessive power. Transparent political processes, and institutional structures that oversee political leaders and hold them accountable for their decisions, are likely to reduce the opportunities for corruption. Democracy's open deliberation process also appeals to investors because public discussion of important economic and political issues allows international investors to recognize the important issues a country faces to see how the public responds to them. This aids in predicting directions in policymaking. Open discussion also allows people in a society to reconcile their different interests in a peaceful way, helping countries in economic trouble to avoid the escalation of social conflict. The checks and balances usual in democracies are also important, particularly for discouraging populism.

The findings of this chapter suggest that democratic systems have positive credibility-building effects on the credit ratings of leftist governments, but not for non-leftist governments. Greater transparency in policy-related information further helps the credit ratings of left-wing governments, but no such relationship is found for others. Moreover, negative institutional changes also have a significant association with left-wing governments' credit ratings. One may interpret these empirical findings as showing that democratic virtues – such as reducing corruption, providing for the rule of law, constraining arbitrary executive power, discouraging populism, and respecting public deliberative processes – are particularly effective when a leftist party is in power. A leftist government's move away from democratic principles is perceived as risky for fear that it is leading toward populist economic policies. Populist leaders typically ignore the rule of law, relying on their mandate directly from the people. If a country lacks effective institutions to constrain the whims of its political leader, that leader may try to exercise power autocratically. Historically, many leftist governments have reversed their pledges to pursue free-market policies and privatization and instead have infringed private property. Investors may greatly appreciate democratic rules that provide greater transparency in the policymaking process and lead to fewer arbitrary policy changes made by political leaders.

Notes

1 For example, refer to Fishkin (1991, 2009).

2 Some political leaders in Latin America have successfully combined populism with neoliberal market reforms, but they have been reluctant to firmly

institutionalize the reforms and have continued to interfere with the economy for political reasons (Weyland 1999a, 1999b). Thus, political risk is still present, because populism inherently aims to reduce institutional checks on political leaders to enhance their power.

3 In this regard, although there are concerns about rising (right-wing) populism in Europe and the US, such populists are not likely to be allowed to pursue extreme policies as fascists did in the past because well-established democratic procedures, institutions, and civil society provide people with opportunities to express their voice against any extreme measures proposed by populists (Berman 2016).

4 For a discussion of democratic recession, refer to Diamond (2015).

5 See Maddala (1986) for further explanation of the model.

6 The results are reported in Table A4.1 in Appendix 4. Other credit ratings have too few observations to yield statistically significant findings in this analysis.

7 The treatment effects model prohibits the interaction of an endogenous variable (democracy) and another explanatory variable in the second stage, so that leftist and non-leftist governments are estimated separately in the model. In contrast, the pooled model allows the use of an interaction term, thus interacting government partisanship with democracy. Using such an interaction term is superior to running two separate regressions for left and non-left governments, because the term can estimate whether the effect of democracy is conditional on the ideology of the government and whether the effect of ideology can be mitigated by democratic institutions.

8 They apply a minimalist definition of democracy, which is contested elections for executive and legislative offices (Cheibub et al. 2010).

9 For model 2, the results based on the two-stage least squares methods are presented in Table A4.2 in Appendix 4.

10 As noted earlier, the credit rating data are log-transformed so the interpretation is based on the original rating scale of 0–100.

11 Whereas the effects of democracy on sovereign credibility are statistically significant for left-wing governments, there is no significant association between democracy and sovereign credibility for any type of government when other ratings are used. This may be due to the small samples containing far fewer observations of left-wing governments that are democracies. Another possible explanation is that the signaling effects of democratic institutions are not as strongly reflected in those other ratings because the ratings' components may focus relatively less on a country's political institutions.

12 Results using the two-stage least squares model is presented in TableA4.3 in Appendix 4.

13 The results for other credit ratings are reported in Table A4.4 in Appendix 4.

14 The negative effects of institutional deterioration on leftist governments' ratings seem to be substantively larger in other ratings so that an additional episode of deterioration in the past five years, for example, is associated with a 2.2- to 5.6-point decline in ratings. This may also suggest that these other ratings are more sensitive to institutional changes than to more stable institutions, such as a stable democracy or autocracy.

15 The results for other credit ratings are reported in Table A4.5 in Appendix 4.

5 Political constraints and sovereign creditworthiness

In 2012, Argentina surprised the world by nationalizing Yacimientos Petrolíferos Fiscales (YPF). YPF had been Argentina's biggest state-run oil and gas company and was privatized in 1993. Following the privatization, the Spanish company Repsol increased its share holdings to more than 50 percent of the YPF shares, an asset estimated to be worth over US$10 billion (BBC, December 4, 2012). YPF and other oil companies subsequently limited investment because they felt energy prices were low, leading to Argentina's changing from an energy exporter to being an energy importer. Argentina's President Cristina Fernández de Kirchner then nationalized the firm, accusing it of making too little investment in Argentina's oil production to meet the country's energy requirements. She further claimed that Argentina was one of the few countries that did not control its oil resources.

The nationalization was praised in Argentina, but it chilled investor sentiment. Argentina's move was problematic not only because the nationalization itself would discourage billions of dollars of private investment, but also because it showed a lack of effective checks on Kirchner's political leadership. The legislation was proposed by Kirchner, and the legislature was dominated by her Justicialist Party. The bill to nationalize YPF received predominant support from both the senate and the lower house. Scholars expressed concern over the structure of the government, arguing that Argentina's democracy might be threatened because there was no effective opposition party and the nationalization displayed institutional weakness through the lack of horizontal accountability and legislative ineffectiveness (Levitsky and Murillo 2009).

Standard and Poor's warned that it would downgrade Argentina's ratings because the nationalization would undermine the country's economic situation and deter potential investors (*The Times*, April 24, 2012). It in fact revised its outlook for Argentina from stable to negative, noting that the decision to nationalize YPF underscored the weakening system of checks and balances in the country. It further stated that better respect for the rule of law and protection of property rights was needed (*Washington Times*, April 27, 2012).

This example shows that institutional investors and rating agencies consider political constraints on political leaders to be an important determinant of sovereign risk. For many investors, a government's ability to craft a credible commitment to its existing policies is an important political variable of great interest. Institutional checks operate as a mechanism to prevent arbitrary and abrupt policy changes, thereby creating a more credible investment environment. Thus, as the findings in the previous chapter show, investors worry about governments that do not have effective checks on their political leadership or show any signs of deterioration in such institutions.

At the same time, however, investors may react sharply when a political system puts too many constraints on the executive. That can generate policy gridlock that hampers improvements in public debt management and restricts economic reform and growth. Such concerns over the political dynamics of checks against the executive appear to be sharper when the political leader is left-oriented. Too few checks on a left-wing leader may lead to unfettered populism that works against business interests, but too many may lock in leftist policies or delay market-friendly reform if left-wing forces are entrenched in a positon to veto them. Accordingly, the markets' perceptions of a country's credibility are likely to depend on its current state. If, for example, a leftist party is pursuing market-friendly policies, the markets may adjudge excessive constraints to be bad for market liberalization, and investors may then prefer fewer of them. If, on the other hand, a left-wing leader is not reform-minded or even market-averse, investors may prefer stronger checks on the executive power.

An influential body of work has analyzed the relationship between political constraints and economic outcomes.[1] A decision-making system with few checks on the executive has the advantage of being decisive. Policies can be made more swiftly and implemented with fewer hurdles, but such swiftness may undermine policy credibility (Haggard 2000). In contrast, a highly constrained system allows bargaining through the process of checks and balances. Such a system is more stable but less decisive. Extreme political constraints may generate policy gridlock, and a stalemate can significantly undermine a government's ability to implement necessary policies, particularly when the economy is in crisis (Haggard 2000).

This chapter, therefore, proceeds one step further from comparing democracies and non-democracies to explore how political checks and balances affect sovereign credibility and, more importantly, how such credibility effects are influenced by the executive's ideological orientation. The previous chapter shows that investors tend to favor a certain degree of political constraints against left-wing leaders in developing countries. The findings in this chapter show that there is an inverted U-shaped association between political constraints and sovereign credibility of left-wing governments in developing countries. In other words, there is a positive relationship between the degree of political constraints and sovereign credit ratings when a system has a very weak to a moderate degree of political constraints. The relationship becomes negative, however, after reaching a certain level of political constraints. This seems to be particularly true when the left-wing government pursues market liberalization. Because of the leftist party label, investors may want to see a certain degree of political constraints on a left-wing executive even if the government pursues market-oriented reform, as investors may be concerned about policy reversals. Whereas this inverted U-shaped association between the degree of political constraints and sovereign credibility exists for left-wing governments in developing countries, no significant association is found for others. A case study of India, which for decades has had a series of coalition governments, shows that markets are particularly concerned about excessive political constraints in left-wing governments because such constraints undermine market-friendly reform efforts.

Political constraints and policy changes

The literature on political checks and balances builds on the idea that a polity's ability to change or to commit to a policy depends on the separation of powers. Cox and McCubbins (2001) and Tsebelis (1995, 2002) analyze political systems using the concept of veto points or veto players, which reflect the number of individuals or collective actors whose agreement is necessary for a change in the status quo, and the conflicts of interests between these actors. Policy change becomes more difficult when the number of veto players or the degree of political constraints is greater and policy preferences are more widely separated. As a result, a higher degree of political constraints creates a more stable and predictable policy environment because policy change requires the agreement of more independent actors (Tsebelis 1995, 2002).

Beyond the number of veto points, the actors' preferences are another important consideration. Significant policy changes are easier when there are few and ideologically compatible veto players. A larger number of veto players with significant ideological differences will result in greater policy stability or maintenance of the status quo (Tsebelis 2002). But of course the status quo does not necessarily involve market-friendly policies (Jensen 2006). For that, the veto players' preferences must align to some extent with those of investors.

Policy stability can be understood in terms of credibility (or resoluteness) and decisiveness. North and Weingast (1989) have focused on credibility, investment, and growth in Europe, and they have persuasively demonstrated that stable and secure protection of property rights is crucial for credibility. Europe's political institutions prevent political leaders from making arbitrary policy changes, and this reassures investors that political leaders will adhere to their promised policies (North and Weingast 1989; Root 1989). Another way to view policy stability is to understand it as a political system's inability to respond to economic and political changes. When there is an economic shock, governments are expected to be adaptable and flexible in responding quickly. If political checks and balances hinder timely adjustment efforts, an economy can be stuck in an undesirable status quo (Haggard 2000). A significant amount of research on this problem has been devoted to explaining the economic performance of coalition governments. Coalition governments often have the problem of heterogeneity and the inability to last long. These features impede their ability to make necessary reforms and adjust to shocks. In certain situations, decisiveness in making policy is called for, and coalition governments often have difficulty responding.

There is also a moderated view of these two extremes that balances the importance of credible commitment with that of adaptability and flexibility. MacIntyre (2001, 2003), for example, argues that both credibility and flexibility matter. His argument is that investors prefer credibility and stability in certain situations, such as in macroeconomic policies, whereas flexibility and timely response are important in other cases, such as post-crisis adjustment and stabilization. He contends that the relationship between veto players and investors' preferences is an inverted U-shape. More numerous veto players reduce the possibility of abrupt policy changes, but there is a point of inflection beyond which additional veto players promote policy gridlock. For investors, in other words, having too few veto players implies policy volatility, but having too many suggests policy rigidity (MacIntyre 2001).

Because the concept of political constraints involves the status quo versus change, research that uses this concept naturally investigates the effects of political constraints on changes in various economic outcomes. Scholars have shown a negative association between a large number of veto players and budget deficits (Franzese 2002; Hallerberg and von Hagen 1999; Kontopoulos and Perotti 1999; Roubini and Sachs 1989a, 1989b; Alesina and Drazen 1991; Alesina and Perotti 1994). Fragmented political systems also seem to impede exchange rate adjustments (Keefer and Stasavage 2002; Haggard 2000; Haggard and Kaufman 1992), and may undermine economic reform (Cox and McCubbins 2001), whereas Gehlbach and Malesky (2010) have shown that more numerous veto players encourage economic reform by weakening the power of special interests. Others have found that greater political constraints tend to promote central bank independence (Lohmann 1998; Moser 1999), investment (Jensen 2006; Stasavage 2002), and growth (Henisz 2000).[2] Falaschetti (2003) and Zheng (2011) found that an intermediate number of veto players tends to correlate with greater investment.

Political constraints and sovereign credibility

Based on the discussion so far, one might expect political constraints to send mixed signals to the markets about economic conditions and thus about sovereign credibility. Although few studies directly test the effects of political constraints on sovereign credibility, one may draw implications from earlier works that examine the effects of political constraints on actual episodes of sovereign default.[3] Some scholars argue that tight political constraints help to prevent default so that coalition governments, for example, are less likely to default than are majoritarian governments (Saiegh 2009; Van Rijckeghem and Weder 2004). The reasoning is that a majoritarian government pursues policies that benefit voters and will thus decide to default if that is what the majority of voters prefer, whereas the leaders of a coalition government must accommodate other coalition members' demands, which may protect the interests that prefer debt repayment. Similarly, Kohlscheen (2004) has presented evidence that parliamentary democracies tend to have a lower propensity to reschedule debt. Contrary to the expectation that parliamentary governments tend to be short-lived and thus are more likely to default on sovereign debt, in fact they actually tend to honor debt obligations more reliably because the checking mechanism of a coalition government deters the executive from reneging on debt obligations. When a government possesses concentrated power, there may be greater fluctuation in policies, including those on debt obligations, whereas coalition governments or a system with shared powers may experience less scope for such policy instability (Breen and McMenamin 2013).

Others argue that political polarization deters efficient policymaking and thus undermines a government's ability to repay sovereign debt. Political polarization may cause policy preferences to be formed according to very narrow private interests (Haggard and McCubbins 2001). In addition, when there are high degrees of political constraints, the government's ability to make timely adjustments becomes difficult, increasing the risk of default. A presidential system may provide greater security of tenure than a parliamentary system, allowing the executive to pursue unpopular policies, such as implementing austerity budgets (Eichler 2014).

Regarding sovereign credibility, Jensen (2006) has tested how veto players and federalism affect sovereign lending risks, and found that veto players do not have a significant influence, whereas federalism is positively associated with credit ratings. Eichler and Hofmann (2013) have shown that a federal system is associated with an increased risk of default. But no published study has yet investigated how political constraints and government orientation might interact to influence market perceptions. This is an important omission, because institutional arrangements may have significantly different effects on investor perceptions depending on what sorts of actors are involved.

As noted earlier, the concept of political constraints naturally involves change versus the status quo. As a result, the sovereign credibility of a country is likely to be shaped by investors' expectations about how an economy's political constraints are likely to affect their investment given the government's orientation. Investors may view excessive political constraints as just as undesirable as too few constraints. News reports about financial market responses to political constraints seem to support this belief, so that more political constraints, as occur with coalition governments, are generally translated into more hurdles in the process of making and implementing policies. Instances from Eastern Europe, Latin America, and India of markets falling when a coalition government is formed seem to support the idea that investors are typically concerned when there are excessive veto players or coalition partners. Polarization induces uncertainty over future policy and thus reduces the expected returns on investments (Frye 2002).

Consideration of a government's orientation further complicates matters. If the decision to default is politically driven, calculations relating to the probability of default may depend on expectations regarding which type of government is more likely to choose default given the degree of political constraints. In developing countries where most government debt is likely to be held by foreign investors, governments may be more tempted to default, particularly when the majority of society prefers it. At the same time, leftist governments are more likely to resort to default than right-wing governments, particularly in times of economic difficulty, because their support base may prefer the government to default and use the funds instead for public expenditure domestically. In that case, a leftist government in coalition is likely to face particularly strong pressure from other leftist veto players in the coalition. Clearly, investors may prefer a moderate degree of political constraints when such governments are in power.

Based on the discussion thus far, I test the following hypotheses.

H5.1: Governments too tightly or too loosely constrained are likely to have lower credit ratings than those with a moderate degree of political constraints.

H5.2: The credibility-building effects of a moderate degree of political constraints are likely to be stronger for left-wing governments than for their right-wing counterparts.

H5.3: For left-wing governments, the negative effects of excessive political constraints are likely to be greater for those that pursue market-oriented reform than for those less interested in reform.

Quantitative and qualitative evidence

The measure of political constraints is *Checks* by the Database of Political Institutions (DPI). *Checks* measures the number of parties in government coalitions, the ideological affinities between the governing party and the coalition members in parliamentary systems, the number of legislative chambers in presidential systems, the existence of competitive elections, and whether an opposition party controls the legislature (Beck et al. 2001). The index ranges from 1 to 18, with a higher score indicating stronger political constraints. If there is a positive relationship between the degree of political constraints and sovereign credit ratings as one moves from a very low to a moderate degree of political constraints, then a negative relationship thereafter (as shown in Figure 5.1), it

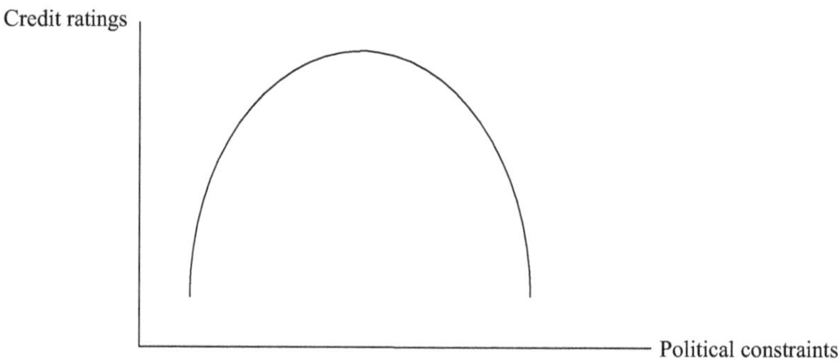

Figure 5.1 The hypothesized relationship between the degree of political constraints and credit ratings

should be represented by a second-order polynomial using *Checks* as the predictor. I test this idea with the variable log-transformed.

To test H5.3, I divided the sample into two groups, one with financial reform and the other with no reform. The financial reform data are drawn from Abiad et al. (2008), which measured financial sector liberalization of 91 countries from 1975 to 2005. The authors take into account degrees of financial liberalization in government controls of credit, interest rates, the banking sector, the capital account, and securities markets. The financial liberalization score ranges from 0 to 21, with a higher score indicating greater financial liberalization. I follow the authors' classification of reform countries so that countries with an increase of more than 1 point in their score comprise the reform group, and those with no change or a decrease make up the no-reform group.

The basic model takes the same form as in the previous chapters, with the variables measuring political constraints and their interactions with government ideology added. As before, the major dependent variable is Institutional Investor sovereign credit ratings. The FGLS model with Prais-Winsten transformation and panel-corrected standard errors is specified as follows:

$$
\begin{aligned}
&\ln Credit\ Rating_{it} \\
&\quad = \gamma_0 + \gamma_1 Left\ Party_{i,t-1} + \gamma_2 Political\ Constraint_{i,t-1} \\
&\qquad + \gamma_3\, Political\ Constraint^2_{i,t-1} + \gamma_4 Left\ Party * Political\ Constraint_{i,t-1} \\
&\qquad + \gamma_5\, Left\ Party * Political\ Constraint^2_{i,t-1} + \gamma_6 Budget\ Balance_{i,t-1} \\
&\qquad + \gamma_7 Capital\ \ Account\ Openness_{i,t-1} + \gamma_8 GDP\ Growth_{i,t-1} \\
&\qquad + \gamma_9 Inflation_{i,t-1} + \gamma_{10} Current\ Account\ Balance_{i,t-1} + \gamma_{11} Investment_{i,t-1} \\
&\qquad + \gamma_{12} \ln Reserves_{i,t-1} + \gamma_{13} Debt_{\ i,t-1} + \gamma_{14} \ln Credit\ Rating_{i,t-1} + \epsilon_{it}
\end{aligned}
$$

Political constraints and sovereign credit ratings

Table 5.1 presents the resulting coefficients.[4] They appear to support the argument that an intermediate number of veto players is most conducive to a better credit rating for leftist governments in developing countries but not for others. Model 1 for developing countries shows that coefficients of the terms representing the interaction of political constraints with a leftist party are statistically significant, suggesting that there is indeed a nonlinear, inverted U-shaped association between the degree of political constraints and the credit ratings of leftist governments in the developing world. The quadratic terms are jointly significant at $p < .05$ (two-tailed). For left-wing governments, credit ratings tend to increase as the degree of political constraints increases, but begin to decline once the number of veto players reaches a certain level (a constraint score of about 4).[5] Figure 5.2 shows the inverted U-shaped relationship between the degree of political constraints and Institutional Investor ratings of leftist governments, based on the results in model 1. There is no such significant association for governments which are not leftist. Other control variables, such

Table 5.1 Political constraints, government partisanship, and credit ratings

	Model 1 *Developing Countries*	*Model 2* *Developed Countries*
Left party	–0.045**	0.047
	(0.021)	(0.035)
Checks	–0.006	–0.017
	(0.020)	(0.033)
Left party* Checks	0.062**	–0.061
	(0.031)	(0.048)
Checks^2	0.003	0.004
	(0.012)	(0.012)
Left party* Checks^2	–0.025*	0.019
	(0.014)	(0.016)
Capital account openness	0.020***	0.000
	(0.004)	(0.002)
Investment	0.001*	–0.000
	(0.001)	(0.001)
Budget balance	0.001	0.000
	(0.001)	(0.000)
GDP growth	0.005***	0.002***
	(0.001)	(0.001)
Reserves (log)	0.042***	0.000
	(0.005)	(0.000)
Inflation	0.000	–0.001***
	(0.000)	(0.000)
Current account balance	0.001*	0.002***
	(0.001)	(0.000)
Debt	0.000	–0.000
	(0.000)	(0.000)
Rating in the previous year	0.800***	0.916***
	(0.015)	(0.023)
Constant	0.339***	0.385***
	(0.074)	(0.096)
Observations	1,275	483
R-squared	0.97	0.98

Notes: ***$p < .01$; **$p < .05$; *$p < .10$ (two-tailed). The dependent variable is Institutional Investor and is log-transformed.

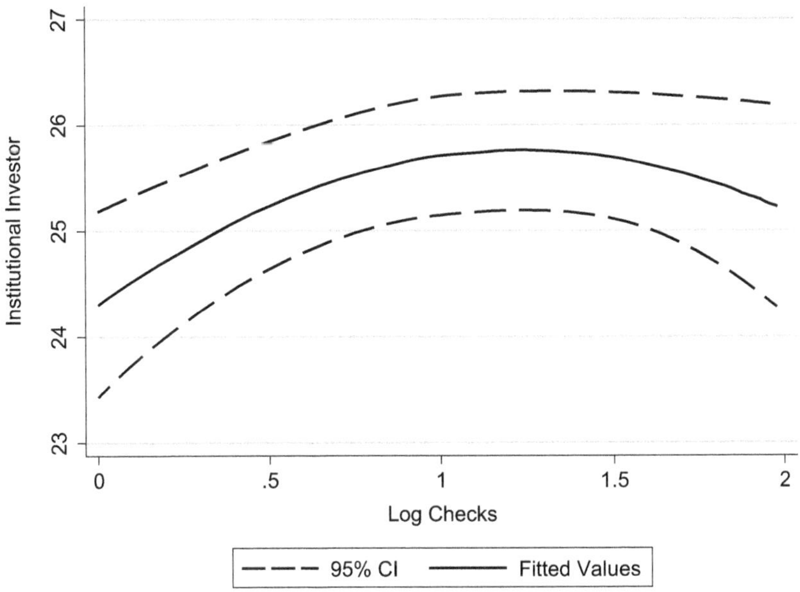

Figure 5.2 Political constraints and credit ratings of leftist governments in developing countries

as capital account openness, investment, economic growth, foreign reserves, and the current account balance, are also influential.

To compare with developing countries, I present in model 2 the regression results of the effects of political checks on Institutional Investor ratings for developed countries. The results show that there is no statistically significant association between political constraints and sovereign credibility for any type of advanced economies.[6] These findings are in line with the information obtained through interviews with financial market experts, who assert that the degree of political constraints does not seriously affect their investment decisions regarding advanced economies. One expert, for example, explained that although investors have been paying more attention to government formation following the Eurozone debt crisis because of issues associated with budget deficits, they still tend to be much less worried about coalition politics in developed countries (Interview 16).

Political constraints, status quo, and sovereign credibility

Finally, Table 5.2 shows models examining how political constraints and government ideology in developing countries interact to affect sovereign credibility in different situations using Institutional Investor ratings.[7] As noted earlier, I divided the countries into two groups: one which undertook financial reforms and the other which did not, using the classification by Abiad et al. (2008). The results in model 3 show that for leftist governments with no financial reform, the

Table 5.2 Political constraints, government partisanship, and credit ratings of developing countries with and without financial reform

	No Reform	*Reform*
	Model 3	*Model 4*
Left party	–0.092***	–0.096**
	(0.033)	(0.040)
Checks	0.001	–0.000
	(0.034)	(0.027)
Left party* Checks	0.095*	0.100**
	(0.057)	(0.049)
$Checks^2$	–0.014	0.005
	(0.022)	(0.013)
Left party* $Checks^2$	–0.020	–0.033*
	(0.028)	(0.018)
Capital account openness	0.026***	0.022***
	(0.005)	(0.007)
Investment	0.002**	0.001
	(0.001)	(0.002)
Budget balance	0.002	0.003*
	(0.001)	(0.002)
GDP growth	0.005***	0.006***
	(0.001)	(0.001)
Reserves (log)	0.038***	0.039***
	(0.008)	(0.011)
Inflation	–0.000*	0.000
	(0.000)	(0.000)
Current account balance	0.003***	0.002*
	(0.001)	(0.001)
Debt	–0.000	–0.001
	(0.001)	(0.001)
Rating in the previous year	0.815***	0.792***
	(0.021)	(0.027)
Constant	0.367***	0.415***
	(0.090)	(0.124)
Observations	626	353
R-squared	0.97	0.98

Notes: ***$p < .01$; **$p < .05$; *$p < .10$ (two-tailed). The dependent variable is Institutional Investor and is log-transformed.

stronger the political constraints, the higher their ratings tend to be. For left-wing governments pursuing financial reform (model 4), however, the inverted U-shaped association appears once again. The quadratic terms are again jointly significant at $p < .05$ (two-tailed).

These findings are interesting, as they tend to confirm that markets may perceive too much constraint on a market-friendly left-wing executive to undermine market liberalization and thus increase sovereign risk. But because of the leftist party label, investors may not fully trust such governments, so an intermediate level of political constraints is most preferred. For a leftist leader who does not implement financial liberalization, however, the markets may prefer strong checks on the executive power. These findings too are confirmed by financial market experts. Those I have interviewed commented that when an extremely leftist leader is unchecked, they feel very worried. They would definitely prefer to see some institutional checks on such leaders. They also clearly indicate that although dictatorships are risky, they also dislike excessive checks and opposition to the government, particularly when market-oriented reform is pursued, because they significantly increase uncertainty about its implementations (Interviews 15, 16, 19, 20).

Case study: India's United Front versus National Democratic Alliance

Of those countries that are perceived to be problematic because of excessive political constraints, the one most frequently mentioned by the interviewees is India. I examine the Indian case to identify how coalition politics in the country has led to negative market perceptions. Although India has a long history of democracy, the market experts I have interviewed did not appreciate democracy's virtues in India's case; instead, they talked about how the political system slows economic reform and keeps state controls in place.

India's long history of democracy is a unique feature given that its neighbor countries tend to be autocracies or new democracies. India also has extensive experience with coalition governments. For decades, Indian politics were dominated by the Congress Party, which started as an organized social movement and became a political party in the 1940s. After 1977, the Congress-dominated one-party system weakened, and regional parties began to gain importance. Indian votes were split between central and regional parties, resulting in a series of minority and coalition governments.

Economically, India had maintained a command economy with strict regulations and myriad controls. In 1991, the country started to restructure the economy. Economic reform continued as the government's orientation varied between left and right, generating quite different market reactions. The negative market response to left-wing governments was stronger than that on the right. I thus discuss India's coalition governments in the late 1990s, because these serve as a good example of how investors perceive coalition politics and how the markets' response differs depending on the ideological orientation of the government.

After the 1996 general election, a left-oriented United Front (UF) coalition government was formed. Initially, the Bharatiya Janata Party (BJP) – a Hindu-nationalist, right-of-center party – formed a government because it had won the most seats, but it held nowhere near enough to rule alone, and that government lasted only 13 days. A center-left-oriented UF coalition that included several major regional parties and the Left Front of the communist parties then took office in June 1996. The key political parties in the coalition were Janata Dal, the Communist Party of India (Marxist) (CPI(M)), the Communist Party of India (CPI), and other regional parties.

The coalition's Prime Minister, H.D. Deve Gowda, and his finance and industry ministers supported economic reform. However, the coalition was ideologically polarized on economic issues. The Janata Dal, and especially the Left Front, had always been very critical of economic liberalization in India. They were particularly opposed to the privatization of public sector entities (Nayar 1999). Fierce opposition to economic liberalization arose from the CPI and CPI(M) with their strong links with workers and trade unions and their strong ideological preference for a planned economy (Nayar 1999).

The resulting internal conflicts had a negative influence on investor perceptions of India. Investors were worried that economic reform would slow down under the left-wing coalition, though in fact the Gowda administration rapidly processed a huge backlog of investment proposals. Between July and December 1996, it approved more than 800 applications worth almost US$5 billion in total, a significant milestone since India's 1991 reforms (*Journal of Commerce*, February 12, 1997). In April 1997, Inder Kumar Gujral became prime minister and promised that he would continue to liberalize the economy. Although Gujral's administration only lasted until December 1997, a significant step to extend the reforms was made by liberalizing outward investment. However, despite the government's pledge to continue with reforms and the country's being able to avoid the shocks resulting from the Asian financial crisis, the government faced significant credibility problems because of continuing doubt about its ability and willingness to carry out reforms. Investors applauded the UF's market liberalization efforts, but were confused by the communist parties' commitment to opposing reform and the conflicts arising between ministers (*Financial Times*, May 9, 1997). Furthermore, foreign investors feared the possibility of the government imposing new conditions on projects that had already been cleared by the Foreign Investment Promotion Board. Commentators noted that Indian politics was upsetting foreign investor sentiment (*Financial Times*, May 9, 1997). So despite the reform measures undertaken by the UF government, India's sovereign credit rating remained largely stagnant.

The markets' perceptions of the UF government contrast with their view of the National Democratic Alliance (NDA) that followed the UF government. In March 1998, following India's 12th general election, a coalition of 16 parties led by the BJP secured a majority of seats and formed a national government. In 1999, the BJP-led coalition was returned in another general election. Political conflict with Pakistan helped the nationalist BJP, with Prime Minister Vajpayee's firm stand against Pakistan contributing to the coalition's victory.

The largely center-right NDA government continued with its reform efforts and had better credentials than the former UF. Prime Minister Vajpayee and his ministers were committed to economic reform and worked hard to forge a national consensus supporting it. This time, however, the coalition government experienced so much conflict between its center and center-right factions that "the fact that the Left parties are not in the NDA may not be such a blessing after all" (*The Hindu*, October 9, 1999). The BJP-led coalition government faced problems not only with stakeholders such as the state bureaucracy, unions, and beneficiaries of government subsidies, but also with right-wing nationalists who were reluctant to see economic reform unfold. As a result, privatization and sectoral reform stagnated (Economist Intelligence Unit, June 16, 2000). The strongest opponent of reform was the opposition Congress Party, which was once a pioneer of Indian economic reform. The Congress Party threatened to undermine the reform of public sector disinvestment (*The Hindu*, July 19, 2000; *The Economic Times*, May 29, 2001).

However, India's credit ratings did not suffer significantly. Although the Institutional Investor rating fell in 1998 because of nuclear tests and the ensuing tension between India and Pakistan (*Institutional Investor*, September 1998), it recovered the following year and soared by 5 points in 2000 despite the political conflict over economic reform. The rating fell the following year, but the fall was not limited to India, as a slowing US economy had a negative influence on the economic prospects of other countries around the world (*Institutional Investor*, March 2000). Only 22 of 145 countries had at least a 1-point increase in their rating, and those of 75 countries fell at least 1 or more points (*Institutional Investor*, March 2000).

This case shows that although investors may be concerned about a constrained government's ability to implement economic reforms, they tend to be more optimistic about a coalition government if the executive is not leftist. Investors may have more confidence that a right-leaning executive will push on with reforms despite opposition, whereas a more leftist leader would find it more difficult to ignore his or her base of support.

Conclusions

In this chapter, I have examined how the degree of political constraints affects country credit ratings for leftist governments in developing countries, comparing the results with those for non-leftist governments and advanced economies. I have further explored how markets respond to political constraints against left-wing governments with financial market reform versus those without reform. This chapter's results suggest that an inverted U-shaped relationship exists between political constraints and sovereign credit ratings for leftist governments in the developing world. Having more than one veto player is likely to increase a country's credit ratings through reducing policy volatility, but once the number of veto players reaches a certain point, then there is a falling inflection after which additional political checks seem to serve only to promote policy rigidity. No such relationship is observed with other types of government.

The positive effects of an intermediate level of constraints on credibility are greater when a leftist government pursues financial liberalization. Leftist governments that do not pursue financial reform tend to show a monotonic relationship between political constraints and sovereign credibility. The finding that there is an inverted U-shaped relationship between the degree of political constraints and the credit ratings of reform-minded leftist governments may suggest that the markets need a certain degree of political constraints on such governments due to their party label, but at the same time they regard excessive constraints as undermining reform. A balance between policy credibility and policy flexibility seems to be required to boost market confidence.

Notes

1 For example, Tsebelis (1995, 2002); Cox and McCubbins (2001); and Haggard (2000).
2 In a similar vein, the effects of federalism on economic outcomes, such as the fiscal balance (Neyapti 2010; Baskaran 2010; Goodspeed 2002; Rodden 2002; Bordignon et al. 2001; de Mello 2000; Fornasari et al. 2000) and inflation (Treisman 2000), have also been extensively studied.
3 Previous studies of the political economy of sovereign debt have tended to emphasize the commitment-enhancing effects of the separation of powers. For example, North and Weingast (1989) explain how checks and balances developed along with common-law courts ruling on economic matters after the Glorious Revolution, and how they reduced the risk that the English king would not repay sovereign debt. Stasavage (2003; 2007) extended their work by concluding that although a system with multiple veto players can improve credibility, the partisan composition of the players, the number of policies, and policy delegation are also important. Stasavage argued that the development of cohesive political parties – the Whigs and the Tories – and political conflict between them were the major causes of the British government's improved credibility in the financial markets. The Whigs represented "moneyed interests" and, according to Stasavage, it was the Whig supremacy in Parliament that was the major source of government credibility in terms of repaying debt.
4 The results obtained for developing countries using other ratings are presented in Appendix 5.
5 The highest credit rating score is obtained when *Checks* is approximately 4 (its logarithm is about 1.24). That falls at roughly the 75th percentile of the sample.
6 Using other credit ratings generates the same conclusion.
7 Other credit ratings have too few observations to yield statistically significant findings for each group in this analysis.

6 The IMF and sovereign creditworthiness

Financial crises are a recurrent feature of the world economy. From the Mexican Tequila Crisis of 1994 to the global financial crisis of 2008 and the European sovereign debt crises of 2010, the past two decades have been marked by a significant number of major crises. Although their causes range from problems with macroeconomic fundamentals to risky lending practices, financial crises are exacerbated by speculative attacks based on market sentiment or herding behavior (Obsfelt 1996; Radelet and Sachs 1998). The shock of such crises can be particularly strong in emerging markets, where they often have enormous economic, social, and political costs.

In times of economic crisis, restoring financial market confidence is essential to prevent further capital flight. However, international investors often lack complete information about the preferences and policy directions of foreign governments (Tomz 2007). Furthermore, the task of predicting policy outcomes can be difficult in developing countries due to the lack of good data and transparency in the policymaking process (Rodrik 1989; Broz 2002; Vaaler et al. 2006). Uncertainty over policy and its associated risks are likely to have a negative influence on a country's creditworthiness. Unlike lenders in domestic credit markets, lenders in the international credit market have little recourse if borrowers do not repay their debts, and there are few direct legal sanctions that can be used against such borrowers, especially when they are sovereign countries (Tomz 2007). Thus, signs of uncertain economic and political outcomes can often result in massive asset sell-offs and financial market turbulence.

If crisis-hit governments fail to restore investor confidence, can international institutions lend a helping hand? The designated role of the IMF is to help countries in severe economic difficulty by lending them money and providing policy advice on economic restructuring. By providing liquidity, IMF-backed lending may guarantee debt repayment, thereby attracting capital inflow (Fischer 1999; Lane and Phillips 2000; Corsetti et al. 2006). The IMF further claims that the policy prescriptions attached to IMF loans performs an important signaling function by assuring investors that the borrowing country is committed to economic reform, thereby halting investor panic and speculative attacks (IMF 1997).

This chapter tests whether the perceived effects and benefits of IMF programs differ depending on the governing party's ideology, such that the positive signaling effect of these programs in improving perceived creditworthiness is greater for leftist than non-leftist governments. The IMF promotes a neoliberal reform agenda that does not accord well with leftist rhetoric on economic programs, which emphasizes redistributive policies and the creation of employment at the expense of inflation control. Thus, leftist governments may seem less likely candidates for the adoption of IMF programs. However, by adopting such programs, their subsequent policy reforms may actually have greater credibility, because market participants perceive the agreement to be indicative of a strong motivation and commitment to undertake economic reform. Furthermore, the high level of enforcement power and reputation costs that IMF programs carry with them enhance the signals that leftist governments send to markets about their commitment to policy reforms.

The positive effect of IMF programs being conditional on government partisanship can be summarized by the metaphor "Only Nixon can go to China." This logic implies that market-oriented IMF reforms are more credible for market participants when leftist parties adopt them than when right-wing parties do so, because the proclaimed ideological position of the former is further away from IMF philosophy. The possible result of adopting IMF programs is a boost in the credibility of leftist governments in international financial markets.

I test for the existence of the "Nixon-Goes-to-China" effect in IMF agreements by exploring whether there is a greater increase in the perceived creditworthiness of leftist governments relative to their non-leftist counterparts following the signing of such an agreement. I first employ the treatment effects model to detect any potential self-selectivity in the participating countries. If no selection bias is identified, I then run a FGLS model using a difference-in-differences design to analyze the sovereign credit ratings of developing countries. Consistent with the "Nixon-Goes-to-China" hypothesis, my findings suggest that IMF programs improve the credibility of leftist governments, but not that of their non-leftist counterparts.

The findings contribute to the literature by demonstrating that the IMF's signaling effect is dependent on the borrowing government's ideological label. Earlier work on the signaling and catalytic effects of the IMF has not focused exclusively on how IMF programs influence investors' perceptions of governing parties with different ideologies.[1] The literature has thus failed to consider the potential significance of government partisanship. Studies that have taken ideology into account have largely focused on how ideological differences among borrowing countries influence IMF program participation and implementation.[2] This chapter combines these two streams of research by addressing the partisan consideration of IMF participation and the catalytic role of the IMF in improving investor perceptions. Given that IMF programs can help governments to gain credibility through the IMF's neoliberal ideology and through conditionality, the results suggest that governments do not necessarily need both to earn investor confidence. To the best of my knowledge, no study to date has offered significant analysis of the effect of IMF programs on sovereign credibility to determine whether participation in these programs affects the credibility of leftist and non-leftist governments in different ways. Given the earlier literature's mixed findings on IMF programs' catalytic effects on economic outcomes, this study contributes to the debate by showing that program effectiveness hinges, at least partially, on government ideology.

Investor confidence and IMF conditionality

In the sovereign debt market, as in many other markets, political events have a significant impact on the profitability of private investment. Investors fear that political events and decisions may affect the business climate such that they will lose money or make less money, and they consider both political and economic factors in assessing a government's ability and willingness to repay its debts (Kobrin 1982).

To reassure market participants about future policy stability and to gain credibility in the financial markets, governments may rely on commitment mechanisms that are conducive to market-friendly policies and property rights protection. The IMF is designed to provide such mechanisms in countries with economic difficulties. It influences the economic policies of recipient countries by attaching specific reform requirements to loans, which is known as conditionality. The IMF has long been a proponent of neoliberal economic policy, which it considers the only means of appeasing market sentiment (Chwieroth 2010). IMF conditionality, therefore, typically requires the borrowing government to reduce its budget deficit through expenditure cuts and tax increases, to increase interest rates to reduce the money supply, and to devalue its currency to increase exports and earn more foreign currency (Vreeland 2003, 2007). More specific and deeper policy reforms are usually imposed under a "structural adjustment" program that includes the privatization of national assets and state-owned industries, trade liberalization, deregulation of businesses and prices, and changes in social welfare policies (Vreeland 2007). Through conditionality, the IMF has become increasingly involved in the national policies of debtor countries with the stated intent of correcting their economic problems. Unlike other international institutions, the IMF has significant enforcement power and can withdraw its support if its policy prescriptions are not observed. By taking IMF conditionality lightly, a country risks not only the significant benefits afforded by adherence but also its reputation as a trustworthy borrower (Stone 2002).

However, the Fund's actions are not without controversy. Some scholars argue that if conditionality is expected to do more harm than good in a troubled economy, then investors will lose confidence in that economy.[3] Although such concerns assume that borrowing governments actually comply with IMF conditionality, some have suggested that the degree of program implementation and compliance may affect economic outcomes.[4] In this regard, Bird (2002) and Bird and Rowlands (2002) argue that programs that are not fully implemented or complied with can be a negative signal about a government's credibility, which undermines investor confidence. Similarly, Edwards (2005) finds that failed programs cause portfolio capital flight.[5] Others see the signing of an IMF agreement as indicative of the debtor country's poor economic performance in both the present and the future, thus transmitting a negative signal about the borrowing country's economic conditions (Conway 1994; Knight and Santaella 1997; Bird 2002).

Despite the increased criticism of IMF programs in recent years, many still believe that the organization boosts the credibility of borrowing governments in financial markets. It entices capital inflows by acting as an international lender of last resort and by providing liquidity in times of crisis. Investors may retain their investment in a country under an IMF program because they believe that the IMF is, in effect, insuring that investment (Tomz 2007: 233–236). Although critics denounce IMF-backed funding as creating "moral hazard," proponents interpret such externally induced confidence as desirable (Fischer 1999; Lane and Phillips 2000; Corsetti et al. 2006). They argue that the insurance against liquidity risks provided by the IMF defends the financial systems of fledgling economies from speculative attacks and encourages them to implement reform policies (Marchesi 2003; Corsetti et al. 2006; Dreher and Walter 2010). The IMF further helps to coordinate the expectations of other official lenders, who extend their financial support to borrowing countries when an IMF program is agreed upon (Broome 2008).

Proponents of IMF programs further argue that an IMF agreement acts as a signaling device that reduces uncertainty and provides information about future policies (Cottarelli and Giannini 1997; Dhonte 1997; Mosley 2003: 116). Governments can commit to similar policies outside the IMF framework, but such commitment will have relatively little credibility in international capital markets because of the greater opportunity to renege. Investors perceive the risk of policy reversal to be greater in developing countries than in advanced industrial democracies (Mosley 2003). IMF conditionality, with its intrusive reform agreements and monitoring, is intended to identify the risk of policy reversals and to push countries forward with economic reform (Diwan and Rodrik 1992; Drazen 2002; Stone 2002). By agreeing to an IMF program, a government strongly signals its intention to stabilize its economy and promote growth (Marchesi and Thomas 1999; Broome 2008).[6] Copelovitch (2010) contends that such signaling effects now constitute the IMF's key policy goals, particularly since the Latin American debt crisis of the 1980s. In addition to conditionality, the Fund's policy advice and technical assistance further help to reduce uncertainty and facilitate reform, because they are often publicly discussed and influence the economic policies and politics of borrowing countries (Killick 1994; Chwieroth 2010). Thus, even when IMF programs are classified as failures with respect to their specific goals, they may nevertheless change attitudes in developing countries and influence their long-term policy directions (Boockmann and Dreher 2003; Dreher and Walter 2010). The IMF's consistent market-oriented policy stance further provides a "seal of approval" to program participants (Boockmann and Dreher 2003; Chwieroth 2010). For these reasons, some believe that the mere existence of IMF-backed programs enhances investor confidence (Dreher and Walter 2010; Gray 2010).

When the IMF negotiates a stabilization program with a government, imposes policy conditions, and provides technical support and advice, it creates a focal point for investor expectations. It allows decentralized market participants to coordinate their behavior, which plays a crucial role in volatile capital markets. In addition, the IMF's resources are magnified, as the world's capital markets often become available to countries that receive "the IMF's seal of approval" (Stone 2002: 11). These favorable conditions can result in a synergetic cycle in which IMF intervention, government policies, and international investments reinforce one another.

IMF programs and investor confidence: the role of government partisanship

Given the contending arguments on the effectiveness of IMF programs for borrowing countries, the question is whether the programs' effects are conditional on a country's governing party. Leftist governments face a brand name effect whereby they receive a biased reaction in the markets, regardless of their stated intentions and policies. Such a general perception about leftist governments leads to the expectation that the ideological costs of commitment to the IMF's neoliberal policies will be much greater for politicians on the left than for those on the right. IMF intervention usually involves trade liberalization, privatization, budget cuts, and inflation control, all of which fit better with right-wing economic rhetoric.[7] Leftist governments may attract severe criticism and resistance from domestic constituents in adopting IMF programs, because such programs tend to be costlier for lower-income sectors and the working class (Pastor 1987; Vreeland 2003; Pop-Eleches 2009).[8]

However, IMF program adoption may enhance the credibility of leftist governments in the financial markets and may even help them to implement neoliberal policies that are unpopular among their domestic constituents (Stokes 2001; Vreeland 2003; Mukherjee and Singer 2010).[9] The "Nixon-Goes-to-China" hypothesis argues that the ability to promote the desirability of a right-wing policy to private-sector decision makers is greater in a left-wing than in a right-wing government, given that the general public has much less information about the state of the economy than the politicians and has imperfect information about the politicians' exact preferences. In this context, private-sector decision makers perceive a market-oriented policy to constitute a greater deviation from the policies traditionally pursued by left-wing governments. They then infer that the new policy must be good for the country's economic welfare, because leftist governments would not pursue extreme right-wing policies because of their ideological tendencies. Therefore, by entering into an agreement with the IMF, leftist governments commit themselves to deviation from their espoused ideology and signal to investors their commitment to overcoming economic crises. IMF programs strengthen the effects because of the IMF's significant enforcement power and requirement that countries sacrifice policy autonomy in most cases. Consequently, investors are likely to attach greater credence to the agreements that leftist governments sign relative to those signed by their rightist counterparts.

To test this sovereign credibility effect of IMF programs, I generate the main hypothesis from the foregoing discussion, as follows.

> H6.1: The effects of IMF programs on improving the creditworthiness of developing countries are greater among leftist governments than among their non-leftist counterparts.

Quantitative and qualitative evidence

To determine the appropriate empirical analysis for hypothesis testing, I first test for the presence of selection bias, as not all countries participate equally in IMF programs (for example, countries typically join IMF programs when they are in economic crisis). Any observed differences in credit ratings may thus stem from differences in the circumstances of countries that do and do not adopt IMF programs, rather than from the effects of those programs alone (Vreeland 2003). Accordingly, it is important to consider the non-random nature of participation in IMF programs when testing their effect on economic outcomes.[10] The treatment effects model of selectivity uses the standard Heckman two-stage procedure by first estimating a program participation equation and then estimating the effects of IMF programs on credit ratings. The results of the treatment effects model indicate that there is no selection bias.[11]

I then adopt the FGLS model with Prais-Winsten transformation, as in the previous chapters, and employ a difference-in-differences design to examine whether the effects of IMF programs on sovereign creditworthiness are more positive for leftist than non-leftist governments.[12] The model is specified as follows:

$$
\begin{aligned}
&\ln \mathit{Credit\ Rating}_{it} \\
&\quad = \gamma_0 + \gamma_1 \mathit{IMF}_{i,t-1} + \gamma_2 \mathit{Left\ Party}_{i,t-1} + \gamma_3 \mathit{IMF}_{i,t-1} * \mathit{Left\ Party}_{i,t-1} \\
&\qquad + \gamma_4 \mathit{Democracy}_{i,t-1} + \gamma_5 \mathit{Budget\ Balance}_{i,t-1} \\
&\qquad + \gamma_6 \mathit{Capital\ Account\ Openness}_{i,t-1} + \gamma_7 \mathit{GDP\ Growth}_{i,t-1} \\
&\qquad + \gamma_8 \mathit{Inflation}_{i,t-1} + \gamma_9 \mathit{Current\ Account\ Balance}_{i,t-1} + \gamma_{10} \mathit{Investment}_{i,t-1} \\
&\qquad + \gamma_{11} \ln \mathit{Reserves}_{i,t-1} + \gamma_{12} \mathit{Debt}_{i,t-1} + \gamma_{13} \mathit{Fixed\ Exchange\ Rate}_{i,t-1} \\
&\qquad + \gamma_{14} \ln \mathit{Credit\ Rating}_{i,t-1} + \epsilon_{it}
\end{aligned}
$$

In the model, *IMF* indicates IMF program participation and is coded 1 when a conditioned IMF agreement is in force, and 0 otherwise.[13] The variable of interest is the difference-in-differences coefficient captured by *IMF*Left Party*, γ_3. The major dependent variable is the sovereign credit ratings by Institutional Investor.[14] I also include GDP growth, government budget balance, current account balance, inflation, level of investment, foreign reserves, debt, capital account openness, and the level of democracy. I further include the fixed exchange rate in the model. The exchange rate regime may influence a country's propensity to borrow money from the IMF, as a country with a fixed exchange rate regime is more likely to turn to IMF when they experience foreign reserve deficiency (Trudel 2005).

A preliminary look at the data seems to support the main hypothesis. Figures 6.1 and 6.2 trace the credit ratings of countries in financial crisis to see how their ratings differ depending on whether they signed an IMF agreement.[15] The data in Figure 6.1 show that leftist signatories and non-signatories both tend to experience a decrease in credit ratings prior to crises, but that IMF program participants have an immediate and faster post-crisis recovery compared with non-participants. However, program participation makes little difference to the credit ratings of non-leftist governments, as shown in Figure 6.2. The preliminary evidence supports my hypothesis that IMF programs have a greater effect on improving credibility when the signatory is a left-leaning government.

Impact of IMF programs on sovereign credibility

The results of model 1 in Table 6.1 show the effect of IMF programs and government partisanship on borrowing countries' credibility when other covariates are controlled for. Government budget balance, capital account openness, current account balance, economic growth, investment, and foreign reserves have a statistically significant association with creditworthiness in the expected directions.

Table 6.2 summarizes the effects of IMF program participation and government partisanship on credibility as reported in model 1 of Table 6.1. The numbers are calculated from the coefficients in Table 6.1 with the assumption that other covariates represent their mean values. As the credit rating data are log-transformed, the numbers are converted to fit the original rating scale of 0–100. Leftist governments that do not participate in IMF programs are perceived as riskier than their non-leftist counterparts (3.5 points lower on the rating scale). Among participating countries, however, the credit ratings of leftist governments catch up with those of non-leftist governments to narrow the ratings gap to 0.9 points. Among leftist governments, program participants are perceived to be more creditworthy than non-participants (2.4 points higher on the rating scale, with the difference being statistically significant at $p < 0.05$, two-tailed). Among non-leftist governments, IMF program participants have a slightly lower rating than non-participants (–0.2 points), but the difference is statistically insignificant. More importantly, the difference in credit ratings between leftist participants and non-participants is 2.6 points higher than that between non-leftist participants and non-participants (that is, the difference-in-differences), and the difference-in-differences is statistically significant at $p < 0.05$.

Figure 6.3 provides a visual representation of the effects reported in Table 6.2, with the difference-in-differences illustrated as the difference in the slopes of leftist and non-leftist governments. The figure shows a contrast between the

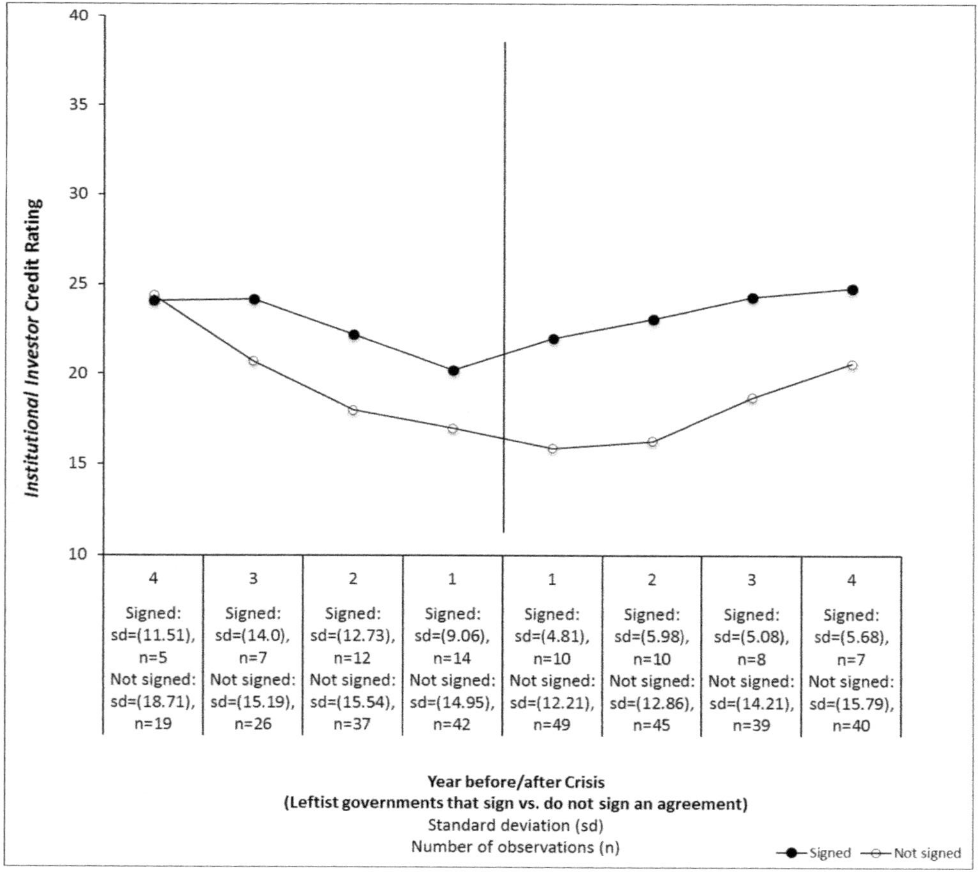

Figure 6.1 Credit ratings before and after a crisis: leftist governments

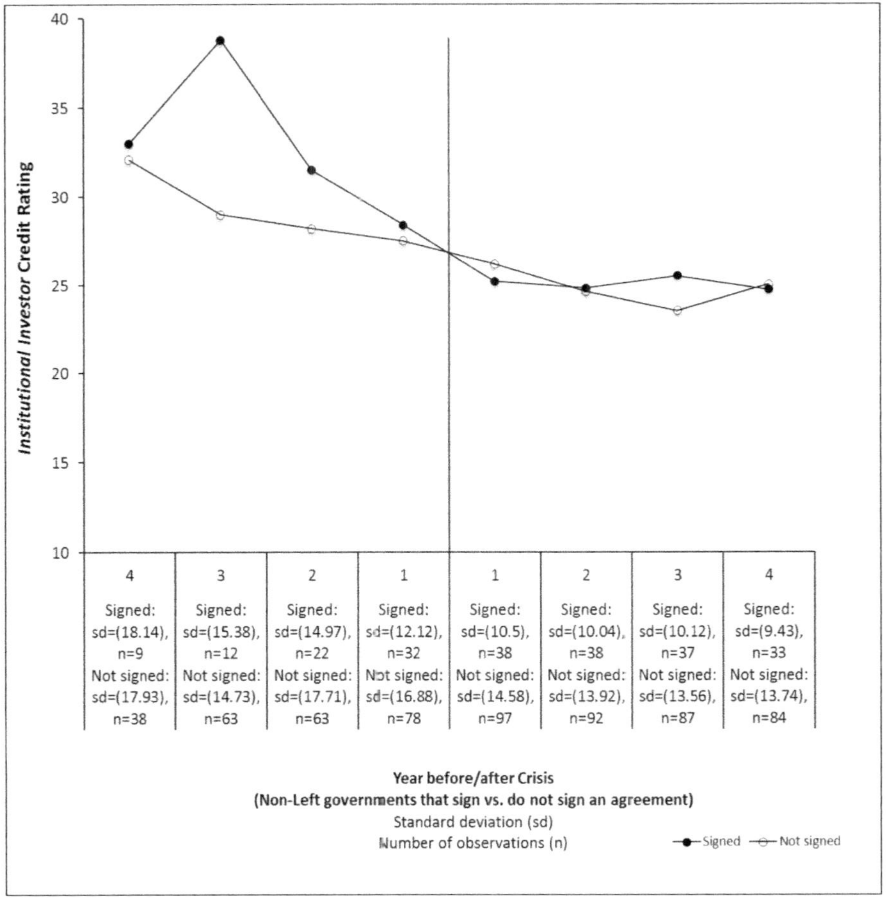

Figure 6.2 Credit ratings before and after a crisis: non-leftist governments

Table 6.1 IMF programs, government partisanship, and credit ratings of developing countries

	Model 1	*Model 2*
IMF	−0.002	0.011
	(0.007)	(0.009)
Left party	−0.035***	−0.038***
	(0.011)	(0.011)
IMF* Left party	0.026**	0.030**
	(0.013)	(0.014)
Noncompliance		−0.020**
		(0.009)
Democracy	0.001	0.000
	(0.001)	(0.001)
Budget balance	0.002**	0.002*
	(0.001)	(0.001)
Capital account openness	0.019***	0.019***
	(0.004)	(0.004)
GDP growth	0.005***	0.005***
	(0.001)	(0.001)
Inflation	0.000	0.000
	(0.000)	(0.000)
Current account balance	0.002***	0.002**
	(0.001)	(0.001)
Investment	0.002**	0.002***
	(0.001)	(0.001)
Reserves (log)	0.039***	0.041***
	(0.005)	(0.006)
Debt	−0.000	−0.000
	(0.000)	(0.000)
Fixed exchange rate	−0.003	−0.000
	(0.009)	(0.009)
Rating in the previous year	0.800***	0.807***
	(0.015)	(0.016)
Constant	0.326***	0.290***
	(0.075)	(0.077)
Observations	1,288	1,141
R-squared	0.97	0.97

Notes: ***$p < .01$; **$p < .05$; *$p < .10$ (two-tailed). The dependent variable is Institutional Investor and is log-transformed.

Table 6.2 IMF programs, government partisanship, and credit ratings of developing countries (summary)

	Government Partisanship		*Difference*
	Leftist	*Non-Leftist*	*(Leftist) – (Non-Leftist)*
IMF program participation			
No	46.23	49.73	**-3.5**
Yes	48.63	49.53	-0.9
Difference (IMF participation) – (IMF non-participation)	**2.4**	-0.2	**2.6** (Difference-in-Differences)

Notes: The effects are presented as the number of points on Institutional Investor's 100-point rating scale, with other covariates at their mean values. Statistically significant figures are in bold.

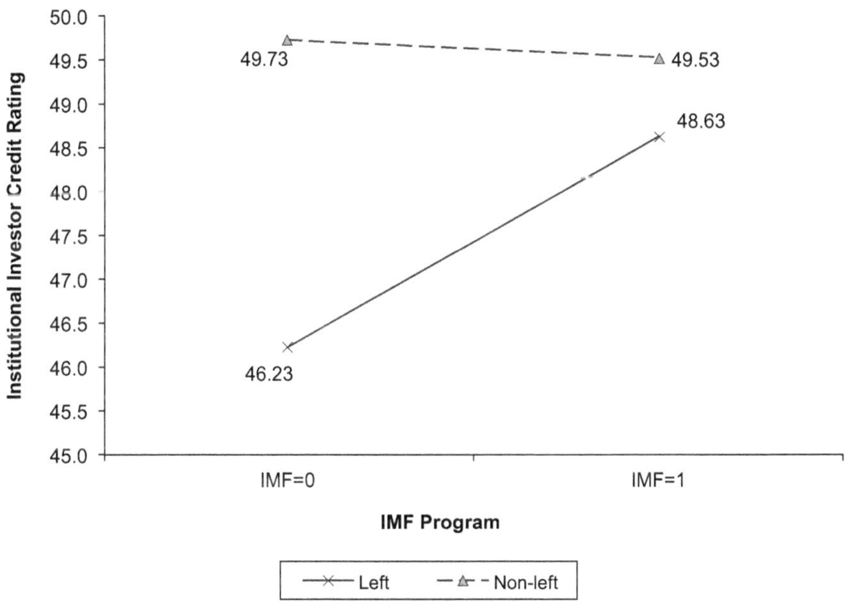

Figure 6.3 Effects of IMF programs on credit ratings

slopes for the two, with that for leftist governments showing an increase in ratings and that for non-leftist governments showing a slightly downward trend. Such contrasting outcomes may imply that IMF programs appeal to investors primarily due to their market-friendly ideology.

Model 2 of Table 6.1 includes a borrowing country's IMF program compliance. Some earlier work has argued that programs that are not fully implemented or complied with may undermine government credibility (Bird 2002; Bird and

Rowlands 2002; Edwards 2005). The results show that countries that do not comply with IMF conditionality tend to have lower ratings than countries that do comply (2 points lower on the rating scale), although this does not affect the Nixon-Goes-to-China dynamics found in the basic model.[16]

The evidence presented in Tables 6.1 and 6.2 and Figure 6.3 is consistent with the common belief that investors feel greater concern about investing in countries with leftist governments than in their non-leftist counterparts. Such concern appears to be reduced, however, when the former join IMF programs, at which point their credit ratings catch up with those of non-leftist governments, regardless of the latter's program participation. Leftist governments that participate in IMF programs enjoy significantly higher ratings than those that do not, as the unlikely match between policymaker and policy may boost credibility. The non-leftist governments in such programs, in contrast, enjoy no such advantage over their non-participating counterparts. Center and center-right governments are perceived to be already in line with the IMF in terms of their policy preferences, and so ideological differences confer no added benefit in terms of credibility. It can thus be concluded that IMF programs have differential effects on the credibility of different types of governments in a manner consistent with the "Nixon-Goes-to-China" hypothesis.

Effects of signing a new IMF program on sovereign credibility

To further investigate the dynamics of the "Nixon-Goes-to-China" effect, I test whether the positive effect of IMF signaling also exists when a country signs up to a new IMF program. I use an OLS model and adopt a first-difference specification to examine how the signing of a new IMF agreement and government partisanship are associated with a *change* in Institutional Investor ratings. The dependent variable and control variables take the first-difference form, and the variable *IMF* in the model on page 96 is replaced by *IMF signed*, which is coded as 1 if a new IMF agreement is signed in the country-year, and 0 otherwise.[17]

Table 6.3 presents the results. Among the control variables, capital account openness, GDP growth, and reserve change have a significant association with a change in investor perceptions in the expected directions. A change in the current account balance is negatively associated with a credit rating change. This negative association may be counterintuitive at first glance, but is in fact plausible because an increase in capital borrowing may reduce the risk of external financing, at least in the short term (Beers and Cavanaugh 2008).

Signing an IMF program is positively associated with the credit ratings of left-wing governments, whereas it is negatively associated with the ratings of right-leaning governments. In model 3, the change in ratings for a leftist government when an IMF agreement is signed is greater than that when none is signed (a 1.3-point difference), and the difference is statistically significant at $p < .10$ (one-tailed). Turning to the main focus of difference-in-differences, the results clearly indicate that the difference in credit-rating changes arising from leftist governments' IMF agreements is significantly greater than that arising

Table 6.3 Effects of signing an agreement with the IMF and government partisanship on *change* in credit ratings of developing countries

Variables	*Model 3*	*Model 4*
IMF signed	-0.018**	-0.016*
	(0.008)	(0.008)
Left party	-0.013	-0.015
	(0.010)	(0.010)
IMF signed* Left party	0.031*	0.037**
	(0.017)	(0.018)
Noncompliance		-0.013*
		(0.007)
Democracy	0.001	0.001
	(0.001)	(0.001)
Δ Budget balance	-0.001	-0.001
	(0.001)	(0.001)
Δ Capital account openness	0.026***	0.024***
	(0.006)	(0.006)
GDP growth	0.007***	0.007***
	(0.001)	(0.001)
Δ Inflation	-0.000	-0.000
	(0.000)	(0.000)
Δ Current account balance	-0.002**	-0.002**
	(0.001)	(0.001)
Δ Investment	-0.001	-0.001
	(0.001)	(0.001)
Δ Reserves (log)	0.044***	0.035***
	(0.008)	(0.008)
Δ Debt	0.000	0.000
	(0.000)	(0.000)
Fixed exchange rate	-0.005	-0.003
	(0.008)	(0.009)
Previous year's rating	-0.101***	-0.095***
	(0.012)	(0.013)
Constant	0.227**	0.072
	(0.104)	(0.080)
Observations	1,225	1,090
R-squared	0.49	0.48

Notes: ***$p < .01$; **$p < .05$; *$p < .10$ (two-tailed). The dependent variable is Institutional Investor and is log-transformed and first-differenced.

from the agreements of non-leftist governments (a statistically significant difference of 3.1 points). The results for model 4 further show that the Nixon dynamic exists even when program noncompliance is included in the model.

As the first-difference specification examines the impact of *signing* an agreement on the change of ratings, the results imply that investors' negative reaction may be particularly sharp when a right-wing government signs a new agreement. Given some earlier studies' findings that IMF programs may indicate the poor economic condition and problems of borrowing countries, not only in the present but also in the future, and that IMF programs have a negative impact on capital flows (Conway 1994; Knight and Santaella 1997; Bird 2002; Vreeland 2007: 55–62; Jensen 2006), signing an agreement may initially highlight the negative aspects of borrowing countries. For leftist governments, however, investors may expect the IMF's neoliberal economic reform programs and policy advice to effect positive changes in these governments over and above those predicted by extant theories. That is, leftist governments have the Nixon-Goes-to-China effect to offset the signal about poor economic conditions. For center and center-right governments that are perceived to be already in line with the IMF in terms of policy preferences, in contrast, the IMF's ideological support confers no additional credibility gain.

The findings so far are largely consistent with the opinions of the financial market experts that I interviewed. When asked how they perceive a country that borrows money from the IMF because of economic problems, the market experts noted that IMF lending is a positive sign, particularly when extensive reform is expected (Interviews 3, 20). Accordingly, left-wing governments, for whom IMF-led reform is typically more extensive than for non-leftist governments, may benefit more in terms of building credibility from borrowing from the IMF than non-leftist governments do. Investors expect a borrowing country's economy to improve with an IMF reform program and are assured that their investment will be safe (Interviews 6, 20). Some interviewees commented that IMF lending would give them greater assurance than no such lending for a country experiencing economic difficulties (Interviews 6, 15). When an international institution as influential as the IMF lends money to a country, investors see an opportunity to get a higher return from their investments. As a result, countries with IMF-led major reforms are attractive investment destinations (Interview 20).

Case study: a tale of two Hungaries

The example of Hungary in the 1990s illustrates how turning to the IMF for financial assistance by two ideologically different governments supports the presence of a "Nixon-Goes-to-China" effect. In the 1990s, the former communist countries of Eastern and Central Europe experienced a number of economic difficulties during their transition to a market economy. Reform in the region focused on the liberalization of government-controlled prices and trade, macroeconomic stabilization, and institutional reform of the market economy, and the IMF became the central promoter of such reform.

Like other countries in the region, Hungary had a high level of foreign debt, a large budget deficit, and a low level of international reserves. The center-right Hungarian Democratic Forum that came to office in 1990 signed an agreement with the IMF in early 1991. With Eastern Europe's highest per-capita foreign debt, Hungary needed such an agreement to secure the Fund's help and to persuade other institutions to keep lending (*New York Times*, February 22, 1991). The government borrowed US$1.6 billion from the IMF on the condition that it would reduce its budget and current account deficits. Although the loan was expected to ease the country's post-communist transition, it met with a cold response. The country fell from 41st to 42nd place in the country creditworthiness ranking, with its Institutional Investor rating declining by 2.7 points compared to the previous year. The reason cited for the downgrade was the country's level of foreign debt (*MTI Econews*, November 4, 1991).

The Hungarian Socialist Party, which had strongly opposed the center-right government's free-market reforms, faced fresh challenges from the budget crisis of 1993 and 1994 when it came to power. Hungary's external debt had declined to 35 percent of GDP from its 1990 high of 45 percent, but deteriorating economic conditions again saw it exceed 45 percent in 1994, with public debt rocketing to more than 85 percent (Cottarelli et al. 1998). The country's external current account deficit deteriorated to roughly 10 percent of GDP, and structural reform came to a near halt (IMF 1996). One of Hungary's main economic problems was its huge budget deficit, which was primarily the result of a large amount of welfare spending. To reverse the negative trend, the newly elected socialist government implemented an extensive adjustment package, including the privatization of the public sector, exchange-rate adjustment to increase exports, and austerity measures to reduce the budget deficit. Hungary's economic performance began to turn around in 1995, as reflected in the country's significantly reduced current account deficits (which fell from approximately 11 percent and 10 percent of GDP in 1993 and 1994, respectively, to 6 percent in 1995), an increase in foreign reserves (from roughly US$6.8 billion in 1993 and 1994 to US$12 billion in 1995), and a moderate reduction in external debt (Cottarelli et al. 1998). Still, the markets were not impressed, as Hungary's credit rating saw no improvement between 1995 and 1996.

However, when the socialist government signed a two-year standby agreement with the IMF for about US$387 million in 1996, the market reacted positively. The agreement led the country's credit rating to increase by five points in the following year. The agreement was intended to support the government's 1995 adjustment package, and consequently it retained the key features of the earlier reform package (IMF 1996). Under the terms of the agreement, Hungary promised to keep its budget deficit under 4 percent of GDP, external debt at around 37 percent of GDP, current account deficit under US$2 billion, and inflation at around 12 percent (IMF 1996). The government signed the agreement, but declared that it would not need to draw on the standby loan. According to the Hungarian officials who negotiated it, the agreement itself was more important than the financial support that accompanied it because of the effect that it was likely to have on Hungary's evaluation in the financial markets (*MTI Econews*, June 17, 1996). The country succeeded in keeping its current account deficit under US$2 billion and external debt under 37 percent of GDP, as agreed; its budget deficit at 4.8 percent of GDP, which was near the agreed level of 4 percent; and inflation at 18.3 percent, which was far beyond the agreed level of 12.7 percent but considerably reduced compared to earlier levels (IMF 2000). The IMF deemed Hungary's structural reform and stabilization successful in its final review of the program (*MTI Econews*, June 25, 1997).

Conclusions

This chapter explored the effects of IMF programs and government partisanship on investor perceptions of governments in the developing world. I find the positive effect of IMF signals to be present among leftist governments but not among their non-leftist counterparts. When other economic and political factors are controlled for, leftist governments participating in IMF programs tend to have higher credit ratings than their non-participating counterparts. However, these programs have no significant effect on investor perceptions of non-leftist governments. Similarly, signing an agreement with the IMF has a positive effect on the credit ratings of leftist governments, but not on those of non-leftist governments.

These findings suggest that the greater boost in investor confidence for leftist governments stems from the stronger economic reform signal that an IMF agreement with such a government sends to the market. When political uncertainty exists, investors perceive these governments to be more likely to engage in inflationary measures and increase government debt than their right-wing counterparts. However, as the "Nixon-Goes-to-China" effect implies, when leftist governments agree to IMF conditionality, which is characterized by neoliberal, market-friendly policies with a significant level of enforcement power, they may reassure investors that they are willing to make a more serious commitment to IMF-backed policy reforms than non-leftist governments and will provide a more favorable and predictable market environment for investors. As a result, the IMF's positive influence in providing policy credibility may be more powerful for leftist than non-leftist governments.

The findings in fact show that investors do not necessarily respond positively to IMF program participation when non-leftist governments are the signatories. Given that these governments are perceived already to be in line with the IMF with respect to their ideological tendency, the benefit of IMF signals as a commitment device disappears. This differing effect of IMF programs, conditional on government partisanship, may at least partially explain the mixed findings in the literature on the catalytic effects of these programs. When government partisanship is taken into consideration, the Nixon-Goes-to-China framework predicts that IMF programs will benefit leftist governments to a greater extent than their non-leftist counterparts because investors anticipate that the IMF's neoliberal economic reform programs and policy advice will effect greater positive change in the former. The results presented here support such an expectation. They suggest that governments adopting IMF programs benefit via neoliberal ideology or conditionality, but do not necessarily require both to send a credible signal to the markets.

The findings in this chapter contribute to the literature by broadening our understanding of the IMF's catalytic role in developing countries and of how that role may be influenced by government partisanship. Its findings have broader lessons for the study of international institutions and for more general analyses of the effects of IMF programs. More specifically, they have important implications for the politics of selecting and complying with IMF agreements. There is serious doubt about the role played by the IMF in international financial markets. The findings reported here imply that despite their ideological differences with the IMF, leftist governments in economic distress may find it beneficial to rely on the signaling effect provided by the Fund to prevent capital outflows and market disturbances. IMF programs can also serve as a strategic tool for leftist governments that hope to pursue domestically unpopular economic reform. The IMF may minimize adverse economic reactions, such as investor panic and contagion across countries. By boosting investor confidence, IMF programs may play a catalytic role by providing an opportunity for improved financial market access.

Notes

1 See Dhonte (1997), Bird and Rowlands (2002), Marchesi (2003), Mody and Saravia (2003), and Edwards (2006).

2 See Vreeland (2007), Pop-Eleches (2009), and Caraway et al. (2012). Pop-Eleches (2009), for example, provides in-depth analysis of partisan politics and the initiation and implementation of IMF programs in Latin America and Eastern Europe.

3 Studies on IMF programs and economic outcomes show mixed results. Killick et al. (1992), Schadler et al. (1993), and Conway (1994) find a positive effect of these programs on budget balances and government consumption. Mody and Saravia (2003) conclude that IMF programs have catalytic effects when they are viewed as likely to succeed. In contrast, other studies find negative associations between IMF programs and economic growth (Przeworski and Vreeland 2000; Vreeland 2002, 2003), investment (Edwards 2006; Jensen 2006), social spending (Nooruddin and Simmons 2006), and income inequality (Nooruddin and Vreeland 2010). Radelet and Sachs (1998) assert that the IMF's one-size-fits-all policies undermine investor confidence, whereas Gould (2006) and Stone (2008) disagree. See Joyce (2004), Vreeland (2007), Steinwand and Stone (2008), and Dreher (2009) for recent surveys of the literature.

4 The findings regarding the effects of program noncompliance on economic outcomes are mixed. Mercer-Blackman and Unigovskaya (2000) and Stone (2002) find a positive impact of program compliance on economic growth and inflation, respectively. Dreher (2006) shows that IMF programs reduce economic growth, although compliance seems to mitigate their negative impact. Killick (1995) and Nsouli et al. (2004) obtain mixed results using different macroeconomic indicators. Dreher and Walter (2010) find the existence of Fund programs to lead to exchange rate stability, but report their result to be driven by neither Fund loans nor compliance. See Joyce (2004) and Vreeland (2006, 2007) for a further review of the literature.

5 Biglaiser and DeRouen (2010) and Dreher and Walter (2010), however, argue that even if IMF programs are not successfully implemented, investors are still likely to expect greater market-oriented reforms in countries under such programs than in those that are not, because they perceive the IMF to have some influence over policy implementation through market-oriented policy advice and other indirect channels. Similarly, Stone (2002) finds the IMF to be an important lender of credibility in international financial markets, even though programs are sometimes not successfully implemented. Gray (2010) finds that investors are responsive to initial program announcements but not to subsequent program revisions or even suspensions.

6 In a similar vein, studies on the IMF's Articles of Agreement argue that governments sign Article VIII of the Agreement, which obligates signatories to maintain an open current account, to signal their future policy intentions to markets (Simmons 2000; von Stein 2005; Nelson 2010).

7 In fact, many left-leaning politicians have criticized the IMF for its incompatibility with their own policy preferences. Examples include Presidents Hugo Chávez of Venezuela, Evo Morales of Bolivia, and Rafael Correa of Ecuador.

8 Stone (2002) and Pop-Eleches (2009) find that a government's ideological stance operates as a filter in the acceptance of IMF programs, with left-leaning governments less likely to sign an IMF deal than their right-leaning counterparts. Caraway et al. (2012), in contrast, report leftist and non-leftist governments to be equally responsive to the domestic labor movement when they negotiate loan conditions with the IMF. The "Nixon-Goes-to-China" effect is likely to be stronger when leftist governments are less likely to turn to the IMF for assistance, and I find evidence consistent with Stone (2002) and Pop-Eleches' (2009) findings. The results are presented in Table A6.1 in Appendix 6.

9 Some governments may rely on the IMF to push unpopular policies and then lay the blame at the Fund's doorstep (Stokes 2001; Vreeland 2003). IMF programs may thus further enhance the signaling effect, as they are seen as reducing the political costs of implementing neoliberal policies in leftist governments. Pop-Eleches (2009) finds that although leftist governments are less likely to sign an IMF agreement, once in a program they are more effective than their right-wing counterparts in handling crisis situations following high inflation levels.

10 The neglect of the problem poses a serious inferential problem. See Vreeland (2003) for further discussion.

11 The results are reported in Table A6.2 in Appendix 6.

12 As explained in Chapter 4, the treatment effects model prohibits the interaction of an endogenous variable (the IMF) and another explanatory variable in the second stage, whereas the pooled model allows the use of an interaction term, thus interacting government partisanship with the IMF. Using such an interaction term is superior to running two separate regressions for left and non-left governments, because the term can estimate whether the IMF programs' effect is conditional on the ideology of the government and whether the effect of ideology can be mitigated by these programs.

13 The IMF has several credit arrangements, including regular facilities (such as standby arrangements and Extended Fund Facilities), concessional facilities for low-income countries, and special facilities. Following Przeworski and Vreeland (2000) and Vreeland (2003), I do not distinguish among them because they share same fundamental objectives. The data are obtained from Vreeland (2007).

14 The results using other credit ratings appear in Table A6.3 in Appendix 6.

15 Countries in financial crisis are defined as i) countries with inflation rates of 40 percent or above, following Bruno and Easterly (1998); or ii) countries in banking, currency, and debt crises as classified in the IMF financial crises data

by Laeven and Valencia (2008). The number of cases may be small because these graphs are based on crisis years only, but they still support the hypothesis.

16 *Noncompliance* is coded 1 if more than 25 percent of the amount agreed in an IMF program remained undrawn at program termination, following Dreher and Walter (2010). Although not without its problems, this is the most commonly used measure of program compliance (Vreeland 2006) and provides a relatively larger number of observations than other compliance measures.

17 The variable is coded by the author using the IMF's data (www.imf.org/external/country).

7 Conclusion

Partisan politics and credibility in global financial markets

Greater market integration brings benefits to participating countries, but also exposes them to increased economic vulnerability. The contemporary international political economic system has led many societies around the world to experience severe market turbulence and economic shocks, which in turn have had significant political and social consequences such as strikes and protests, government changes, and even regime changes. Some studies conclude that such economic shocks have increased the gap between rich and poor, as financial crises tend to increase income inequality in crisis-hit countries through various channels (Atkinson et al. 1992; Friedman and Levinson 2002; Habib et al. 2010; Jenkins et al. 2012). As one financial market expert I have interviewed noted (Interview 1), the policy emphases traditionally associated with left-wing ideologies, such as creating more jobs and redistribution of wealth, may be useful for governments experiencing economic difficulties and attempting to redress economic wounds and promote recovery. However, left-wing governments suffer from the brand name effect, as investors tend to be wary of leftist policies and to suspect the ability of any left-wing government to manage the economy properly. So although left-wing governments may be able to win support from the domestic public, they are typically a source of concern for international investors. One of this book's messages is that by embracing institutional constraints that commit a government to protecting property rights and respecting the rule of law, a left-wing government can gain better policy credibility and predictability which may give it greater policy autonomy in the long term without posing a threat to investors.

Investors' perceptions have important market consequences. The finance literature contains studies of investor behavior over several centuries, but the persistent financial crises since the 1990s and the recent European debt crisis demonstrate once again the importance of understanding investor behavior (Reinhart and Rogoff 2011). When uncertainty makes financial decision-making significantly challenging, assessing outcome probabilities is generally difficult and investors may be unaware of all of the possible outcomes (Ackert 2014). In a state of imperfect information, a rational investor may rely on information shortcuts that allow decision-making based on risk perceptions. In that situation, how a country is perceived in international markets carries much more weight than might be expected, because perceptions guide market behavior. Studies have shown that perceptions indeed significantly influence economic outcomes (Kaminsky and Schmukler 2002; Albuquerque 2003). International private investors' increased interest in the sovereign debt of developing countries has become a source of greater instability, because such investors tend to be less tolerant of policy uncertainty and may choose to exit the market to pursue other options. Because investors perceive developing countries to pose greater default risks than developed economies, it is important for developing countries to build credible market environments.

I have discussed why international investors distrust left-wing governments, particularly in the developing world, and the consequences of such perceptions. Due to the historical association of left-wing governments with expansionary policies, neglect of debt obligations, and aggressive populist policies that threaten private investment in particular, such governments tend to suffer credibility problems and face continual suspicion about their true motives, even when they claim to pursue market-friendly policies. Such brand name effects, together with the negativity bias, influence investment decisions. From investors' perspective, being cautious about left-wing governments is only rational, particularly when they have diversified investment portfolios and have little in-depth information about each investment destination. The governing party's ideological orientation then becomes a useful cue for investors' decision-making.

I have argued that institutions that constrain political leaders are a particularly important signal of leftist governments' credibility. Furthermore, any significant changes in a country's institutional arrangements, such as deterioration of democracy or joining an international organization, have a greater impact on the perceived creditworthiness of a left-wing government. This is an important departure from earlier scholarship addressing institutions and investment. Earlier studies have neglected the fact that the effects of institutions depend on an important domestic political condition – who governs. Moreover, scholars have not sufficiently examined how changes in the institutional landscape interact with domestic political conditions to affect market perceptions.

I have empirically examined the effects of domestic political and international institutions on investors' perceptions of the sovereign credibility of leftist governments. I asked two sets of questions in a logical sequence. I first tested whether financial market participants perceive leftist governments to be less creditworthy in sovereign bond markets when other important economic and political conditions are taken into consideration. I then explored the effects of political institutions that constrain political leaders in credibly committing to market-friendly policy to show that such institutions and changes have greater credibility-building effects for left-wing governments than for others. Specifically, I discussed the credibility-building effects of democratic institutions and the degree of political constraints. I further explored the effects of IMF conditionality.

Thus, in Chapter 3, I first tested whether the government's political orientation affects a country's creditworthiness when other important economic conditions are controlled for. Despite the efforts of many left-wing governments to reassure investors about their commitment to market-friendly policies, investors tend to perceive such governments – particularly those in the developing world – as posing greater political risk and default risk. Statistical data analysis and interviews with financial market experts revealed that markets do tend to perceive left-wing governments to be more risky than other types of government, and that a longer tenure in office does not necessarily enhance the policy credibility of a left-wing government because investors suspect that it may still reverse its policies to meet domestic political demands.

Given that the financial markets perceive leftist governments in developing countries to be less creditworthy, I turned to the question of whether political institutions can help a leftist government build investor confidence. Chapter 4 tested whether democratic institutions counter the depressing effects of a leftist government on sovereign credit ratings. Democracy is believed to better protect property rights, to provide executive accountability, to be more transparent in policymaking, and tends to better limit corruption. Strong democracies may also discourage populism better than weak democracies or autocracies, and deliberative democracy allows investors to understand and better predict policy directions. These features are particularly important for developing countries where left-wing populism has been particularly threatening to investors. Therefore, one might expect that any strengthening or deterioration in democracy would also be more significant for a left-wing government in developing countries.

I used a statistical procedure correcting for potential endogeneity and selection bias to test the relationship between democracy and sovereign credit ratings. I found that democratic institutions tend to accompany better creditworthiness for leftist governments. I also found that any deterioration in democracy tends to undermine market confidence, with the results suggesting that such negative effects are likely to be stronger for left-wing governments. These results indicate that investors particularly appreciate democracy when the government is left-wing. Venezuela and Peru exemplify the contrasting market responses to deteriorating democracy in different countries. Both countries experienced serious threats to democracy during the presidency of populist leaders, leftist Chávez in Venezuela and right-leaning Fujimori in Peru, but the deterioration had a larger negative effect on the sovereign credibility of Venezuela than on that of Peru.

Investors react sharply to a leftist government's movement away from democratic principles. Some leftist leaders' move toward populism – in which political leaders ignore the rule of law, believing that they have a mandate from the people, and act like dictators – alienates investors. If a country lacks effective institutions to constrain such a populist leader, it is difficult to prevent the leader from exercising autocratic political authority. However, if leftist leaders are restricted by democratic institutions, they need to compromise with their opponents. Considering that many leftist governments have reversed pledges to pursue free-market policies and infringed on private property rights, investors may greatly appreciate democratic rules that provide for greater transparency in policymaking and constrain arbitrary policy changes.

While Chapter 4 showed the advantages of democracy for maintaining sovereign credibility, Chapter 5 demonstrated that having too many political constraints in a democracy actually undermines sovereign credibility. A decision-making system which concentrates power and applies few constraints on executive decisions has the advantage of being decisive, but it risks the policymaking process being dominated by a few political leaders. In contrast, a system with multiple political constraints has the advantage of checks and balances, which induce deliberation and bargaining. The downside of a system in which power is dispersed, however, is a risk of policy gridlock. Too much political constraint may undermine sovereign credibility, particularly when a chief executive tries to pursue market-oriented reform but has to deal with political opposition.

My data analysis has shown that there is an inverted U-shaped association between the degree of political constraints and the credit ratings of leftist governments in developing countries. This trend appears stronger if a leftist government is pursuing market-oriented financial liberalization. The findings suggest that both policy stability and policy flexibility are important for investment in such situations. Political constraints on a leftist government which are too weak may lead to arbitrary policy changes and non-accountability. However, investors may also fear that excessive political constraints could lock in unfavorable leftist policies.

The findings also show that the degree of political constraints and government partisanship are not significantly associated with sovereign credibility in advanced economies. Regardless of political orientation, such countries have already gained a certain level of market confidence about government policy. As a result, there is less concern about arbitrary policy changes. These findings imply that market participants are considerably sophisticated in estimating the effect of political dynamics on the investment environment.

The case of India clearly shows that markets tend to be concerned about over-constrained coalition governments. Markets tend to be more critical about such constraints when a left-wing coalition is in power. Although coalition governments of both the left and the right experienced severe policy gridlock in the late 1990s due to opposition within the coalition, the leftist United Front coalition suffered greater credibility problems than the right-wing coalition government of the National Democratic Alliance.

In Chapter 6, I examined the role of international institutions in building sovereign credibility. I specifically examined the role of the IMF. Some argue that IMF programs send a positive signal to investors because IMF financing will tend to increase debt liquidity in markets with a catalytic effect on investment. Others disagree, concluding that IMF programs worsen the economic conditions of borrowing countries. Because IMF conditionality emphasizes fiscal austerity and deregulation, it is incompatible with traditional leftist politics. This tends to make the ideological costs of compliance much greater for left-wing governments than for others. That, however, benefits left-wing governments signing to an IMF agreement, because in their case it sends a stronger signal of commitment to economic reform and market-friendly policies.

Using a statistical model which corrected for the biased sample selection commonly associated with studies of IMF program participation, I found that IMF programs tend to have a positive effect on the credit ratings of leftist governments. However, I did not find a significant association between IMF conditionality and the credit ratings of governments which could not be termed leftist. The IMF's emphasis on fiscal austerity, reducing inflation, privatization, and market liberalization seems to appeal especially to investors when the recipient government is leftist. At the same time, leftist governments can more easily convince investors of their motivation to carry out reforms, because their ideological stance is normally incompatible with the IMF's terms. As a result, the positive impact of the IMF in providing policy credibility may be greater for leftist governments than for others.

The case of Hungary provides a good example. The center-right Hungarian Democratic Forum government and the left-wing Hungarian Socialist government each signed an agreement with the IMF in the early 1990s, but the left-wing government's signing sent a stronger positive signal about sovereign credibility than such an agreement with a right-wing government.

The quantitative and qualitative evidence of this book has shown that left-wing governments are perceived to pose a greater default risk, and domestic political and international institutions that constrain political leaders work as a contingent signal so that they send strong positive signals about left-wing governments' credibility in international financial markets.

Implications for scholars: conditional effects of institutions on market perceptions

There is ongoing debate about whether or not domestic political institutions such as democracy and autocracy, presidential and parliamentary systems, veto players, and electoral rules matter in terms of economic performance. Similarly, there is debate about whether international institutions such as the IMF, the World Bank, the United Nations, the proliferating regional institutions and the newly established New Development Bank (formerly the BRICS bank), and the Asian Infrastructure Investment Bank matter for economic outcomes. Studies examining these issues usually ignore any interaction with political conditions, particularly the ideological orientations of the governments being studied. As a result, the literature on sovereign credibility and investment suggests that domestic political and international institutions are an important determinant of sovereign credibility of national governments, but few studies have explored how political parties influence the effect of such institutions on credibility.

The lack of consideration of partisanship in the discussion on political and international institutions is problematic, because the ideological orientation of political parties and leaders significantly influences domestic politics. Political parties are the essential element of real-world politics, with clear influence over national and international policy choices. The financial market experts that I have interviewed clearly emphasize the importance of political parties in predicting a country's policy directions, and those predictions shape investment decisions.

An important conclusion, then, is that the effects of institutions – both domestic and international – depend on a government's orientation, a finding that has been overlooked in earlier research. My findings suggest that when it comes to sovereign credibility, institutions may matter less – or at least differently – for governments which are not left-wing, but for governments which are left-wing, the effects have actually been underestimated. Scholars have pooled leftist governments with others in their analyses, and so have missed the fact that left-wing governments rely much more heavily than others on commitment devices, at least regarding sovereign credibility.

Another important point which has been neglected is that important changes in a country's institutional arrangements – especially a transition to or a breakdown of democracy, or joining an institutional organization such as the IMF that significantly influence domestic politics – have important effects on investment decisions. Scholars have treated institutional settings as static, failing to account for the dynamics and their effects on investment decisions. At the same time, changes in the institutional setting are likely to interact with domestic political conditions to affect market perceptions.

By addressing these important yet largely neglected research questions, this book contributes to the field of international political economy by enriching the relatively sparse body of literature on the relationship between political ideology, political institutions, and investor perceptions.

Implications for policymakers: embracing constraints for greater policy autonomy

In recent decades, some have adjudged that left-wing ideology is withering and that big government is declining because of the increasing significance of mobile international capital in international markets (Huber and Stephens 1998; Kurzer 1993; Mishra 1999; Moses 2000; Pierson 1995, 2001; Rodrik 1997; Ross 2000). This "convergence" argument surrounding the discussion about declining welfare states contends that the forces of globalization undermine sovereign autonomy with respect to macroeconomic and social policies so that governments have to adopt business-friendly policies to remain a viable destination for foreign investment.

Although an emphasis on the welfare state, employment, and redistribution may be required in societies suffering from the aftermath of economic crisis, the problem, as shown by this book, is that investors tend to be suspicious of a leftist government's intentions and policy directions. Such distrust leads to market fluctuation and disruption when a leftist government comes to power. Left-wing governments often become scapegoats of perception, losing credibility in international financial markets because of their labels even when they are prudently managing the economy. Losing market confidence can disadvantage such governments by making them more vulnerable to market reaction.

As shown by the findings in this book, however, such governments can improve market sentiment with the help of domestic and international institutions which send positive signals about their policy credibility. Paradoxically, left-wing governments that constrain themselves through institutional arrangements may have greater long-term autonomy in pursuing their leftist policies. With strong institutional foundations that constrain and credibly commit itself, a leftist government may pursue welfare policies without threatening the market. Such institutional arrangements can also help them to achieve stable economic growth by reducing the economic turbulence caused by market responses.

Regarding developing countries' policy reforms, recent years have seen increased emphasis on good governance. In particular, international institutions such as the World Bank have promoted good governance, backed by the rule of law and property rights protection, as an important condition for achieving stable economic growth. But not everyone agrees. Rodrik (2008), for example, has argued that developing countries should aim for second-best institutions, because best-practice institutions – such as formal institutions that guard the rule of law, property rights, independent courts, contract enforcement, and accountability – are hard to achieve, and trying to build them may actually undermine a country's economic performance. Similarly, Dixit (2004) argues that trying to build formal institutions at an early stage of development may be too costly for a developing country. These authors argue that for developing countries, it is better to aim for second best: that is, getting "desirable institutions" may be ideal, but dealing with developing countries' institutional design requires a second-best approach. Some scholars emphasize the role of informal institutions in promoting economic activities and growth (Helmke and Levitsky 2004; Pejovich 1999; de Soysa and Jütting 2007). These informal institutions, such as informal business practices and norms, may play an important role in supplementing formal institutions in certain circumstances.

However, the findings I have discussed emphasize the importance of building best-practice institutions. It may be difficult, but they are the fundamental basis for shaping market-friendly economic institutions, and they play an important signaling role in the international financial markets, especially for left-wing governments. Interviews with financial market experts clearly reveal that they greatly value the rule of law, protection of property rights, and contract enforcement, and that institutional arrangements that provide these qualities boost investors' confidence in an economy. As noted in earlier works, an important way in which institutions play a role in economic performance is by sending signals to markets about the content and direction of future policy (Cukierman et al. 1992; Schultz and Weingast 2003; Nooruddin 2011). Informal institutions are not likely to have such strong credibility-building power, in part, perhaps, because they are often not obvious to outsiders. They may work well, but they signal less effectively. Signaling is very important, particularly when an economy is in difficulty. If investors can be confident about the ability of a country's institutions to limit even a left-wing government to prudent economic policies, the government will have more freedom to address problems without losing market confidence.

Turning to the effects of international institutions, there has been serious doubt about the role of the IMF in international financial markets. The findings reported here imply that, despite ideological disagreements, leftist governments in economic distress may find it beneficial to seek support from the IMF. IMF support can also be a useful tool for a leftist government finding itself obliged to pursue domestically unpopular economic reforms (Vreeland 2003). More importantly, the IMF involvement may minimize adverse economic reactions, such as investor panic and contagion across countries. By increasing investor confidence, an IMF program may play a catalytic role by providing an opportunity for improved access to financial markets.

Building credibility in international financial markets is essential for a country wishing to maintain financial market stability and achieve stable, long-term economic growth. In international financial markets where market perception of sovereign credibility is critical, domestic political and international institutions that constrain political leaders send a positive signal about sovereign credibility, particularly for left-wing governments that need to work harder to gain market confidence. Ironically, because these governments face greater problems regarding credibility, embracing institutional constraints may allow left-wing governments greater policy autonomy in the long run through earning market confidence.

Appendix 1

Interviews with financial market experts

Invitation emails were sent out to 116 financial market experts specializing in emerging market investments. The list was drawn predominantly from experts in Hong Kong, one of the three major financial centers in the world along with New York and London. Hong Kong is a major financial center for developing countries, so much of the experts' business involved dealing with emerging markets. Those who replied and agreed to an interview were then interviewed face-to-face.

Each interview lasted 60 to 90 minutes. In each interview, the expert was asked the same set of open-ended questions soliciting his/her opinions. The questions asked (1) how they gather information regarding political conditions in the countries where they considered investing; (2) what they considered important political factors in making their investment decisions; (3) what political factors they considered most important in reducing policy uncertainty and increasing policy credibility in a country; (4) whether or not their perception of a political leader's ideological orientation (pro-business or pro-labor, or left or right) and party label was important in making investment decisions; and (5) whether or not their perceptions about the role of political institutions (the rule of law, the policymaking process, checks and balances) and international organizations (especially the IMF) influenced their assessment of governments and investment. The subsequent questions then depended on the experts' answers.

List

(Most of the interviewees were high-level executives and I do not specify details of their positions for the sake of privacy.)

Interviewee 1 (November 12, 2013) Coface, France
Interviewee 2 (November 15, 2013) KDB Daewoo Securities, Hong Kong
Interviewee 3 (November 22, 2013) CLSA Capital Partners, Hong Kong Limited
Interviewee 4 (November 25, 2013) Credit Suisse, Hong Kong

Interviewee 5 (November 26, 2013) Financial Supervisory Service, Hong Kong
Interviewees 6, 7, 8, and 9 (November 26, 2013) KB Kookmin Bank, Hong Kong Limited
Interviewee 10 (November 27, 2013) Ping-An of China Asset Management (Hong Kong) Co. Limited
Interviewee 11 (November 29, 2013) Woori Investment & Securities, Hong Kong Limited
Interviewees 12 and 13 (December 3, 2013) Moody's, Hong Kong
Interviewee 14 (December 4, 2013) Pacific Century Insurance, Hong Kong
Interviewees 15 and 16 (December 5, 2013) Samsung Asset Management, Hong Kong Limited
Interviewees 17 and 18 (December 6, 2013) Hyundai Securities, Hong Kong/Asia Limited
Interviewee 19 (December 6, 2013) UBS, Hong Kong
Interviewee 20 (December 16, 2013) Calista Capital, Hong Kong
Interviewees 21 and 22 (December 18, 2013) Baring, Hong Kong
Interviewee 23 (December 20, 2013) Cathay Conning, Hong Kong
Interviewee 24 (January 3, 2014) Woori Investment & Securities, Korea

Appendix 2.1

Data sources and summary statistics

Table A2.1.1 Data sources

Variable	*Source*
Credit ratings	Institutional Investor, Moody's, Standard and Poor's, and Fitch, various years.
Left party	*Database of Political Institutions* (Beck et al. 2001).
Checks	*Database of Political Institutions* (Beck et al. 2001).
Years in office	*Database of Political Institutions* (Beck et al. 2001).
Democracy	Cheibub et al. (2010), Polity IV (Marshall et al. 2009).
Budget balance	Central government deficit or surplus as a percentage of GDP. *International Financial Statistics* and *World Development Indicators*, various years.
GDP growth	GDP growth, annual percentage. *World Development Indicators* and OECD Economic Outlook, various years.
Current account balance	Current account balance as a percentage of GDP. *World Development Indicators*, various years.
Inflation	Inflation, GDP deflator (annual percentage). *World Development Indicators*, various years.
Investment	Investment as a share of GDP. *Penn World Tables 6.2 & 7.2* (Heston et al. 2006).
Debt	Total debt service as a share of exports of goods, services, and income (for developing countries); central government debt per GDP (for developed countries). *World Development Indicators* and *OECD Economic Outlook*, various years.
Reserves	Foreign reserves as a percentage of external debt (for developing countries); total reserves in US dollars (for developed countries). *World Development Indicators* and OECD Economic Outlook, various years.
Fixed exchange rates	1 = fixed, 0 = flexible. Following Broz and Plouffe (2010), I recode Ilzetzki et al. (2017)'s *de facto* exchange rate regime classification into a binary variable.
Capital account openness	Higher values indicate more open capital accounts. Chinn and Ito (2006).
IMF	Vreeland (2007).

Table A2.1.1 Continued

Variable	*Source*
IMF signed	Coded by the author using the IMF's data (www.imf.org/external/country/).
Noncompliance	Coded by the author using the IMF's data (www.imf.org/external/country/).
UN voting	The percentage of votes within a year that are in line with the United States in the United Nations General Assembly. Dreher and Sturm (2012).
Years in IMF program (since 1951)	The cumulative number of years of program participation. Vreeland (2007).
Number of other countries in IMF program	Vreeland (2007).
Average level of democracy in the region	Author's calculation based on Polity score of Polity IV.
Transparency	Hollyer et al. (2014).
Natural resources	Total natural resource rents as a percentage of GDP. *World Development Indicators* (2010).

Table A2.1.2 Summary statistics, developing countries

	Mean	*SD*	*Min*	*Max*
Institutional Investor	31.25	15.29	4.3	77.6
Moody's	5.89	2.92	1	13
Standard and Poor's	6.21	2.88	1	17
Fitch	6.23	2.72	1	12
Left party	0.26	0.44	0	1
Checks	2.76	1.87	1	18
Years in office	7.16	7.85	1	46
GDP growth	3.97	4.44	-19.01	27.46
Inflation	70.07	605.21	-23.48	13611.63
Current account	−3.04	6.61	−42.89	32.54
Budget balance	−2.93	4.83	−49.94	40.43
Capital account openness	−0.26	1.38	−1.86	2.46
Fixed exchange rates	0.39	0.49	0	1
Democracy (Polity IV)	12.37	6.47	0	20
Democracy (Cheibub et al. 2010)	0.53	0.50	0	1
Reserves	38.75	115.59	0.122	1946.159
Debt	22.70	15.35	0.28	152.27

(Continued)

Table A2.1.2 Continued

	Mean	*SD*	*Min*	*Max*
IMF	0.54	0.50	0	1
IMF signed	0.20	0.40	0	1
Years in IMF program (since 1951)	13.58	8.87	0	38
Noncompliance	0.28	0.45	0	1
UN voting	0.24	0.12	0	0.72
Number of other countries in IMF program	59.79	8.64	42	75
Average level of democracy in the region	11.49	4.61	2.25	19.67
Transparency	1.53	1.63	-0.94	8.35
Natural resources	7.07	9.32	0	52.25
Investment	21.59	9.66	-34.02	71.02

Table A2.1.3 Summary statistics, developed countries

	Mean	*SD*	*Min*	*Max*
Institutional Investor	80.75	11.39	48.8	98.3
Moody's	15.81	1.70	8	17
Standard and Poor's	15.82	1.77	8	17
Fitch	15.69	1.79	8	17
Left party	0.42	0.49	0	1
Checks	4.27	1.33	2	11
GDP growth	2.74	2.17	-5.99	11.49
Inflation	4.216	3.489	-.707	21.276
Current account	-0.45	3.81	-14.85	16.12
Budget balance	-2.64	4.08	-14.16	15.37
Capital account openness	1.74	1.09	-1.85	2.45
Reserves	19,199.09	33,864.55	58	447,229
Debt	49.13	25.33	6.02	156.81
Investment	22.68	4.04	14.51	42.85

Appendix 2.2

Countries in the sample*

Table A2.2.1 Developing countries in the sample

Country	*Sample start year*	*Sample end year*	*Years of leftist government*	*Years of democracy*	*Years in IMF programs*
Albania	1996	2007	1998–2005	1996–2007	1996, 98–2007
Argentina	1981	2005	2004–05	1983–2005	1983–2005
Armenia	2004	2007		2004–07	2004–07
Bangladesh	1987	2007	1991	1987–2006	1987–93, 2003–07
Belarus	1997	2007			
Bolivia	1981	2007	1983–85, 90–93, 2006–07	1982–2007	1981, 86–2006
Botswana	1993	2004			
Brazil	1981	2007	1995–2007	1985–2007	1983–86, 88–90, 92–93, 98–2005
Bulgaria	1995	2007	1995–96, 2006–07	1995–2007	1995–2007
Burkina Faso	1994	2007	2005–2007		1994–2007
Burundi	2001	2004			2004
Cameroon	1983	2000			1988–92, 94–2000
Chile	1981	2007	1994–2007	1990–2007	1983–90
China	1985	2005	1985–2005		1986–87
Colombia	1981	2007		1981–2007	1999–2006
Costa Rica	1981	2004	1983–90, 95–98	1981–2007	1981–97
Cote d'Ivoire	1985	2005	2001–05		1985–92, 1994–2005
Dominican Republic	1981	2007	1981–86, 2001–04	1981–2007	1983–86, 91–94, 2003–07
Ecuador	1981	2004	1982–84, 89–92, 98–2002	1981–99, 2002–04	1983–92, 94–96, 2000–01, 03–04

(Continued)

Table A2.2.1 Continued

Country	*Sample start year*	*Sample end year*	*Years of leftist government*	*Years of democracy*	*Years in IMF programs*
Egypt	1981	2007			1981, 87–88, 91–98
El Salvador	1982	2007		1984–2007	1982–83, 90–2000
Ethiopia	1983	2007	1983–91, 2005–07		1992–99, 2001–04
Gabon	1981	1992			1981–82, 86–92
Georgia	1998	2007		2004–07	1998–99, 2001–07
Ghana	1993	2007		1993–2007	1995–2006
Guatemala	1982	2007		1986–2007	1982–84, 88–90, 92–94, 2002–04
Haiti	1993	2004			1995–99
Honduras	1982	2007		1982–2007	1982–83, 90–97, 99–02, 04–07
India	1981	2007	1981–98, 2005–07	1981–2007	1981–84, 91–93
Indonesia	1982	2007		1999–2007	1997–2003
Iran	1981	1983			
Jamaica	1981	2007	1990–2007	1981–2007	1981–1996
Jordan	1981	2007			1989–99, 2001–04
Kazakhstan	1997	2007			1997–99, 2001–02
Kenya	1981	2007		1998–2008	1981–86, 88–94, 96–99, 2001–03, 05–07
Kyrgyz Republic	2001	2004			2001–04
Latvia	2006	2007		2006–07	
Lebanon	2003	2007			
Lesotho	2001	2007	2001–2007		2001–04
Lithuania	1997	2007		1997–2007	1997, 2000–03
Malawi	1982	1991			1982–86, 88–91
Malaysia	1981	2007			

Table A2.2.1 Continued

Country	*Sample start year*	*Sample end year*	*Years of leftist government*	*Years of democracy*	*Years in IMF programs*
Mali	1994	2007		1994–2007	1994–2007
Mauritius	1982	2004	1982–95	1982–2004	1982–86
Mexico	1981	2002	1981–82	2000–02	1983–93, 95–97, 99–00
Moldova	2004	2007	2004–07	2004–07	2006–07
Morocco	1981	2007			1981–93
Nepal	1989	2006	1992–2002	1990–2001	1989–90, 92–95, 2003–06
Nicaragua	1981	2007	1981–90, 2007	1984–2007	1991–2007
Niger	2006	2007		2006–07	2006–07
Nigeria	1984	2007		1999–2007	1987–92, 2001
Pakistan	1981	2007	1989–90, 94–96	1988–98	1981–83, 88–91, 93–2004
Panama	1981	2002		1989–2002	1981–87, 92–2002
Papua New Guinea	1984	2003		1984–2003	1990–92, 95–97, 2000–01
Paraguay	1981	2007		1989–2007	2003–07
Peru	1981	2007	1986–90, 2007	1981–89, 2001–07	1982–85, 93–2007
Philippines	1981	2007		1986–2007	1981, 83–2000
Romania	1988	2007	1988–89, 92–96, 2001–04	1990–2007	1991–2006
Russia	1997	2007			1997–2000
Rwanda	2004	2004			2004
Senegal	1981	2002	1981–2000	2000–2002	1981–92, 94–2002
Sierra Leone	1981	2007	1981–92, 97–07	1996, 1998–2007	1981–89, 94–98, 2002–07
South Africa	1995	2007	1995–2007		
Sri Lanka	1983	2007	1995–2005	1989–2007	1983–84, 88–95, 2001–06
Sudan	1981	2000		1986–88	1981–85
Swaziland	1989	2004			
Syria	1996	2000			
Tanzania	1990	2004	1989–2004		1990–94, 96–2004
Thailand	1981	2007		1981–90, 92–2005	1981–83, 85–86, 97–2000

(Continued)

Table A2.2.1 Continued

Country	*Sample start year*	*Sample end year*	*Years of leftist government*	*Years of democracy*	*Years in IMF programs*
Togo	1995	2007			1995–98
Tunisia	1987	2007	1987–2007		1987–92
Turkey	1981	2007	2000–02	1983–2007	1981–85, 94–96, 2000–07
Uganda	1984	2007	1984–85	1984	1984, 87–2006
Ukraine	2000	2007		2000–07	2000–02, 04–05
Uruguay	1981	2007	2005–07	1985–2007	1981–87, 90–93, 96–2006
Venezuela	1981	2006	1984–88, 99–2006	1981–2006	1989–93, 96–97
Zambia	1981	2007	1981–2007		1981–87, 95–2007
Zimbabwe	1985	1995			1992–95

Table A2.2.2 Developed countries in the sample

Country	*Sample start year*	*Sample end year*	*Years of leftist government*
Australia	1981	2007	1984–96
Austria	1981	2007	1981–99, 2007
Belgium	2003	2007	
Canada	1982	2007	1982–84, 94–2006
Denmark	1981	2007	1981–82, 94–2001
Finland	1991	2007	1996–02
France	1993	2007	1993, 1998–2002
Germany	1981	2007	1981–82, 1999–2005
Greece	1994	2007	1994–2004
Iceland	1981	2007	
Ireland	1991	2007	
Israel	1999	2007	
Italy	1981	2007	1984–87, 93–94, 2007
Japan	1981	2007	1995–96
Netherlands	1982	2007	1995–2003
New Zealand	1993	2007	2000–07
Norway	1983	2007	1987–89, 91–97, 2006–07
Portugal	1981	2007	1984–85, 96–2002, 2006–07
Spain	1981	2007	1983–96, 2005–07
Sweden	1981	2007	1983–91, 95–2006
United Kingdom	1999	2007	1999–2007
United States	1981	2007	1993–2000

*These are comprehensive lists, and some observations are dropped in individual regressions depending on data availability.

Appendix 3

Supplements to Chapter 3

Table A3.1 Government partisanship and credit ratings of developing countries (Moody's, Fitch, and Standard and Poor's ratings)

	Moody's					*Fitch*					*Standard and Poor's*[1]
	(1)	*(2)*	*(3)*	*(4)*	*(5)*	*(6)*	*(7)*	*(8)*	*(9)*	*(10)*	*(11)*
Left party	−0.117**	−0.118**	−0.115**	−0.121**	−0.132**	−0.118**	−0.118**	−0.127**	−0.118**	−0.193***	0.004
	(0.059)	(0.059)	(0.058)	(0.059)	(0.065)	(0.054)	(0.054)	(0.054)	(0.054)	(0.065)	(0.045)
Resources		0.002					0.004				
		(0.005)					(0.005)				
Fixed			−0.098*					0.117**			
			(0.054)					(0.059)			
Regime				0.005					0.000		
				(0.008)					(0.011)		
Years in office					0.008*					0.002	
					(0.004)					(0.006)	
Years* left party					−0.010					0.010	
					(0.009)					(0.010)	

Budget	0.003	0.003	0.003	0.003	0.001	0.003	0.002	0.003	0.003	0.000	0.002
	(0.005)	(0.005)	(0.005)	(0.005)	(0.005)	(0.004)	(0.004)	(0.004)	(0.004)	(0.004)	(0.004)
Growth	0.007*	0.006	0.007*	0.007	0.008*	0.002	0.002	0.002	0.002	0.002	0.002
	(0.004)	(0.004)	(0.004)	(0.004)	(0.004)	(0.004)	(0.004)	(0.004)	(0.004)	(0.004)	(0.004)
Capital	0.027	0.027	0.029	0.027	0.050*	0.102***	0.104***	0.100***	0.102***	0.129***	0.099***
	(0.029)	(0.029)	(0.029)	(0.029)	(0.029)	(0.025)	(0.026)	(0.025)	(0.026)	(0.026)	(0.022)
Invest	0.017***	0.017***	0.018***	0.018***	0.012**	0.017***	0.016***	0.019***	0.017***	0.016***	0.014***
	(0.005)	(0.005)	(0.006)	(0.005)	(0.006)	(0.005)	(0.005)	(0.005)	(0.005)	(0.005)	(0.005)
Current	–0.005	–0.006	–0.005	–0.004	–0.007	0.001	–0.001	0.001	0.001	0.002	0.002
	(0.004)	(0.004)	(0.005)	(0.005)	(0.005)	(0.004)	(0.004)	(0.004)	(0.004)	(0.004)	(0.004)
Inflation	–0.000	–0.000	–0.000	–0.000	–0.000	–0.000	–0.000	–0.000	–0.000	–0.000	–0.000***
	(0.000)	(0.000)	(0.000)	(0.000)	(0.000)	(0.000)	(0.000)	(0.000)	(0.000)	(0.000)	(0.000)
Reserves (log)	0.190***	0.190***	0.198***	0.187***	0.226***	0.305***	0.306***	0.317***	0.304***	0.346***	0.218***
	(0.045)	(0.045)	(0.045)	(0.045)	(0.047)	(0.051)	(0.051)	(0.051)	(0.050)	(0.055)	(0.040)
Debt	0.001	0.001	0.001	0.001	0.002	0.002	0.001	0.001	0.001	0.002	0.001
	(0.002)	(0.002)	(0.002)	(0.002)	(0.002)	(0.002)	(0.002)	(0.002)	(0.002)	(0.002)	(0.002)
Constant	0.426	0.410	0.447	0.322	0.377	–0.306	–0.318	–0.444	–0.307	–0.393	1.523***
	(0.268)	(0.275)	(0.274)	(0.298)	(0.269)	(0.307)	(0.309)	(0.301)	(0.357)	(0.300)	(0.379)
Observations	431	431	426	428	406	346	346	342	343	324	487
R-squared	0.76	0.76	0.76	0.76	0.77	0.78	0.78	0.79	0.78	0.80	0.50

Notes: $^{***}p < .01$; $^{**}p < .05$; $^{*}p < .10$ (two-tailed). The dependent variables are log-transformed.

Table A3.2 Government partisanship and credit ratings of developed countries (Moody's, Fitch, and Standard and Poor's ratings)

	Moody's	*Fitch*	*Standard and Poor's*
Left party	0.005	0.003	0.002
	(0.005)	(0.005)	(0.004)
Budget	0.002	0.001	0.001
	(0.001)	(0.001)	(0.001)
Growth	0.000	-0.002	-0.000
	(0.001)	(0.001)	(0.001)
Capital	0.016***	0.041***	0.013***
	(0.005)	(0.013)	(0.004)
Invest	0.001	0.006**	0.001
	(0.002)	(0.003)	(0.002)
Current	-0.001	0.002	-0.001
	(0.001)	(0.002)	(0.001)
Inflation	-0.002**	-0.003**	-0.001**
	(0.001)	(0.001)	(0.001)
Reserves (log)	0.000***	-0.000	0.000
	(0.000)	(0.000)	(0.000)
Debt	-0.002***	-0.001**	-0.002***
	(0.000)	(0.000)	(0.000)
Constant	2.750***	2.554***	2.763***
	(0.048)	(0.071)	(0.040)
Observations	414	270	438
R-squared	0.98	0.99	0.99

Notes: ***p < .01; **p < .05; *p < .10 (two-tailed). The dependent variables are log-transformed.

Note

1 For Standard and Poor's ratings, models including additional control variables (i.e. natural resources, fixed exchange rates, regime type, and years in office) do not significantly change the findings as shown in this model (model 11).

Appendix 4

Supplements to Chapter 4

Effects of democracy on sovereign credibility (the treatment effects model, Table A4.1)

The treatment effects model corrects for selection bias by measuring the correlation between the errors that result from selection and those that result from performance, and then including this correlation (called the hazard rate) in the second stage. A statistically significant hazard rate indicates the existence of selection bias. The model is specified as follows:

$$\begin{aligned}
&Democracy_{i,t-1} \\
&\quad = \alpha_0 + \alpha_1 GDP\,Growth_{i,t-2} + \alpha_2 Investment_{i,t-2} + \alpha_3 Debt_{i,t-2} \\
&\qquad + \alpha_4 Average\ Level\ of\ Democracy\ of\ Other\ Countries\ in\ the\ Region_{i,t-2} \\
&\qquad + \alpha_5 Democratic\ Breakdown\ in\ the\ Past_{i,t-2} + \alpha_6 Multilateral\ Lending_{i,t-2} \\
&\qquad + \alpha_7 Natural\ Resources_{i,t-2} + \mu_{it}
\end{aligned}$$

$$\begin{aligned}
&\ln Credit\ Rating_{it} \\
&\quad = \beta_0 + \beta_1 Democracy_{i,t-1} + \beta_2 Budget\ Balance_{i,t-1} \\
&\qquad + \beta_3 Capital\ Account\ Openness_{i,t-1} + \beta_4 GDP\,Growth_{i,t-1} \\
&\qquad + \beta_5 Inflation_{i,t-1} + \beta_6 Current\ Account\ Balance_{i,t-1} \\
&\qquad + \beta_7 Investment_{i,t-1} + \beta_8 \ln Reserves_{i,t-1} + \beta_9 Debt_{i,t-1} \\
&\qquad + \beta_{10} \ln Credit\ Rating_{i,t-1} + \beta_{11} \rho_{it} + \epsilon_{it}
\end{aligned}$$

In the first stage, in addition to economic determinants of democracy such as economic growth, investment, and debt levels, I include the following variables:

Past transitions to authoritarianism. This variable measures the sum of past transitions to authoritarianism in a country. According to Przeworski et al. (2000), the political history of regimes has an important role in affecting the chances that the current regime will survive or die. The expectation is that countries that have had more democratic breakdowns in the past are less likely to have democratic regimes.

Oil-exporting countries. The income generated from natural resources such as oil may create less pressure for democratization than income associated with the accumulation of human and physical capital (Barro 1999: 164; Ross 2001: 327). Resource-rich governments use low tax rates and patronage to relieve pressures for greater accountability. The measure estimates the volume of oil production.

Multilateral lending. The literature on recent waves of democratization in developing countries argues that multilateral lending by the Western

Table A4.1 Democracy and credit ratings of developing countries, treatment effects model

	Democracy Indicator (Cheibub et al. 2010)	
	Leftist	*Non-leftist*
Democracy	0.006	0.002
	(0.031)	(0.012)
Budget balance	0.003***	0.000
	(0.001)	(0.001)
Capital account openness	0.011*	0.019***
	(0.006)	(0.004)
GDP growth	0.001	0.006***
	(0.001)	(0.001)
Current account balance	−0.002	0.002**
	(0.001)	(0.001)
Investment	−0.001	0.002*
	(0.001)	(0.001)
Reserves (log)	0.035***	0.050***
	(0.010)	(0.006)
Inflation	0.000	0.000
	(0.000)	(0.000)
Debt service	−0.001	0.000
	(0.000)	(0.000)
Rating in the previous year	0.751***	0.814***
	(0.032)	(0.015)
Constant	0.586***	0.173**
	(0.107)	(0.070)
Hazard	−0.003	−0.003
	(0.017)	(0.009)
Observations	313	978

Notes: ***$p < .01$; **$p < .05$; *$p < .10$ (two-tailed). The second stage results are presented. The dependent variable is Institutional Investor and is log-transformed.

developed countries and international institutions requires the borrowing countries to adopt democratic process in order to receive the financial aid.

Average level of democracy of other countries in the region. The expectation is that the more democratic other countries in the region are, the more likely a given country is also a democracy.

Table A4.2 Democracy (continuous variable), partisanship, and credit ratings of developing countries, two-stage least squares model

	Polity IV
Left party	–0.283**
	(0.130)
Democracy	0.004
	(0.004)
Left party* democracy	0.017**
	(0.008)
Budget balance	0.002**
	(0.001)
GDP growth	0.005***
	(0.001)
Capital account openness	0.817***
	(0.015)
Investment	0.002***
	(0.001)
Current account	0.002***
	(0.001)
Inflation	0.000
	(0.000)
Reserves (log)	0.035***
	(0.005)
Debt	–0.000
	(0.000)
Rating in the previous year	0.817***
	(0.015)
Constant	0.443***
	(0.077)
Observations	1,341
R-squared	0.95

Notes: ***$p < .01$; **$p < .05$; *$p < .10$ (two-tailed). The dependent variable is Institutional Investor and is log-transformed.

Table A4.3 Government transparency, partisanship, and credit ratings of developing countries, two-stage least squares model

Left party	–0.163***
	(0.055)
Transparency	0.074*
	(0.045)
Left party* transparency	0.092***
	(0.033)
Budget balance	0.002**
	(0.001)
GDP growth	0.004***
	(0.001)
Capital account openness	0.008
	(0.006)
Investment	0.003**
	(0.001)
Current account	0.003***
	(0.001)
Inflation	0.000
	(0.000)
Reserves (log)	0.052***
	(0.008)
Debt service	–0.001
	(0.000)
Rating in the previous year	0.802***
	(0.020)
Constant	0.474***
	(0.070)
Observations	1,265
R-squared	0.92

Notes: ***p < .01; **p < .05; *p < .10 (two-tailed). The dependent variable is Institutional Investor and is log-transformed.

Table A4.4 Institutional deterioration, government partisanship, and credit ratings of developing countries

	Deterioration in Past 5 Years			*Deterioration in Past 10 Years*		
	Moody's	*Standard and Poor's*	*Fitch*	*Moody's*	*Standard and Poor's*	*Fitch*
Left party	–0.032	0.050	–0.058	0.061	0.068	–0.045
	(0.062)	(0.047)	(0.063)	(0.069)	(0.055)	(0.074)
Deterioration	–0.050	–0.127***	–0.006	–0.043	–0.084***	0.036
	(0.054)	(0.047)	(0.048)	(0.027)	(0.027)	(0.029)
Left party* deterioration	–0.266***	–0.142*	–0.128**	–0.060	–0.094**	–0.059*
	(0.101)	(0.075)	(0.063)	(0.048)	(0.041)	(0.033)
Budget balance	0.002	0.001	0.003	–0.001	0.003	0.003
	(0.005)	(0.003)	(0.003)	(0.005)	(0.004)	(0.003)
GDP growth	0.007*	0.002	0.004	0.009**	0.002	0.006
	(0.004)	(0.004)	(0.004)	(0.004)	(0.005)	(0.005)
Capital account	0.036	0.090***	0.076***	0.028	0.072***	0.082***
	(0.028)	(0.021)	(0.022)	(0.023)	(0.022)	(0.023)
Investment	0.018***	0.012***	0.008*	0.012***	0.012**	0.006
	(0.005)	(0.005)	(0.005)	(0.004)	(0.005)	(0.005)
Current account	–0.002	0.002	–0.001	0.001	0.000	–0.002
	(0.004)	(0.003)	(0.004)	(0.004)	(0.004)	(0.004)
Inflation	–0.000	–0.000***	–0.000	0.000	–0.000**	–0.000
	(0.000)	(0.000)	(0.000)	(0.000)	(0.000)	(0.000)

(Continued)

Table A4.4 Continued

	Deterioration in Past 5 Years			*Deterioration in Past 10 Years*		
	Moody's	*Standard and Poor's*	*Fitch*	*Moody's*	*Standard and Poor's*	*Fitch*
Reserves (log)	0.137***	0.167***	0.218***	0.179***	0.142***	0.238***
	(0.044)	(0.036)	(0.039)	(0.040)	(0.035)	(0.040)
Debt	0.000	0.000	0.001	–0.000	–0.000	0.001
	(0.002)	(0.002)	(0.002)	(0.002)	(0.002)	(0.002)
Crisis in past 5 years	0.016	0.000	–0.039			
	(0.023)	(0.021)	(0.028)			
Crisis in past 10 years				–0.014	0.038	0.007
				(0.024)	(0.025)	(0.034)
Constant	0.538**	1.607***	0.193	1.976***	0.470*	0.090
	(0.264)	(0.362)	(0.314)	(0.246)	(0.284)	(0.324)
Observations	415	471	330	408	460	312
R-squared	0.78	0.74	0.78	0.63	0.70	0.79

Notes: $^{***}p < .01$; $^{**}p < .05$; $^{*}p < .10$ (two-tailed). The dependent variables are log-transformed.

Table A4.5 Institutional improvement, government partisanship, and credibility of developing countries

	Improvement in past 5 years			*Improvement in past 10 years*		
	Moody's	*Standard and Poor's*	*Fitch*	*Moody's*	*Standard and Poor's*	*Fitch*
Left Party	–0.100	–0.100	–0.126**	–0.017	–0.020	–0.088
	(0.063)	(0.063)	(0.058)	(0.068)	(0.060)	(0.065)
Improvement	–0.005	–0.095***	–0.077**	–0.008	–0.040	–0.036
	(0.032)	(0.031)	(0.035)	(0.032)	(0.032)	(0.035)
Left party* improvement	–0.034	0.030	0.041	0.029	0.050	0.011
	(0.057)	(0.040)	(0.040)	(0.046)	(0.030)	(0.035)
Budget balance	0.000	–0.000	0.001	–0.001	–0.001	0.002
	(0.005)	(0.004)	(0.003)	(0.005)	(0.003)	(0.003)
GDP growth	0.007*	0.003	0.004	0.009**	0.002	0.004
	(0.004)	(0.004)	(0.004)	(0.004)	(0.004)	(0.005)
Capital account openness	0.020	0.093***	0.088***	0.031	0.094***	0.101***
	(0.032)	(0.021)	(0.025)	(0.023)	(0.020)	(0.025)
Investment	0.016***	0.011**	0.011**	0.011**	0.007	0.006
	(0.005)	(0.004)	(0.005)	(0.004)	(0.005)	(0.005)
Current account	–0.006	0.001	–0.001	0.000	–0.002	–0.003
	(0.005)	(0.003)	(0.004)	(0.004)	(0.004)	(0.004)
Inflation	0.000	–0.000***	–0.000	0.000	–0.000***	–0.000
	(0.000)	(0.000)	(0.000)	(0.000)	(0.000)	(0.000)

(Continued)

Table A4.5 Continued

	Improvement in past 5 years			*Improvement in past 10 years*		
	Moody's	*Standard and Poor's*	*Fitch*	*Moody's*	*Standard and Poor's*	*Fitch*
Reserves (log)	0.071*	0.170***	0.234***	0.179***	0.214***	0.282***
	(0.039)	(0.036)	(0.044)	(0.040)	(0.037)	(0.047)
Debt	0.001	0.001	0.001	0.001	0.000	0.000
	(0.002)	(0.002)	(0.002)	(0.002)	(0.002)	(0.002)
Crisis in past 5 years	0.025	0.003	–0.031			
	(0.022)	(0.021)	(0.028)			
Crisis in past 10 years				–0.015	0.037	0.016
				(0.025)	(0.024)	(0.032)
Constant	0.374	1.749***	0.126	1.998***	1.782***	0.023
	(0.264)	(0.364)	(0.292)	(0.252)	(0.369)	(0.298)
Observations	415	471	330	408	460	312
R-squared	0.74	0.74	0.80	0.62	0.75	0.82

Notes: ***$p < .01$; **$p < .05$; *$p < .10$ (two-tailed). The dependent variables are log-transformed.

Appendix 5
Supplements to Chapter 5

Table A5.1 Political constraints, government partisanship, and credit ratings of developing countries

	Fitch	*Moody's*	*Standard and Poor's*
Left party	-0.859***	-0.587*	-0.140
	(0.299)	(0.316)	(0.133)
Checks	-0.044	0.022	0.160
	(0.253)	(0.161)	(0.178)
Left party*Checks	0.858**	0.493	-0.006
	(0.376)	(0.395)	(0.186)
Checks^2	-0.001	0.016	-0.075
	(0.086)	(0.061)	(0.067)
Left party*Checks^2	-0.216*	-0.114	0.050
	(0.115)	(0.107)	(0.063)
Capital account openness	0.132***	0.048*	0.120***
	(0.025)	(0.029)	(0.022)
Investment	0.015***	0.015***	0.014***
	(0.005)	(0.005)	(0.005)
Budget balance	0.008	0.002	0.005
	(0.006)	(0.005)	(0.006)
GDP growth	0.001	0.008**	0.002
	(0.004)	(0.004)	(0.004)
Reserves (log)	0.336***	0.238***	0.245***
	(0.055)	(0.047)	(0.043)
Inflation	-0.000	-0.000	-0.000***
	(0.000)	(0.000)	(0.000)
Current account balance	0.002	-0.005	0.003
	(0.004)	(0.005)	(0.004)

(Continued)

Table A5.1 Continued

	Fitch	*Moody's*	*Standard and Poor's*
Debt	0.002	0.002	0.002
	(0.002)	(0.002)	(0.002)
Constant	−0.255	0.333	1.274***
	(0.341)	(0.276)	(0.389)
Observations	319	405	454
R-squared	0.80	0.78	0.74

Notes: ***p < .01; **p < .05; *p < .10 (two-tailed). The dependent variables are log-transformed.

Appendix 6
Supplements to Chapter 6

Table A6.1 Government partisanship and IMF programs participation, developing countries

Dependent variable: IMF program participation (1 = participation, 0 = no participation)	
Left party	–0.267***
	(0.097)
Budget balance	0.014
	(0.009)
GDP growth	–0.020**
	(0.009)
Inflation	–0.000
	(0.000)
Current account balance	–0.029***
	(0.007)
Fixed exchange rate	–0.106
	(0.089)
Debt	0.009***
	(0.003)
Investment	–0.009*
	(0.005)
Reserves (log)	–0.292***
	(0.048)
Democracy	0.003
	(0.007)
UN voting	0.721***
	(0.219)
Years in program	0.013**
	(0.005)
Number of other countries in program	0.012**
	(0.005)
Constant	–0.130
	(0.394)
Observations	1,181

Notes: robust standard errors are in parentheses. *** $p < .01$; ** $p < .05$; * $p < .1$ (two-tailed).

Effects of IMF programs on sovereign credibility (treatment effects model) (Table A6.2)

The treatment effects model corrects for selection bias by measuring the correlation between the errors that result from selection and those that result from performance, and then including this correlation (called the hazard rate) in the second stage. A statistically significant hazard rate indicates the existence of selection bias. The model is specified as follows:

$$
\begin{aligned}
IMF_{i,t-1} = {} & \alpha_0 + \alpha_1 Budget\ Balance_{i,t-2} + \alpha_2 GDP\ Growth_{i,t-2} \\
& + \alpha_3 Inflation_{i,t-2} + \alpha_4 Current\ Account\ Balance_{i,t-2} \\
& + \alpha_5 Fixed\ Exhange\ Rate_{i,t-2} + \alpha_6 \ln Reserves_{i,t-2} + \alpha_7 Debt_{i,t-2} \\
& + \alpha_8 Investment_{i,t-2} + \alpha_9 UN\ Voting_{i,t-2} \\
& + \alpha_{10} Years\ in\ Program_{i,t-2} + \alpha_{11} Number\ of\ Other\ Countries_{i,t-2} + \mu_{it}
\end{aligned}
$$

$$
\begin{aligned}
& \ln Credit\ Rating_{it} \\
& = \beta_0 + \beta_1 IMF_{i,t-1} + \beta_2 Democracy_{i,t-1} + \beta_3 Budget\ Balance_{i,t-1} \\
& \quad + \beta_4 Capital\ \ Account\ Openness_{i,t-1} + \beta_5 GDP\ Growth_{i,t-1} + \beta_6 Inflation_{i,t-1} \\
& \quad + \beta_7 Current\ Account\ Balance_{i,t-1} + \beta_8 Investment_{i,t-1} + \beta_9 \ln Reserves_{i,t-1} \\
& \quad + \beta_{10} Debt_{i,t-1} + \beta_{11} \ln Credit\ Rating_{i,t-1} + \beta_{12} \rho_{it} + \epsilon_{it}
\end{aligned}
$$

The first-stage equation includes *UN Voting*, which measures a country's UN General Assembly voting pattern. Earlier studies find that developing countries with closer ties with the United States tend to vote in line with the States (Thacker 1999; Vreeland 2007; Dreher and Jensen 2007). Given the earlier argument that IMF conditionality is more relaxed for politically important countries, especially to the United States (Broz and Hawes 2006; Dreher and Jensen 2007; Edwards 2005; Stone 2002, 2004), such countries are more likely to participate in IMF programs. The variable *Years in Program* (the cumulative number of years of program participation) assumes that countries are more likely to sign up to an IMF program if they have participated in such a program in the past, with that likelihood increasing with lengthier periods of past program participation. The variable *Number of Other Countries* is the number of other countries in a program, as the more countries that are currently participating in an IMF program, the more likely it is that a particular country will continue to participate (Vreeland 2003).[1]

Table A6.2 IMF programs and credit ratings of developing countries, in treatment effects model

Variables	*Institutional Investor*	
	Leftist governments	*Non-leftist governments*
IMF	0.048***	0.016
	(0.016)	(0.012)
Democracy	0.000	0.001**
	(0.001)	(0.001)
Budget balance	0.002	0.001
	(0.001)	(0.001)
Capital account openness	0.005	0.003
	(0.006)	(0.003)
GDP growth	0.001	0.006***
	(0.002)	(0.001)
Inflation	0.000	0.000
	(0.000)	(0.000)
Current account balance	-0.000	0.001
	(0.001)	(0.001)
Fixed exchange rate	-0.004	-0.013
	(0.014)	(0.008)
Investment	0.000	0.000
	(0.001)	(0.000)
Reserves (log)	0.029***	0.023***
	(0.009)	(0.005)
Debt	-0.000	-0.000
	(0.000)	(0.000)
Rating in the previous year	0.945***	0.906***
	(0.017)	(0.011)
Constant	0.107**	0.238***
	(0.051)	(0.035)
Hazard	-0.018	0.003
	(0.013)	(0.009)
Wald Chi-Sq	10007.91	14685.24
Prob>Chi-Sq	0.0000	0.0000
Observations	223	748

Notes: *** $p < .01$; ** $p < .05$; * $p < .1$. The second-stage results are presented. The dependent variable is Institutional Investor and is log-transformed.

Table A6.3 IMF programs, government partisanship, and credit ratings of developing countries

	Moody's	*Standard and Poor's*	*Fitch*
IMF	-0.129**	-0.097*	-0.053
	(0.059)	(0.056)	(0.066)
Left party	-0.264***	-0.031	-0.095
	(0.092)	(0.057)	(0.083)
Left party* IMF	0.179*	0.229***	0.000
	(0.107)	(0.083)	(0.109)
Noncompliance	0.012	-0.009	-0.038
	(0.060)	(0.054)	(0.073)
Democracy	0.008	0.001	-0.012
	(0.013)	(0.011)	(0.017)
Budget balance	-0.000	0.026***	0.008
	(0.006)	(0.008)	(0.008)
GDP growth	0.008*	0.011**	0.001
	(0.005)	(0.005)	(0.005)
Capital account openness	0.010	0.035*	0.109***
	(0.035)	(0.020)	(0.028)
Investment	0.022***	0.002	0.020**
	(0.007)	(0.006)	(0.008)
Current account	-0.005	0.008	-0.002
	(0.007)	(0.006)	(0.008)
Inflation	0.000	0.000	0.000
	(0.000)	(0.000)	(0.000)
Foreign reserves	0.142***	0.129***	0.441***
	(0.046)	(0.039)	(0.062)
Debt service	0.003	0.001	0.003
	(0.002)	(0.002)	(0.002)
Fixed exchange rate	-0.122**	0.027	0.083
	(0.057)	(0.039)	(0.060)
Constant	0.033	-0.003	-0.561
	(0.362)	(0.299)	(0.446)
Observations	354	363	265
R-squared	0.74	0.85	0.79

Notes: ***$p < .01$; **$p < .05$; *$p < .10$ (two-tailed). The dependent variables are log-transformed.

Note

1 Signing an IMF agreement can be costly for the governments that do so because they have to ascribe to IMF conditionality, thus sacrificing a degree of sovereignty in return for a loan (Vreeland 2003: 11). These sovereignty costs are reduced when many countries are subject to the conditions of IMF programs (Vreeland 2003: 11).

References

Abdelal, Rawi, and Mark Blyth. 2015. "Just Who Put You in Charge? We Did: CRAs and the Politics of Ratings." In Alexander Cooley and Jack Snyder (eds.), *Ranking the World: Grading States as a Tool of Global Governance*. Cambridge: Cambridge University Press, pp. 39–59.

Abiad, Abdul, Enrica Detragiache, and Thierry Tressel. 2008. "A New Database of Financial Reforms." IMF Working Paper WP/08/266.

Acemoglu, Daron, Simon Johnson, and James Robinson. 2005. "Institutions as a Fundamental Cause of Long-Term Growth." In Philippe Aghion and Steven Durlauf (eds.), *Handbook of Economic Growth*, Vol. I. Amsterdam: Elsevier, pp. 386–472.

Acemoglu, Daron, Suresh Naidu, Pascual Restrepo, and James A. Robinson. 2014. "Democracy Does Cause Growth." NBER Working Paper No. 20004.

Acemoglu, Daron, and James Robinson. 2001. "A Theory of Political Transitions." *American Economic Review* 91(4): 938–963.

Acemoglu, Daron, and Thierry Verdier. 2000. "The Choice Between Market Failures and Corruption." *American Economic Review* 90(1): 194–211.

Achen, Christopher. 2000. "Why Lagged Dependent Variables Can Suppress the Explanatory Power of Other Independent Variables." Paper presented at the Annual Meeting of Political Methodology, University of California, Los Angeles.

Ackert, Lucy. 2014. "Traditional and Behavioral Finance." In H. Kent Baker and Victor Ricciardi (eds.), *Investor Behavior – The Psychology of Financial Planning and Investing*. Hoboken, NJ: John Wiley & Sons, pp. 25–41.

Afonso, António, Davide Furceri, and Pedro Gomes. 2012. "Sovereign Credit Ratings and Financial Markets Linkages: Application to European Data." *Journal of International Money and Finance* 31: 606–638.

Afonso, António, Pedro Gomes, and Philipp Rother. 2011. "Short- and Long-run Determinants of Sovereign Debt Credit Ratings." *International Journal of Finance and Economics* 16(1): 1–15.

Aguero, Felipe. 1992. "The Military and the Limits to Democratization in South America." In Scott Mainwaring, Guillermo O'Donnell, and J. Samuel Valenzuela (eds.), *Issues in Democratic Consolidation*. South Bend: University of Notre Dame Press, pp. 153–198.

Akhtar, Shumi, Robert Faff, Barry Oliver, and Avanidhar Subrahmanyam. 2011. "The Power of Bad: The Negativity Bias in Australian Consumer Sentiment Announcements on Stock Returns." *Journal of Banking and Finance* 35: 1239–1249.

Albuquerque, Rui. 2003. "The Composition of International Capital Flows: Risk Sharing Through Foreign Direct Investment." *Journal of International Economics* 61(2): 353–383.

Alesina, Alberto, and Alan Drazen. 1991. "Why Are Stabilization Delayed?" *American Economic Review* 81(5): 1170–1188.

Alesina, Alberto, and Roberto Perotti. 1994. "The Political Economy of Budget Deficits." NBER Working Paper No. 4637.

Alesina, Alberto, and Dani Rodrik. 1994. "Distributive Politics and Economic Growth." *Quarterly Journal of Economics* 109: 465–490.

Alesina, Alberto, Nouriel Roubini, and Gerald Cohen. 1997. *Political Cycles and the Macroeconomy*. Cambridge, MA: MIT Press.

Altenkirch, Carmen. 2005. "The Determinants of Sovereign Credit Ratings: A New Empirical Approach." *South African Journal of Economics* 73(3): 462–473.

Archer, Candace, Glen Biglaiser, and Karl DeRouen. 2007. "Sovereign Bond Ratings and Democracy: The Effects of Regime Type in the Developing World." *International Organization* 61(1): 341–365.

Arslanalp, Serkan, and Takahiro Tsuda. 2014. "Tracking Global Demand for Emerging Market Sovereign Debt." IMF Working Paper 14/39.

Association for Financial Professionals Risk Survey. 2013. Available at: http://www.oliverwyman.com/content/dam/oliver-wyman/global/en/files/archive/2013/2013_AFP_Risk_Survey_-_Final.pdf. (Accessed October 1, 2016)

Atkinson, Anthony, Francois Bourguignon, and Christian Morrisson. 1992. "Empirical Studies of Earnings Mobility." In J. Lesourne and H. Sonnenschien (eds.), *Fundamentals of Pure and Applied Economics*, Vol. 52. Reading, UK: Harwood Academic.

Aytac, Erdem, and Ziya Onis. 2014. "Varieties of Populism in a Changing Global Context: The Divergent Paths of Erdogan and Kirchnerismo." *Comparative Politics* 47(1): 41–59.

Bacmann, Jean-Francois, and Guido Bolliger. 2001. "Who Are the Best? Local Versus Foreign Analysts on Latin American Stock Markets." Working Paper. University of Neuchatel, Neuchatel, Switzerland.

Bagashka, Tanya, and Randall Stone. 2013. "Risky Signals: The Political Costs of Exchange Rate Policy in Post-Communist Countries." *International Studies Quarterly* 57(3): 519–531.

Bailey, John, and Arturo Valenzuela. 1997. "The Shape of the Future." *Journal of Democracy* 8(4): 43–57.

Baker, Andy, and Kenneth Greene. 2011. "The Latin American Left's Mandate: Free-Market Policies and Issue Voting in New Democracies." *World Politics* 63(1): 43–77.

Balkan, Erol. 1992. "Political Instability, Country Risk, and the Probability of Default." *Applied Economics* 24(9): 999–1008.

Barber, Brad, Reuven Lehavy, Maureen McNichols, and Brett Trueman. April 2001. "Can Investors Profit From the Prophets? Security Analyst Recommendations and Stock Returns." *Journal of Finance* 56: 531–563.

Bardhan, Pranab. 1997. "Corruption and Development: A Review of Issues." *Journal of Economic Literature* 35(3): 1320–1346.

Bardhan, Pranab. 1999. "Democracy and Development." In Ian Shapiro and Casiano Hacker-Cordon (eds.), *Democracy's Value*. Cambridge: Cambridge University Press, pp. 93–111.

Barro, Robert. 1996. "Determinants of Economic Growth: A Cross-country Empirical Study." NBER Working Paper No. 5698.

Barro, Robert. 1999. "Determinants of Democracy." *Journal of Political Economy* 107(6): 158–183.

Baskaran, Thushyanthan. 2010. "On the Link Between Fiscal Decentralization and Public Debt in OECD Countries." *Public Choice* 145: 351–378.

Bates, Robert. 2001. *Prosperity and Violence: The Political Economy of Development.* New York and London: Norton.

Baumeister, Roy, Ellen Bratslavsky, Catrin Finkenauer, and Kathleen Vohs. 2001. "Bad Is Stronger Than Good." *Review of General Psychology* 5(4): 323–370.

Bearce, David. 2003. "Societal Preferences, Partisan Agents, and Monetary Policy Outcomes." *International Organization* 57(2): 373–410.

Beaulieu, Emily, Gary Cox, and Sebastian Saiegh. 2012. "Sovereign Debt and Regime Type: Reconsidering the Democratic Advantage." *International Organization* 66(4): 709–738.

Beck, Nathaniel, and Jonathan Katz. 1996. "Nuisance vs. Substance: Specifying and Estimating Time-Series-Cross-Section Models." *Political Analysis* 6: 1–36.

Beck, Nathaniel, and Jonathan Katz. 2001. "Throwing Out the Baby With the Bath Water: A Comment on Green, Kim, and Yoon." *International Organization* 55: 487–495.

Beck, Nathaniel, and Jonathan Katz. 2009. "Modeling Dynamics in Time-Series-Cross-Section Political Economy Data." California Institute of Technology Division of the Humanities and Social Sciences Working Paper No. 1304.

Beck, Thorsten, George Clarke, Alberto Groff, Philip Keefer, and Patrick Walsh. 2001. "New Tools in Comparative Political Economy: The Database of Political Institutions." *The World Bank Economic Review* 15(1): 165–176.

Beers, David, and Marie Cavanaugh. 2008. *Sovereign Credit Ratings: A Primer.* New York: Standard and Poor's. Available at: www.investinginbondseurope.org/uploadedFiles/Learn_About_Bonds/What_You_Should_Know/Market_and_Economic_Influences_on_Your_Bond_Investments/Sovereign%20Credit%20Ratings%20Primer%20-%20SP.pdf. (Accessed July 28, 2010)

Beetsma, Roel, Massimo Giuliodori, Frank de Jong, and Daniel Widijanto. 2013. "Spread the News: The Impact of News on the European Sovereign Bond Markets During the Crisis." *Journal of International Money and Finance* 34: 83–101.

Benoit, Kenneth, and Michael Laver. 2006. *Party Policy in Modern Democracies.* New York: Routledge.

Berger, Susan. 2000. "Globalization and Politics." *Annual Review of Political Science* 3: 43–62.

Bergoeing, Raphael, Norman Loayza, and Andrea Repetto. 2004. "Slow Recoveries." *Journal of Development Economics* 75(2): 473–506.

Berman, Sheri. 2016. "Populism Is Not Fascism." *Foreign Affairs* 95(6): 39–44.

Bhattacharyya, Sambit, and Roland Hodler. 2010. "Natural Resources, Democracy and Corruption." *European Economic Review* 54(4): 608–621.

Biglaiser, Glen, and Karl DeRouen. 2010. "The Effects of IMF Programs on U.S. Foreign Direct Investment in the Developing World." *The Review of International Organizations* 5(1): 73–95.

Biglaiser, Glen, and Joseph Staats. 2012. "Finding the 'Democratic Advantage' in Sovereign Bond Ratings: The Importance of Strong Courts, Property Rights Protection, and the Rule of Law." *International Organization* 66(3): 515–535.

Bikhchandani, Sushil, and Sunil Sharma. 2000. "Herd Behavior in Financial Markets: A Review." IMF Working Paper WP/00/48.

Bird, Graham. 2002. "The Completion Rate of IMF Programmes: What We Know, Don't Know, and Need to Know." *The World Economy* 25(6): 833–847.

Bird, Graham, and Dane Rowlands. 2002. "Do IMF Programmes Have a Catalytic Effect on Other International Capital Flows?" *Oxford Development Studies* 30(3): 229–249.

Blais, Andre, Donald Blake, and Stephane Dion. 1993. "Do Parties Make a Difference? Parties and the Size of Government in Liberal Democracies." *American Journal of Political Science* 37(1): 40–62.

Bodea, Cristina, and Masaaki Higashijima. 2015. "Central Bank Independence and Fiscal Policy: Can the Central Bank Restrain Deficit Spending?" *British Journal of Political Science* 47(1): 47–70.

Boix, Carles. 2003. *Democracy and Redistribution*. Cambridge: Cambridge University Press.

Boix, Carles, and Susan Stokes. 2003. "Endogenous Democratization." *World Politics* 55: 517–549.

Boni, Leslie, and Kent Womack. 2002. "Wall Street's Credibility Problem: Misaligned Incentives and Dubious Fixes?" *Brookings-Wharton Papers on Financial Services* 1: 93–130.

Boockmann, Bernhard, and Axel Dreher. 2003. "The Contribution of the IMF and the World Bank to Economic Freedom." *European Journal of Political Economy* 19(3): 633–649.

Bordignon, Massimo, Pablo Manasse, and Guido Tabellini. 2001. "Optimal Regional Redistribution Under Asymmetric Information." *American Economic Review* 91: 709–723.

Brands, Hal. 2009. "Dealing With Political Ferment in Latin America: The Populist Revival, the Emergence of the Center, and Implications for U.S. Foreign Policy." Strategic Studies Institute.

Breen, Michael, and Iain McMenamin. 2013. "Political Institutions, Credible Commitment, and Sovereign Debt in Advanced Economies." *International Studies Quarterly* 57(4): 842–854.

Brewer, Thomas, and Pietra Rivoli. 1990. "Politics and Perceived Country Creditworthiness in International Banking." *Journal of Money, Credit, and Banking* 22(3): 357–369.

Broner, Fernando, Tatiana Didier, Aitor Erce, and Sergio Schmukler. 2013. "Gross Capital Flows: Dynamics and Crises." *Journal of Monetary Economics* 60: 113–133.

Brooks, Sarah, and Layna Mosley. 2007. "Risk, Uncertainty and Autonomy: Financial Market Constraints in Developing Nations." Chapter presented at the annual meeting of the American Political Science Association, Chicago, IL, August 30–September 2.

Broome, André. 2008. "The Importance of Being Earnest: The IMF as a Reputational Intermediary." *New Political Economy* 13(2): 125–151.

Broz, J. Lawrence. 2002. "Political System Transparency and Monetary Commitment Regimes." *International Organization* 56(4): 861–887.

Broz, J. Lawrence. 2013. "Partisan Financial Cycles." In David Lake and Miles Kahler (eds.), *Politics in the New Hard Times: The Great Recession in Comparative Perspective*. Ithaca: Cornell University Press.

Broz, J. Lawrence, and Jeffry Frieden. 2001. "The Political Economy of International Monetary Relations." *Annual Review of Political Science* 4: 317–343.

Broz, J. Lawrence, and Michael Hawes. 2006. "US Domestic Politics and International Monetary Fund Policy." In Darren Hawkins, David Lake, Daniel Nielson, and Michael Tierney (eds.), *Delegation and Agency in International Organizations.* Cambridge: Cambridge University Press.

Broz, J. Lawrence, and Michael Plouffe. 2010. "The Effectiveness of Monetary Policy Anchors: Firm-Level Evidence." *International Organization* 64(4): 695–717.

Broz, J. Lawrence, and Stephen Weymouth. 2013. "Government Partisanship and Property Rights: Cross-Country Firm-Level Evidence." *Economics & Politics* 25: 229–256.

Brunetti, Aymo.1997. "Political Variables in Cross-Country Growth Analysis." *Journal of Economic Surveys* 11(2): 163–190.

Brunetti, Aymo, and Beatrice Weder. 1998. "Investment and Institutional Uncertainty: A Comparative Study of Different Uncertainty Measures." *Weltwirtschaftliches Archiv* 134(3): 513–533.

Bruno, Michael, and William Easterly. 1998. "Inflation Crises and Long-Run Growth." *Journal of Monetary Economics* 41(1): 3–26.

Buthe, Tim, and Helen Milner. 2008. "The Politics of Foreign Direct Investment Into Developing Countries." *American Journal of Political Science* 52(4): 741–762.

Butler, Alexander, and Larry Fauver. 2006. "Institutional Environment and Sovereign Credit Ratings." *Financial Management* 35(3): 53–79.

Caballero, Ricardo, and Arvind Krishnamurthy. 2005. "Exchange Rate Volatility and the Credit Channel in Emerging Markets: A Vertical Perspective." *International Journal of Central Banking* 1(1): 207–245.

Caddel, Jeremy, and Nathan Jensen. 2014. "Which Host Country Government Actors Are Most Involved in Disputes With Foreign Investors?" Columbia University Academic Commons. Available at: http://dx.doi.org/10.7916/D8M32SWK.

Calvo, Guillermo, and Enrique Mendoza. 2000. "Rational Contagion and the Globalization of Securities Markets." *Journal of International Economics* 51(1): 79–113.

Calvo, Guillermo, and Ernesto Talvi. 2005. "Sudden Stop, Financial Factors and Economic Collapse in Latin America: Learning From Argentina and Chile." NBER Working Paper No. 11153.

Campello, Daniela. 2015. The Politics of Market Discipline in Latin America: Globalization and Democracy. Cambridge: Cambridge University Press.

Cantor, Richard, and Frank Packer. 1996. "Determinants and Impact of Sovereign Credit Ratings." *Economic Policy Review* 2: 37–54.

Cantor, Richard, and Frank Packer. 1997. "Differences of Opinion and Selection Bias in the Credit Rating Industry." *Journal of Banking and Finance* 21(1997): 1395–1417.

Caraway, Teri, Stephanie Rickard, and Mark Anner. 2012. "International Negotiations and Domestic Politics: The Case of IMF Labor Market Conditionality." *International Organization* 66: 27–61.

Cardoso, Eliana, and Ann Helwege. 1991. "Populism, Profligacy, and Redistribution." In Rudiger Dornbusch and Sebastian Edwards (eds.), *The Macroeconomics of Populism in Latin America.* Chicago: University of Chicago Press.

Carruthers, Bruce. 1996. City of Capital: Politics and Markets in the English Financial Revolution. Princeton: Princeton University Press.

Castaneda, Jorge. May–June 2006. "Latin America's Left Turn." *Foreign Affairs* 85: 28–43.

Castles, Francis. 1989. "Explaining Public Education Expenditure in OECD Nations." *European Journal of Political Research* 17: 431–448.

Cerny, Philip. 1996. "International Finance and the Erosion of State Policy Capacity." In Philip Gummett (ed.), *Globalization and Public Policy*. Cheltenham: Elgar, pp. 83–104.

Cheibub, José Antonio, Jennifer Gandhi, and James Raymond Vreeland. 2010. "Democracy and Dictatorship Revisited." *Public Choice* 143(1–2): 67–101.

Chinn, Menzie, and Hiro Ito. 2006. "What Matters for Financial Development? Capital Controls, Institutions, and Interaction." *Journal of Development Economics* 81(1): 163–192.

Cho, Hye Jee. 2009. "Democracy and Sovereign Credit Ratings: Do Democratic Institutions Boost Investor Confidence?" *Korean Political Science Review* 43(5): 113–135.

Cho, Hye Jee. 2014. "Impact of IMF Programs on Perceived Creditworthiness of Emerging Market Countries: Is There a 'Nixon-Goes-to-China' Effect?" *International Studies Quarterly* 58: 308–321.

Chwieroth, Jeffrey. 2010. *Capital Ideas: The IMF and the Rise of Financial Liberalization*. Princeton: Princeton University Press.

Cole, Harold, and Patrick Kehoe. 1997. "Reviving Reputation Models of International Debt." *Federal Reserve Bank of Minneapolis Quarterly Review* 21(1): 21–30.

Conaghan, Catherine. 2005. *Fujimori's Peru: Deception in the Public Sphere*. Pittsburgh: University of Pittsburgh Press.

Conway, Patrick. 1994. "IMF Lending Programs: Participation and Impact." *Journal of Development Economics* 45(2): 365–391.

Cooley, Alexander. 2015. "The Emerging Politics of International Rankings and Ratings: A Framework for Analysis." In Alexander Cooley and Jack Snyder (eds.), *Ranking the World: Grading States as a Tool of Global Governance*. Cambridge: Cambridge University Press.

Copelovitch, Mark. 2010. The International Monetary Fund in the Global Economy: Banks, Bonds, and Bailouts. London: Cambridge University Press.

Coppedge, Michael. 1997. "A Classification of Latin American Political Parties." Kellogg Institute Working Paper 244.

Corsetti, Giancarlo, Bernardo Guimaraes, and Nouriel Roubini. 2006. "International Lending of Last Resort and Moral Hazard Problems: A Model of IMF's Catalytic Finance." *Journal of Monetary Economics* 53(3): 441–471.

Cortell, Andrew, and James Davis, Jr. 1996. "How Do International Institutions Matter? The Domestic Impact of International Rules and Norms." *International Studies Quarterly* 40(4): 451–478.

Cosset, Jean-Claude, and Jean Roy. 1991. "The Determinants of Country Risk Ratings." *Journal of International Business Studies* 22(1): 134–142.

Cottarelli, Carlo, and Curzio Giannini. 1997. "Credibility Without Rules? Monetary Frameworks in the Post-Bretton Woods Era." IMF Occasional Chapter 154.

Cottarelli, Carlo, Thomas Krueger, Reza Moghadam, Perry Perone, Edgardo Ruggiero, and Rachel van Elkan. 1998. "Hungary: Economic Policies for Sustainable Growth." IMF, Washington.

Cowen, Tyler, and Daniel Sutter. 1998. "Why Only Nixon Could Go to China." *Public Choice* 97: 605–615.

Cowhey, Peter. 1993. "Domestic Institutions and the Credibility of International Commitments: Japan and the United States." *International Organization* 50: 109–139.

Cox, Gary, and Mathew McCubbins. 2001. "The Institutional Determinants of Economic Policy Outcomes." In Stephan Haggard and Mathew D. McCubbins (eds.), *Structure and Policy in Presidential Democracies.* New York: Cambridge University Press.

Crisp, Brian, and Maria Escobar-Lemmon. 2001. "Democracy in Latin America: Individuals in Institutional Contexts." *Latin American Research Review* 36(2): 175–192.

Cruces, Juan. 2006. "Statistical Properties of Country Credit Ratings." *Emerging Markets Review* 7(1): 27–51.

Cukierman, Alex, and Mariano Tommasi. 1998. "When Does It Take a Nixon to Go to China?" *The American Economic Review* 88(1): 180–197.

Cukierman, Alex, Steven Webb, and Bilin Neyapti. 1992. "Measuring the Independence of Central Banks and Its Effect on Policy Outcomes." *The World Bank Economic Review* 6(3): 353–398.

Dahrendorf, Ralf. 1990. *Reflections on the Revolution in Europe.* London: Chatto & Windus.

Davis, Otto, M.A.H. Dempster, and Aaron Wildavsky. 1966. "A Theory of the Budgetary Process." *American Political Science Review* 60(3): 529–547.

Davis, Otto, M.A. Dempster, and Aaron Wildavsky. 1974. "Toward a Predictive Theory of Government Expenditures: U.S. Domestic Appropriations." *British Journal of Political Science* 4: 1–34.

Denzau, Arthur, and Douglass North. 1994. "Shared Mental Models, Ideologies and Institutions." *Kyklos* 47: 3–31.

Dhonte, Pierre. 1997. "Conditionality as an Instrument of Borrower Credibility." IMF Chapters on Policy Analysis and Assessment PPAA/97/2.

Diamond, Larry. 2000. "Developing Democracy in Africa: African and International Imperatives." *Cambridge Review of International Affairs* 14(1): 191–213.

Diamond, Larry. 2002. "Thinking About Hybrid Regimes." *Journal of Democracy* 13(2): 21–35.

Diamond, Larry. 2015. "Facing up the Democratic Recession." *Journal of Democracy* 26(1): 141–155.

Diwan, Ishack, and Dani Rodrik. 1992. "External Debt, Adjustment, and Burden Sharing: A Unified Framework." *Princeton Studies in International Finance* 73: 1–49.

Dixit, Avinash. 2004. *Lawlessness and Economics.* Princeton: Princeton University Press.

Dornbusch, Rudiger, and Sebastian Edwards. 1991. *The Macroeconomics of Populism in Latin America.* Chicago: University of Chicago Press.

Dornbusch, Rudiger, Yung Chul Park, and Stijn Claessens. 2000. "Understanding How It Spreads." *The World Bank Research Observer* 15(2): 177–197.

Downs, Anthony. 1957. "An Economic Theory of Political Action in a Democracy." *Journal of Political Economy* 65(2): 135–150.

Doyle, David. 2011. "The Legitimacy of Political Institutions: Explaining Contemporary Populism in Latin America." *Comparative Political Studies* 44(11): 1447–1473.

Drake, Paul. 1991. "Comment: The Political Economy of Latin American Populism." In Rudiger Dornbusch and Sebastian Edwards (eds.), *The Macroeconomics of Populism in Latin America.* Chicago, IL: University of Chicago Press, pp. 35–40.

Drazen, Allan. 1997. "Towards a Political Economic Theory of Domestic Debt." In Guillermo Calvo and Mervyn King (eds.), *The Debt Burden and Its Consequences for Monetary Policy.* London: Palgrave Macmillan.

Drazen, Allan. 1999. "Political Contagion in Currency Crisis." NBER Working Paper No. 7211.

Drazen, Allan. 2002. "Conditionality and Ownership in IMF Lending: A Political Economy Approach." *IMF Staff Chapters* 49: 36–67.

Dreher, Axel. 2006. "IMF and Economic Growth: The Effects of Programs, Loans, and Compliance With Conditionality." *World Development* 34(5): 769–788.

Dreher, Axel. 2009. "IMF Conditionality: Theory and Evidence." *Public Choice* 141(1): 233–267.

Dreher, Axel, and Nathan Jensen. 2007. "Independent Actor or Agent? An Empirical Analysis of the Impact of US Interests on IMF Conditions." *The Journal of Law and Economics* 50(1): 105–124.

Dreher, Axel, and Jan-Egbert Sturm. 2012. "Do the IMF and the World Bank Influence Voting in the UN General Assembly?" *Public Choice* 151(1): 363–397.

Dreher, Axel, and Stefanie Walter. 2010. "Does the IMF Help or Hurt? The Effect of IMF Programs on the Likelihood and Outcome of Currency Crises." *World Development* 38(1): 1–18.

Drezner, Daniel. 2001. "Globalization and Policy Convergence." *International Studies Review* 3: 53–78.

Duffield, John. 1992. "International Regimes and Alliance Behavior: Explaining NATO Counter Force Levels." *International Organization* 46: 819–855.

Eaton, Jonathan, Mark Gersovitz, and Joseph Stiglitz. 1986. "The Pure Theory of Country Risk." *European Economic Review* 30: 481–513.

Eden, Maya, Aart Kraay, and Rong Qian. 2012. "Sovereign Defaults and Expropriations: Empirical Regularities." The World Bank Policy Research Working Paper 6218.

Edwards, Martin. 2005. "Investor Responses to IMF Program Suspensions: Is Noncompliance Costly?" *Social Science Quarterly* 86(4): 857–873.

Edwards, Martin. 2006. "Signaling Credibility? The IMF and Catalytic Finance." *Journal of International Relations and Development* 9(1): 27–52.

Eichler, Stefan. 2014. "The Political Determinants of Sovereign Bond Yield Spreads." *Journal of International Money and Finance* 46: 82–103.

Eichler, Stefan, and Michael Hofmann. 2013. "Sovereign Default Risk and Decentralization: Evidence for Emerging Markets." *European Journal of Political Economy* 32(4): 113–134.

Elster, Jon. 1998. "Introduction." In Jon Elster (ed.), *Deliberative Democracy.* Cambridge: Cambridge University Press, pp. 1–18.

Falaschetti, Dino. 2003. "Credible Commitments and Investment: Does Opportunistic Ability or Incentive Matter?" *Economic Inquiry* 41(4): 660–674.

Fearon, James. 1994. "Domestic Political Audiences and the Escalation of International Disputes." *American Political Science Review* 88: 577–592.

Feng, Yi. 2003. Democracy, Governance, and Economic Performance: Theory and Evidence. Cambridge: MIT Press.

Fischer, Stanley. 1999. "On the Need for an International Lender of Last Resort." *The Journal of Economic Perspectives* 13(4): 85–104.

Fishkin, James. 1991. Democracy and Deliberation: New Directions for Democratic Reform. New Haven, CT: Yale University Press.

Fishkin, James. 2009. When the People Speak: Deliberative Democracy and Public Consultation. Oxford: Oxford University Press.

Fitch, Ratings. 2002. Fitch Sovereign Ratings – Rating Methodology. New York: Moody's Investor Services.

Fornasari, Francesca, Steven Webb, and Heng-Fu Zou. 2000. "The Macroeconomic Impact of Decentralized Spending and Deficits: International Evidence." *Annals of Economics and Finance* 1(2): 403–433.

Franzese, Robert. 2002. *Macroeconomic Policies of Developed Democracies*. Cambridge: Cambridge University Press.

Friedman, Jed, and James Levinson. 2002. "The Distributional Impacts of Indonesia's Financial Crisis on Household Welfare: A 'Rapid Response Methodology'." *World Bank Economic Review* 16(3): 397–423.

Frye, Timothy. 2002. "The Perils of Polarization." *World Politics* 54(3): 308–337.

Fung, Archon. 2003. "Deliberative Democracy and International Labor Standards." *Governance* 16(1): 51–71.

Garrett, Geoffrey. 1998. *Partisan Politics in the Global Economy*. Cambridge: Cambridge University Press.

Gaubatz, Kurt. 1996. "Democratic States and Commitment in International Relations." *International Organization* 50: 109–139.

Gavin, Michael, and Roberto Perotti. 1997. "Fiscal Policy in Latin America." In Ben Bernanke and Julio Rotemberg (eds.), *NBER Macroeconomics Annual*. Cambridge: MIT Press.

Gehlbach, Scott, and Edmund Malesky. 2010. "The Contribution of Veto Players to Economic Reform." *The Journal of Politics* 72(4): 957–975.

Gelos, R. Gaston, Ratna Sahay, and Guido Sandleris. 2011. "Sovereign Borrowing by Developing Countries: What Determines Market Access?" *Journal of International Economics* 83(2): 243–254.

Giavazzi, Francesco, and Guido Tabellini. 2005. "Economic and Political Liberalizations." *Journal of Monetary Economics* 52(7): 1297–1330.

Ginsburg, Tom. 2005. "International Substitutes for Domestic Institutions: Bilateral Investment Treaties and Governance." *International Review of Law and Economics* 25: 107–123.

Goodspeed, Timothy. 2002. "Bailouts in a Federation." *International Tax and Public Finance* 9: 409–421.

Gould, Erica. 2006. Money Talks: The International Monetary Fund, Conditionality and Supplementary Financiers. Stanford: Stanford University Press.

Gray, Julia. 2010. "Bailouts and Credibility in the European Union." Chapter presented at the annual meeting of the International Political Economy Society, Cambridge, MA, November 12–13.

Gray, Julia. 2013. The Company States Keep: International Economic Organization and Sovereign Risk in Emerging Markets. Cambridge: Cambridge University Press.

Habib, Bilal, Ambar Narayan, Sergio Olivieri, Carolina Sanchez. 2010. "The Impact of the Financial Crisis on Poverty and Income Distribution: Insights From Simulations in Selected Countries." Economic Premise. March 2010. No 7. World Bank, Washington, DC.

Habib, Moshin, and Leon Zurawicki. 2002. "Corruption and Foreign Direct Investment." *Journal of International Business Studies* 33(2): 291–307.

Haendel, Dan. 1979. Foreign Investment and the Management of Political Risk. Boulder: Westview Press.

Haggard, Stephan. 2000. *The Political Economy of Asian Financial Crisis*. Washington: Institute for International Economics.

Haggard, Stephan, and Robert Kaufman. 1992. "Institutions and Economic Adjustment." In Stephan Haggard and Robert Kaufman (eds.), *The Politics of Economic Adjustment: Institutional Constraints, Distributive Conflicts and the State*. Princeton: Princeton University Press.

Haggard, Stephan, and Robert Kaufman. 1995. *The Political Economy of Democratic Transitions*. Princeton: Princeton University Press.

Haggard, Stephan, and Mathew McCubbins, eds. 2001. *Presidents, Parliaments, and Policy*. Cambridge: Cambridge University Press.

Hallerberg, Mark, and Jurgen von Hagen. 1999. "Electoral Institutions, Cabinet Negotiations, and Budget Deficits Within the European Union." In James Poterba and Jurgen von Hagen (eds.), *Fiscal Institutions and Fiscal Performance*. Chicago: University of Chicago Press, pp. 209–232.

Haque, Nadeem, Manmohan Kumar, Nelson Mark, and Donald Mathieson. 1996. "The Economic Content of Indicators of Developing Country Creditworthiness." IMF Working Chapter WP/96/9.

Hawkins, Kirk. 2003. "Populism in Venezuela: The Rise of Chavismo." *Third World Quarterly* 24(6): 1137–1160.

Helliwell, John. 1994. "Empirical Linkages Between Democracy and Economic Growth." *British Journal of Political Science* 24: 225–248.

Helmke, Gretchen, and Steven Levitsky. 2004. "Informal Institutions and Comparative Politics: A Research Agenda." *Perspectives on Politics* 2(4): 725–740.

Henisz, Witold. 2000. "The Institutional Environment for Economic Growth." *Economics and Politics* 12(1): 1–31.

Henisz, Witold, and Bennett Zelner. 2010. "The Hidden Risk in Emerging Markets." *Harvard Business Review* 88(4): 88–95.

Heston, Alan, Robert Summers, and Bettina Aten. 2006. *Penn World Tables*. Philadelphia: University of Pennsylvania.

Hibbs, Douglass. 1977. "Political Parties and Macroeconomic Policy." *American Political Science Review* 71(4): 1467–1487.

Hollyer, James, Peter Rosendorff, and James Vreeland. 2014. "Measuring Transparency." *Political Analysis* 22(1): 413–434.

Howard, Marc, and Philip Roessler. 2006. "Liberalizing Electoral Outcomes in Competitive Authoritarian Regimes." *American Journal of Political Science* 50(2): 365–381.

Huber, Evelyn, and John Stephens. 1998. "Internationalization and the Social Democratic Model: Crisis and Future Prospects." *Comparative Political Studies* 31(3): 353–397.

Huntington, Samuel. 1968. *Political Order in Changing Societies*. New Haven: Yale University Press.

Huntington, Samuel. 1991. *The Third Wave, Democratization in the Late Twentieth Century*. Norman and London: University of Oklahoma Press.

Huntington, Samuel, and Jorge Dominguez. 1975. "Political Development." In Fred Greenstein and Nelson Polsby (eds.), *Handbook of Political Science, vol.3, Macropolitical Theory*. New York: Addison-Wesley, pp. 1–114.

Ilzetzki, Ethan, Carmen M. Reinhart, and Kenneth S. Rogoff. 2017. "Exchange Rate Arrangements Entering the 21st Century: Which Anchor Will Hold?" NBER Working Paper No. 23134.

IMF. 1996. "IMF Approves Stand-By Credit for Hungary." Press Release No.96/10.

IMF. 1997. "IMF Conditionality Can Signal Policy Credibility to Markets." *IMF Survey* 26(6): 81–83.

IMF. September 1998. *International Capital Markets: Developments, Prospects, and Key Policy Issues.* Washington, DC: International Monetary Fund.

IMF. 2000. "Hungary: Selected Issues and Statistical Appendix." Country Report 00/59.

IMF. *International Financial Statistics*, various years. Washington: IMF.

Ismailescu, Iuliana, and Hossein Kazemi. 2010. "The Reaction of Emerging Market Credit Default Swap Spreads to Sovereign Credit Rating Changes." *Journal of Banking and Finance* 34: 2861–2873.

Iversen, Torben. 1999. Contested Economic Institutions: The Politics of Macroeconomics and Wage Bargaining in Advanced Democracies. New York: Cambridge University Press.

Jegadeesh, Narasimhan, and Woojin Kim. 2010. "Do Analysts Herd? An Analysis of Recommendations and Market Reactions." *The Review of Financial Studies* 23(2): 901–937.

Jenkins, Stephen, Andrea Brandolini, John Micklewright, and Brian Nolan. 2012. *The Great Recession and the Distribution of Household Income.* Oxford: Oxford University Press.

Jensen, Nathan. 2006. Nation-States and the Multinational Corporation: A Political Economy of Foreign Direct Investment. Princeton: Princeton University Press.

Jensen, Nathan, Glen Biglaiser, Quan Li, Edmund Malesky, Pablo Pinto, Santiago Pinto, and Joseph Staats. 2012. *Politics and Foreign Direct Investment.* Ann Arbor: University of Michigan Press.

Joyce, Joseph. 2004. "Adoption, Implementation and Impact of IMF Programmes: A Review of the Issues and Evidence." *Comparative Economics Studies* 46(3): 451–467.

Kaminsky, Graciela, Carmen Reinhart, and Carlos Végh. 2004. "When It Rains, It Pours: Procyclical Capital Flows and Macroeconomic Policies." In M. Gertler and K. Rogoff (eds.), *NBER Macroeconomics Annual.* Cambridge, MA: MIT Press.

Kaminsky, Garciela, and Sergio Schmukler. 2002. "Emerging Markets Instability: Do Sovereign Ratings Affect Country Risk and Stock Returns?" World Bank Policy Research Working Paper No. 2678.

Kaplan, Stephen. 2013. *Globalization and Austerity Politics in Latin America.* Cambridge: Cambridge University Press.

Kastner, Scott, and Chad Rector. 2003. "International Regimes, Domestic Veto-Players, and Capital Controls Policy Stability." *International Studies Quarterly* 47: 1–22.

Kaufman, Robert, and Barbara Stallings. 1991. "The Political Economy of Latin American Populism." In Rudiger Dornbusch and Sebastian Edwards (eds.), *The Macroeconomics of Populism in Latin America.* Chicago: University of Chicago Press.

Kaufmann, Daniel, Art Kraay, and Pablo Zoido-Lobaton. 1999. "Governance Matters." World Bank Policy Research Working Paper No. 2196.

Keefer, Philip, and David Stasavage. 2002. "Checks and Balances, Asymmetric Information, and the Credibility of Monetary Commitments." *International Organization* 56(4): 751–774.

Killick, Tony. 1994. "Adjustment and Economic Growth." In James Boughton and K. Sawar Lateef (eds.), *Fifty Years After Bretton Woods – The Future of the IMF and the World Bank.* Washington: International Monetary Fund and World Bank Group.

Killick, Tony. 1995. IMF Programmes in Developing Countries: Design and Impact. London: Routledge.

Killick, Tony, Moazzam Malik, and Marcus Manuel. 1992. "What Can We Know About the Effects of IMF Programmes?" *The World Economy* 15(5): 575–598.
Kim, Suk-Joong, and Eliza Wu. 2011. "International Bank Flows to Emerging Markets: Influence of Sovereign Credit Ratings and Their Regional Spillover Effects." *The Journal of Financial Research* 34(2): 331–364.
Knight, Frank. 1985. *Risk, Uncertainty and Profit.* Chicago: University of Chicago Press.
Knight, Malcolm, and Julio Santaella. 1997. "Economic Determinants of IMF Financial Arrangements." *Journal of Development Economics* 54(2): 405–436.
Kobrin, Stephen. 1982. Managing Political Risk Assessment: Strategic Response to Environmental Change. Berkeley: University of California Press.
Kohlscheen, Emanuel. 2004. "Sovereign Risk: Constitutions Rule." Social Science Research Network Working Paper Series.
Kontopoulos, Yianos, and Roberto Perotti. 1999. "Government Fragmentation and Fiscal Policy Outcomes: Evidence From OECD Countries." In James Poterba and Jurgen von Hagen (eds.), *Fiscal Institutions and Fiscal Performance.* Chicago: University of Chicago Press, pp. 81–102.
Kramer, Gerald H. 1971. "Short-Term Fluctuations in U.S. Voting Behavior, 1896–1964." *American Political Science Review* 65(1): 131–143.
Kraussel, Roman. 2005. "Do Credit Rating Agencies Add to the Dynamics of Emerging Market Crises?" *Journal of Financial Stability* 1(3): 355–385.
Krueger, Anne. 1999. "The World Bank Group in the International Economy." Paper prepared for the International Financial Institution Advisory Commission, Washington, DC.
Krueger, Anne. 2002. *A New Approach to Sovereign Restructuring.* Washington, DC: International Monetary Fund.
Kurzer, Paulette. 1993. Business and Banking: Political Change and Economic Integration in Western Europe. Ithaca: Cornell University Press.
Laeven, Luc, and Fabian Valencia. 2008. "Systemic Banking Crises: A New Database." IMF Working Chapter.
Laffont, Jean-Jacques, and Mathieu Meleu. 2001. "Separation of Powers and Development." *Journal of Development Economics* 64(1): 129–145.
Lane, Philip. 2003. "Business Cycles and Macroeconomic Policy in Emerging Market Economies." *International Finance* 6(1): 89–108.
Lane, Timothy, and Steven Phillips. 2000. "Does IMF Financing Result in Moral Hazard?" IMF Working Chapter WP/00/168.
Lange, Peter, and Geoffrey Garrett. 1985. "The Politics of Growth: Strategic Interaction and Economic Performance in the Advanced Industrial Democracies, 1974–1980." *Journal of Politics* 47: 791–827.
LaPalombara, Joseph. 1994. "Structural and Institutional Aspects of Corruption." *Social Research* 61(2): 325–350.
Leblang, David. 2002. "The Political Economy of Speculative Attacks in the Developing World." *International Studies Quarterly* 46(1): 69–91.
Leblang, David, and William Bernhard. 2000. "The Politics of Speculative Attacks in Industrial Democracies." *International Organization* 54: 291–324.
Lederman, Daniel, Norman Loayza, and Rodrigo Soares. 2005. "Accountability and Corruption: Political Institutions Matter." *Economics and Politics* 17(1): 35.
Leeds, Brett. 1999. "Domestic Political Institutions, Credible Commitments, and International Cooperation." *American Journal of Political Science* 42(4): 979–1002.

Leff, Nathaniel. 1964. "Economic Development Through Bureaucratic Corruption." *American Behavioral Scientist* 8(3): 8–14.

Levich, Richard, Giovanni Majnoni, and Carmen Reinhart (eds.). 2002. *Ratings, Rating Agencies and the Global Financial System*. Boston: Kluwer Academic Publishers.

Levine, Ross, and David Renelt. 1992. "A Sensitivity Analysis of Cross-Country Growth Regressions." World Bank Working Paper # 608.

Levitsky, Steven, and James Loxton. 2013. "Populism and Competitive Authoritarianism in the Andes." *Democratization* 20: 107–136.

Levitsky, Steven, and María Victoria Murillo. 2009. "Variation in Institutional Strength." *Annual Review of Political Science* 12: 115–133.

Levitsky, Steven, and Lucan A. Way. 2002. "The Rise of Competitive Authoritarianism." *Journal of Democracy* 13(2): 51–65.

Li, Quan. 2009. "Democracy, Autocracy, and Expropriation of Foreign Direct Investment." *Comparative Political Studies* 42(8): 1098–1127.

Linz, Juan. 1990. "The Virtues of Parliamentarism." *Journal of Democracy* 1(4): 84–92.

Linz, Juan, and Alfred Stepan. 1996a. "Toward Consolidated Democracies." *Journal of Democracy* 7(2): 14–33.

Linz, Juan, and Alfred Stepan. 1996b. Problems of Democratic Transition and Consolidation: Southern Europe, South America and Post-Communist Europe. Baltimore: Johns Hopkins University Press.

Lipset, Seymour Martin. 1959. "Some Social Requisites of Democracy, Economic Development and Political Legitimacy." *American Political Science Review* 53(1): 69–105.

Loayza, Norman, Romain Ranciere, Louis Serven, and Jaume Ventura. 2007. "Macroeconomic Volatility and Welfare in Developing Countries: An Introduction." *The World Bank Economic Review* 21(3): 343–357.

Lohmann, Susanne. 1998. "Federalism and Central Bank Independence: The Politics of German Monetary Policy, 1957–1992." *World Politics* 50(3): 401–446.

Londregan, John, and Keith Poole. 1990. "Poverty, the Coup Trap, and the Seizure of Executive Power." *World Politics* 42(2): 151–183.

McElroy, Robert. 1992. *Morality and American Foreign Policy*. Princeton: Princeton University Press.

MacIntyre, Andrew. 2001. "Institutions and Investors: The Politics of Economic Crisis in Southeast Asia." *International Organization* 55(1): 81–122.

MacIntyre, Andrew. 2003. The Power of Institutions: Political Architecture and Governance. Ithaca: Cornell University Press.

MacRae, Duncan. 1977. "A Political Model of the Business Cycle." *Journal of Political Economy* 85(2): 239–263.

Maddala, G.S. 1986. *Limited-Dependent and Quantitative Variables in Econometrics*. Cambridge: Cambridge University Press.

March, Luke. 2007. "From Vanguard of the Proletariat to Vox Populi: Left-populism as a 'Shadow' of Contemporary Socialism." *The SAIS Review of International Affairs* 27(1): 63–77.

Marchesi, Silvia. 2003. "Adoption of an IMF Programme and Debt Rescheduling: An Empirical Analysis." *Journal of Development Economics* 70(2): 403–423.

Marchesi, Silvia, and Jonathan Thomas. 1999. "IMF Conditionality as a Screening Device." *The Economic Journal* 109: 111–125.

Marshall, Monty, Ted Gurr, and Keith Jaggers. 2009. *Polity IV Project: Political Regime Characteristics and Transitions.* Vienna, VA: Center for Systemic Peace.

Martinez, Juan, and Javier Santiso. 2003. "Financial Markets and Politics: The Confidence Game in Latin American Emerging Economies." *International Political Science Review* 24(3): 363–395.

Mauro, Paolo. 1996. "The Effects of Corruption on Growth, Investment, and Government Expenditure: A Cross-country Analysis." IMF Working Paper No. 96/98.

Mello Jr., Luiz de. 2000. "Fiscal Decentralization and Intergovernmental Fiscal Relations: ACross-Country Analysis." *World Development* 28(2): 365–380.

Mendoza, Enrique. 1991. "Real Business Cycles in a Small Open Economy." *American Economic Review* 81(4): 797–818.

Mercer-Blackman, Valerie, and Anna Unigovskaya. 2000. "Compliance With IMF Program Indicators and Growth in Transition Economies." IMF Working Chapter 00/47.

Mershon, Carol. 1994. "Expectations and Informal Rules in Coalition Formation." *Comparative Political Studies* 27(1): 40–79.

Milner, Helen, and Bumba Mukherjee. 2009. "Democratization and Economic Globalization." *Annual Review of Political Science* 12: 163–181.

Mishra, Ramesh. 1999. *Globalization and the Welfare State.* Cheltenham: Edward Elgar.

Mo, Pak Hung. 2001. "Corruption and Economic Growth." *Journal of Comparative Economics* 29(1): 66–79.

Mody, Ashoka, and Diego Saravia. 2003. "Catalyzing Capital Flows: Do IMF Programs Work as Commitment Devices?" IMF Working Chapter 03/100.

Moody's. 2012. "Proposed Refinements to the Sovereign Bond Rating Methodology." Moody's Investor Service.

Moser, Peter. 1999. "Checks and Balances, and the Supply of Central Bank Independence." *European Economic Review* 43(8): 1569–1593.

Moses, Jonathan. 2000. "Floating Fortunes: Scandinavian Full Employment in the Tumultuous 1970s–1980s." In Robert Geyer, Christine Ingebritsen and Jonathon W. Moses (eds.), *Globalization, Europeanization and the End of Scandinavian Social Democracy?* Houndmills, Basingstoke, Hampshire: Macmillan.

Mosley, Layna. 2003. *Global Capital and National Governments.* Cambridge: Cambridge University Press.

Mudde, Cas, and Cristobal Kaltwasser. 2012. *Populism in Europe and the Americas: Threat or Corrective for Democracy?* Cambridge: Cambridge University Press.

Mukherjee, Bumba, and David Singer. 2010. "International Institutions and Domestic Compensation: The IMF and the Politics of Capital Account Liberalization." *American Journal of Political Science* 54(1): 45–60.

Multilateral Investment Guarantee Agency (MIGA). 2012. *World Investment and Political Risk.* Washington: World Bank.

Multilateral Investment Guarantee Agency (MIGA). 2013. *World Investment and Political Risk.* Washington: World Bank.

Nadelmann, Ethan. 1990. "Global Prohibition Regimes: The Evolution of Norms in International Society." *International Organization* 44: 479–536.

Navia, Patricio, and Ignacio Walker. 2009. "Political Institutions, Populism, and Democracy in Latin America." In Scott Mainwaring and Timothy Scully (eds.), *Democratic Governance in Latin America.* Stanford: Stanford University Press, pp. 245–268.

Nayar, Baldev Raj. 1999. "Policy and Performance Under Democratic Coalitions: India's United Front Government and Economic Reforms, 1996–98." *Commonwealth & Comparative Politics* 37(2): 22–56.

Nelson, Stephen. 2010. "Does Compliance Matter? Assessing the Relationship Between Sovereign Risk and Compliance With International Monetary Law." *The Review of International Organizations* 5(2): 107–139.

Neyapti, Bilin. 2010. "Fiscal Decentralization and Deficits: International Evidence." *European Journal of Political Economy* 26: 155–166.

Nickell, Stephen. 1981. "Biases in Dynamic Models With Fixed Effects." *Econometrica* 49: 1417–1426.

Nooruddin, Irfan. 2011. Coalition Politics and Economic Development: Credibility and the Strength of Weak Governments. New York: Cambridge University Press.

Nooruddin, Irfan, and Joel Simmons. 2006. "The Politics of Hard Choices: IMF Programs and Government Spending." *International Organization* 60(4): 1001–1033.

Nooruddin, Irfan, and James Vreeland. 2010. "The Effect of IMF Programs on Public Wages and Salaries." In Rorden Wilkinson and Jennifer Clapp (eds.), *Global Governance, Poverty and Inequality*. London: Routledge.

Nordhaus, William. 1975. "The Political Business Cycle." *The Review of Economic Studies* 42(1): 169–190.

North, Douglass. 1990. *Institutions, Institutional Change and Economic Performance*. Cambridge: Cambridge University Press.

North, Douglass, and Barry Weingast. 1989. "Constitutions and Commitment: The Evolution of Institutions Governing Public Choice in 17th-Century England." *Journal of Economic History* 49(4): 803–832.

Nsouli, Saleh, Ruben Atoian, and Alex Mourmouras. 2004. "Institutions, Program Implementation, and Macroeconomic Performance." IMF Working Chapter WP/04/184.

Nye, Joseph. 1987. "Nuclear Leaning and U.S.-Soviet Security Regimes." *International Organization* 41: 371–402.

Obsfelt, Maurice. 1996. "Models of Currency Crises With Self-Fulfilling Features." *European Economic Review* 40: 1037–1047.

Olson, Mancur. September 1993. "Dictatorship, Democracy, and Development." *The American Political Science Review* 87(3): 567–576.

Pandya, Sonal. 2014. "Democratization and Foreign Direct Investment Liberalization, 1970–2000." *International Studies Quarterly* 58(3): 475–488.

Papaioannou, Elias, and Gregorios Siourounis. 2008. "Democratisation and Growth." *The Economic Journal* 118(532): 1520–1551.

Pastor, Manuel. 1987. "The Effects of IMF Programs in the Third World: Debate and Evidence From Latin America." *World Development* 15(2): 249–262.

Pastor, Manuel, and Eric Hilt. 1993. "Private Investment and Democracy in Latin America." *World Development* 21: 489–507.

Pastor, Manuel, and Jae Ho Sung. 1995. "Private Investment and Democracy in Developing Countries." *Journal of Economic Issues* 29: 223–243.

Peeters, Guido, and Janusz Czapinski. 1990. "Positive-Negative Asymmetry in Evaluations: The Distinction Between Affective and Informational Negativity Effects." *European Review of Social Psychology* 1: 33–60.

Pejovich, Svetozar. 1999. "The Effects of the Interaction of Formal and Informal Institutions on Social Stability and Economic Development." *Journal of Markets and Morality* 2(Fall): 164–181.

Pericoli, Marcello, and Massimo Sbracia. 2003. "A Primer on Financial Contagion." *Journal of Economic Surveys* 17(4): 571–608.

Perotti, Roberto, and Yianos Kontopoulos. 2002. "Fragmented Fiscal Policy." *Journal of Public Economics* 86(2): 191–222.

Persson, Torsten. 2005. "Forms of Democracy, Policy and Economic Development." NBER Working Paper No. 11171.

Persson, Torsten, Gerard Roland, and Guido Tabellini. 1997. "Separation of Powers and Political Accountability." *The Quarterly Journal of Economics* 112(4): 1163–1202.

Persson, Torsten, and Guido Tabellini. 1994. "Is Inequality Harmful for Growth?" *American Economic Review* 84(3): 600–621.

Persson, Torsten, and Guido Tabellini. 2006. "Democracy and Development: The Devil in the Details." NBER Working Paper No. 11993.

Persson, Torsten, and Guido Tabellini. 2009. "Democratic Capital: The Nexus of Political and Economic Change." *American Economic Journal: Macroeconomics* 1(2): 88–126.

Pierson, Paul. 1995. Dismantling the Welfare State? Reagan, Thatcher, and the Politics of Retrenchment. Cambridge: Cambridge University Press.

Pierson, Paul, ed. 2001. *The New Politics of the Welfare State.* Oxford: Oxford University Press.

Pinto, Pablo. 2013. Partisan Investment in the Global Economy: Why the Left Loves Foreign Investment, and FDI Loves the Left. New York: Cambridge University Press.

Pinto, Pablo, and Santiago Pinto. 2008. "The Politics of Investment Partisanship and the Sectoral Allocation of Foreign Direct Investment." *Economics and Politics* 20(2): 216–254.

Poirson, Hélène. 1998. "Economic Security, Private Investment, and Growth in Developing Countries." IMF Working Paper WP/98/4.

Pop-Eleches, Grigore. 2009. From Economic Crisis to Reform: IMF Programs in Latin America and Eastern Europe. Princeton: Princeton University Press.

Przeworski, Adam, Michael Alvarez, Jose Cheibub, and Fernando Limongi. 2000. *Democracy and Development: Political Institutions and Wellbeing in the World.* New York: Cambridge University Press.

Przeworski, Adam, and Susan Stokes. 1999. *Democracy, Accountability, and Representation.* Cambridge: Cambridge University Press.

Przeworski, Adam, and James Vreeland. 2000. "The Effect of IMF Programs on Economic Growth." *Journal of Development Economics* 62(2): 385–421.

Radelet, Steven, and Jeffrey Sachs. 1998. "The East Asian Financial Crisis: Diagnosis, Remedies, Prospects." *Brookings Chapter on Economic Activity* 1: 1–90.

Reinhart, Carmen, and Kenneth Rogoff. 2009. *This Time Is Different: Eight Centuries of Financial Folly.* Princeton, NJ: Princeton University Press.

Reinhart, Carmen, and Kenneth Rogoff. 2011. "From Financial Crash to Debt Crisis." *American Economic Review* 101(5): 1676–1706.

Reinhart, Carmen, Kenneth Rogoff, and Miguel Savastano. 2003. "Debt Intolerance." *Brookings Papers on Economic Activity* 34(1): 1–74.

Reisen, Helmut, and Julia von Maltzan. 1999. "Boom and Bust and Sovereign Ratings." OECD Development Centre Working Paper 148.

Resnick, Adam. 2001. "Investors, Turbulence, and Transition: Democratic Transition and Foreign Direct Investment in Nineteen Developing Countries." *International Interactions* 27(4): 381–398.

Riker, William, and David Weimer. 1993. "The Economic and Political Liberalization of Socialism, the Fundamental Problem of Property Rights." *Social Philosophy and Policy* 10: 79–102.

Roberts, Kenneth. 1995. "Neoliberalism and the Transformation of Populism in Latin America: The Peruvian Case." *World Politics* 48(1): 82–116.

Roberts, Kenneth. 2002. "Populism and Democracy in Latin America." Paper presented to a conference at the Carter Center for Democracy, Atlanta, GA.

Roberts, Kenneth. 2007. "Latin America's Populist Revival." *The SAIS Review of International Affairs* 27(1): 3–15.

Roberts, Kenneth. 2012. "Populism and Democracy in Venezuela Under Hugo Chávez." In Cas Mudde and Cristobal Kaltwasser (eds.), *Populism in Europe and the Americas: Threat or Corrective Democracy?* Cambridge: Cambridge University Press, pp. 136–159.

Roberts, Kenneth. 2014. Changing Course in Latin America: Party Systems in Latin America's Neoliberal Era. Cambridge: Cambridge University Press.

Rodden, Jonathan. 2002. "The Dilemma of Fiscal Federalism: Grants and Fiscal Performance Around the World." *American Journal of Political Science* 46(3): 670–687.

Rodrik, Dani. 1989. "Promises, Promises: Credible Policy Reform via Signaling." *The Economic Journal* 99(397): 756–772.

Rodrik, Dani. 1997. *Has Globalization Gone Too Far?* Wshington, DC: Institute for International Economics.

Rodrik, Dani. 2007. One Economics, Many Recipes: Globalization, Institutions, and Economic Growth. Princeton, NJ: Princeton University Press.

Rodrik, Dani. 2008. "Second-best Institutions." NBER Working Paper No. 14050.

Rodrik, Dani, and Romain Wacziarg. 2005. "Do Democratic Transitions Produce Bad Economic Outcomes?" *American Economic Review* 95(2): 50–55.

Rohwer, Anja. 2009. "Measuring Corruption: A Comparison Between Transparency International's Corruption Perceptions Index and the World Bank's Worldwide Governance Indicators." CESifo DICE Report, Ifo Institute – Leibniz Institute for Economic Research at the University of Munich, vol. 7, issue 3, pp. 42–52.

Root, Hilton. 1989. "Tying the King's Hands: Credible Commitments and Royal Fiscal Policy During the Old Regime." *Rationality and Society* 1(2): 240–258.

Rose-Ackerman, Susan. 1999. "Political Corruption and Democracy." Yale Law School Faculty Scholarship Series Paper 592.

Rosendorff, Peter, and Kong Joo Shin. 2015. "Regime Type and International Commercial Agreements." *International Journal of Economic Theory* 11(1): 107–119.

Ross, Fiona. 2000. "Beyond Left and Right: The New Partisan Politics of Welfare." *Governance* 13: 155–183.

Ross, Michael. 2001. "Does Oil Hinder Democracy?" *World Politics* 53: 325–361.

Roubini, Nouriel, and Jeffrey Sachs. May 1989a. "Political and Economic Determinants of Budget Deficits in the Industrial Democracies." *European Economic Review* 33: 903–934.

Roubini, Nouriel, and Jeffrey Sachs. 1989b. "Government Spending and Budget Deficits in the Industrialized Countries." *Economic Policy* 8: 700–732.

Rowland, Peter. 2004. "Determinants of Spread, Credit Ratings and Credit Worthiness for Emerging Market Sovereign Debt: A Panel Data Study." Borradores de Economica #001844.

Ryan, Christopher. 2009. "Discerning the Compliance Calculus: Why States Comply With International Investment Law." *The Georgia Journal of International and Comparative Law* 38: 63–95.

Sachs, Jeffrey. 1989. "Social Conflict and Populist Policies in Latin America." NBER Working Paper No. 2897.

Sachs, Jeffrey, and Felipe Larrain. 1999. "Why Dollarization is More Straightjacket than Salvation." *Foreign Policy* 116 (Autumn): 80–92.

Saiegh, Sebastian. 2005. "Do Countries Have a 'Democratic Advantage'? Political Institutions, Multilateral Agencies, and Sovereign Borrowing." *Comparative Political Studies* 38(4): 366–387.

Saiegh, Sebastian. 2009. "Coalition Governments and Sovereign Debt Crises." *Economics and Politics* 21(2): 232–254.

Salacuse, Jeswald. 2010. *The Law of Investment Treaties.* Oxford: Oxford University Press.

Santiso, Javier. 1999. "Wall Street and the Mexican Crisis: A Temporal Analysis of Emerging Markets." *International Political Science Review* 20(1): 49–72.

Santiso, Javier. 2003. The Political Economy of Emerging Markets: Actors, Institutions, and Financial Crises in Latin America. New York: Palgrave Macmillan.

Schedler, Andreas. 2002. "The Menu of Manipulation." *Journal of Democracy* 13(2): 36–50.

Schadler, Susan, Franek Rozwadowski, Siddharth Tiwari, and David Robinson. 1993. "Economic Adjustment in Low-Income Countries: Experience Under the Enhanced Structural Adjustment Facility." IMF Occasional Chapter No. 106.

Schmidt, Manfred. 1996. "When Parties Matter: A Review of the Possibilities and Limits of Partisan Influence on Public Policy." *European Journal of Political Research* 30: 155–183.

Schultz, Kenneth. 2003. "Could Humphrey Have Gone to China? Measuring the Electoral Costs and Benefits of Making Peace." Unpublished manuscript.

Schultz, Kenneth, and Barry Weingast. 1998. "Limited Governments, Powerful States." In Randolph Siverson (ed.), *Strategic Politicians, Institutions, and Foreign Policy.* Ann Arbor: University of Michigan Press, pp. 15–50.

Schultz, Kenneth, and Barry Weingast. 2003. "The Democratic Advantage: Institutional Foundations of Financial Power in International Competition." *International Organization* 57(1): 3–42.

Shugart, Matthew. 2005. "Semi-Presidential Systems: Dual Executive and Mixed Authority Patterns." *French Politics* 3(3): 323–351.

Simmons, Beth. 2000. "International Law and State Behavior: Commitment and Compliance in International Monetary Affairs." *American Political Science Review* 94(4): 819–835.

Sobel, Andrew. 2002. *State Institutions, Private Incentives, Global Capital.* Ann Arbor: University of Michigan Press.

Soysa, Indra de, and Johannes Jütting. 2007. "Informal Institutions and Development: An Overview." In Johannes Jütting, Denis Dreschler, Sebastian Bartsch, and Indra de Soysa (eds.), *Informal Institutions: How Social Norms Help or Hinder Development.* Paris: OECD.

Standard & Poor's Ratings Direct. 2013. "How We Rate Sovereigns." http://www.spcapitaliq-credit.com/cms/wp-content/uploads/SP_RatingsDirect_HowWeRateSovereigns_12Nov2013.pdf?t=1411739321. (Accessed August 5, 2016)

Stasavage, David. 2002. "Investment and Institutions." *Economics and Politics* 14(1): 41–63.

Stasavage, David. 2003. Public Debt and Birth of the Democratic State: France and Great Britain 1688–1789. Cambridge: Cambridge University Press.

Stasavage, David. 2007. "Partisan Politics and Public Debt: The Importance of the 'Whig Supremacy' for Britain's Financial Revolution." *European Review of Economic History* 2: 123–153.

Stein, Jana von. 2005. "Do Treaties Constrain or Screen? Selection Bias and Treaty Compliance." *American Political Science Review* 99(4): 611–622.

Steinwand, Martin, and Randall Stone. 2008. "The International Monetary Fund: A Review of the Recent Evidence." *Review of International Organizations* 3(2): 123–149.

Stokes, Susan. 2001. Mandates and Democracy: Neoliberalism by Surprise in Latin America. Cambridge: Cambridge University Press.

Stone, Randall. 2002. Lending Credibility: The International Monetary Fund and the Post-Communist Transition. Princeton: Princeton University Press.

Stone, Randall. 2004. "Political Economy of IMF Lending in Africa." *American Political Science Review* 98(4): 577–591.

Stone, Randall. 2008. "The Scope of IMF Conditionality." *International Organization* 62(4): 589–620.

Strange, David, and Patricia Chang. 1993. "The International Labor Organization and the Welfare State: Institutional Effects on National Welfare Spending, 1960–1980." *International Organization* 47: 235–262.

Suleman, Muhammad. 2012. "Stock Market Reaction to Good and Bad Political News." *Asian Journal of Finance and Accounting* 4(1): 299–312.

Summers, Lawrence. May 2000. "International Financial Crises: Causes, Prevention, and Cures." *American Economic Review* 90(2): 1–16.

Sussman, Nathan, and Yishay Yafeh. 2000. "Institutions, Reforms, and Country Risk, Lessons From Japanese Government Debt in the Meiji Era." *Journal of Economic History* 60(2): 442–467.

Tanzi, Vito. 1998. "Corruption Around the World: Causes, Consequences, Scope, and Cures." IMF Working Paper WP/98/63.

Tavits, Margit, and Natalia Letki. 2009. "When Left Is Right: Party Ideology and Policy in Post-Communist Europe." *American Political Science Review* 103: 555–569.

Thacker, Strom. October 1999. "The High Politics of IMF Lending." *World Politics* 52: 38–75.

Tobin, Jennifer, and Susan Rose-Ackerman. 2011. "When BITs Have Some Bite: The Political-Economic Environment for Bilateral Investment Treaties." *The Review of International Organizations* 6(1): 1–32.

Tomz, Michael. 2007. Reputation and International Cooperation: Sovereign Debt Across Three Centuries. Princeton: Princeton University Press.

Tomz, Mike. 2002. "Democratic Default, Domestic Audiences and Compliance With International Agreements." American Political Science Association Annual Meeting.

Treisman, Daniel. 2000. "Decentralization and Inflation: Commitment, Collective Action, or Continuity?" *American Political Science Review* 94(4): 837–857.

Trudel, Robert. 2005. "Effects of Exchange Rate Regime on IMF Program Participation." *Review of Policy Research* 22(6): 919–936.

Tsebelis, George. 1995. "Decision Making in Political Systems: Veto Players in Presidentialism, Parliamentarism, Multicameralism and Multipartyism." *British Journal of Political Science* 25(3): 289–325.

Tsebelis, George. 2002. *Veto Players: How Political Institutions Work*. New York: Russell Sage Foundation and Princeton University Press.

Tufte, Edward. 1975. "Determinants of the Outcomes of Midterm Congressional Elections." *American Political Science Review* 69: 812–826.

Tufte, Edward. 1978. *Political Control of the Economy*. Princeton, NJ: Princeton University Press.

Turnovsky, Stephen, and Marcus Miller. 1984. "The Effects of Government Expenditure on the Term Structure of Interest Rates." *Journal of Money, Credit, and Banking* 16: 16–33.

Vaaler, Paul, Burkhard Schrage, and Steven Block. 2005. "Counting the Investor Vote: Political Business Cycle Effects on Sovereign Bond Spreads in Developing Countries." *Journal of International Business Studies* 36: 62–88.

Vaaler, Paul, Burkhard Schrage, and Steven Block. 2006. "Elections, Opportunism, Partisanship and Sovereign Ratings in Developing Countries." *Review of Development Economics* 10(1): 154–170.

Van Rijckeghem, Caroline, and Beatrice Weder. 2004. *The Politics of Debt Crises*. London: Centre for Economic Policy Research.

Vreeland, James. 2002. "The Effect of IMF Programs on Labor." *World Development* 30(1): 121–139.

Vreeland, James. 2003. *The IMF and Economic Development*. New York: Cambridge University Press.

Vreeland, James. 2006. "IMF Program Compliance: Aggregate Index Versus Policy Specific Research Strategies." *The Review of International Organizations* 1(4): 359–378.

Vreeland, James. 2007. The International Monetary Fund: Politics of Conditional Lending. New York: Routledge.

Weingast, Barry. 1995. "The Economic Role of Political Institutions: Market-Preserving Federalism and Economic Development." *Journal of Law, Economics and Organization* 1(11): 1–31.

Weyland, Kurt. 1996. "Neopopulism and Neoliberalism in Latin America: Unexpected Affinities." *Studies in Comparative International Development* 31(3): 3–31.

Weyland, Kurt. 1999a. "Neoliberal Populism in Latin America and Eastern Europe." *Comparative Politics* 31(4): 379–401.

Weyland, Kurt. 1999b. "Populism in the Age of Neoliberalism." In Michael Conniff (ed.), *Populism in Latin America*. Tuscaloosa: University of Alabama Press, pp. 172–90.

Weyland, Kurt. 2002. The Politics of Market Reform in Fragile Democracies: Argentina, Brazil, Peru, and Venezuela. Princeton, NJ: Princeton University Press.

Weyland, Kurt. 2006. "The Rise and Decline of Fujimori's Neopopulist Leadership." In Julio Carrion (ed.), *The Fujimori Legacy: The Rise of Electoral Authoritarianism in Peru*. University Park: Pennsylvania State University Press, pp. 13–38.

Weyland, Kurt. 2013. "Why Latin America Is Becoming Less Democratic." *Atlantic*, July 15.

Wiesehomeier, Nina, and Kenneth Benoit. 2009. "Presidents, Parties, and Policy Competition." *Journal of Politics* 71(4): 1435–1447.

Williamson, Oliver. 1994. "The Institutions and Governance of Economic Development and Reform." In *Proceedings of the World Bank Annual Conference on Development Economics*. Washington, DC: The World Bank, pp. 171–197.

World Bank. 2001. Developing Government Bond Markets: A Handbook. Washington, DC: World Bank: International Monetary Fund.

World Bank. 2012. *Global Development Finance*. Washington: World Bank.

World Bank. *World Development Indicators*, various years. Washington: World Bank.

Zheng, Yu. 2011. "Credibility and Flexibility: Political Institutions, Governance, and Foreign Direct Investment." *International Interactions* 37(3): 293–319.

Index

www.ingramcontent.com/pod-product-compliance
Ingram Content Group UK Ltd.
Pitfield, Milton Keynes, MK11 3LW, UK
UKHW011016180926
475701UK00004B/767
* 9 7 8 0 3 6 7 2 7 2 8 2 1 *